LOCAL PUBLIC FINANCIAL MANAGEMENT

Introduction to the Public Sector Governance and Accountability Series

Anwar Shah, Series Editor

A well-functioning public sector that delivers quality public services consistent with citizen preferences and that fosters private market-led growth while managing fiscal resources prudently is considered critical to the World Bank's mission of poverty alleviation and the achievement of the Millennium Development Goals. This important new series aims to advance those objectives by disseminating conceptual guidance and lessons from practices and by facilitating learning from one another's experiences on ideas and practices that promote *responsive* (by matching public services with citizens' preferences), *responsible* (through efficiency and equity in service provision without undue fiscal and social risk), and *accountable* (to citizens for all actions) public governance in developing countries.

This series represents a response to several independent evaluations in recent years that have argued that development practitioners and policy makers dealing with public sector reforms in developing countries and, indeed, anyone with a concern for effective public governance could benefit from a synthesis of newer perspectives on public sector reforms. This series distills current wisdom and presents tools of analysis for improving the efficiency, equity, and efficacy of the public sector. Leading public policy experts and practitioners have contributed to this series.

The first 14 volumes in this series, listed below, are concerned with public sector accountability for prudent fiscal management; efficiency, equity, and integrity in public service provision; safeguards for the protection of the poor, women, minorities, and other disadvantaged groups; ways of strengthening institutional arrangements for voice, choice, and exit; means of ensuring public financial accountability for integrity and results; methods of evaluating public sector programs, fiscal federalism, and local finances; international practices in local governance; and a framework for responsive and accountable governance.

Fiscal Management

Public Services Delivery

Public Expenditure Analysis

Local Governance in Industrial Countries

Local Governance in Developing Countries

Intergovernmental Fiscal Transfers: Principles and Practice

Participatory Budgeting

Budgeting and Budgetary Institutions

Local Budgeting

Local Public Financial Management

Performance Accountability and Combating Corruption

Tools for Public Sector Evaluations

Macrofederalism and Local Finances

Citizen-Centered Governance

PUBLIC SECTOR
GOVERNANCE AND
ACCOUNTABILITY SERIES

LOCAL PUBLIC
FINANCIAL
MANAGEMENT

Edited by ANWAR SHAH

THE WORLD BANK
Washington, D.C.

ISBN-10: 0-8213-6937-7
ISBN-13: 978-0-8213-6937-1
eISBN-10: 0-8213-6938-5
eISBN-13: 978-0-8213-6938-8
DOI: 10.1596/978-0-8213-6937-1

Library of Congress Cataloging-in-Publication Data
Local public financial management / edited by Anwar Shah.
    p. cm.
  Includes bibliographical references and index.
  ISBN-13: 978-0-8213-6937-1
  ISBN-10: 0-8213-6937-7
  ISBN-10: 0-8213-6938-5 (electronic)
    1. Local finance. 2. Finance, Public. I. Shah, Anwar.

HJ9105.L616 2007
355.4'215—dc22

                                                                    2006101269

Contents

CHAPTER

7   **External Auditing and Performance Evaluation, with Special Emphasis on Detecting Corruption**   227

Aad Bac

Index   255

BOX

FIGURES

TABLES

Foreword

In Western democracies, systems of checks and balances built into government structures have formed the core of good governance and have helped empower citizens for more than two hundred years. The incentives that motivate public servants and policy makers— the rewards and sanctions linked to results that help shape public sector performance—are rooted in a country's accountability frameworks. Sound public sector management and government spending help determine the course of economic development and social equity, especially for the poor and other disadvantaged groups, such as women and the elderly.

Many developing countries, however, continue to suffer from unsatisfactory and often dysfunctional governance systems that include rent seeking and malfeasance, inappropriate allocation of resources, inefficient revenue systems, and weak delivery of vital public services. Such poor governance leads to unwelcome outcomes for access to public services by the poor and other disadvantaged members of society, such as women, children, and minorities. In dealing with these concerns, the development assistance community in general and the World Bank in particular are continuously striving to learn lessons from practices around the world to achieve a better understanding of what works and what does not work in improving public sector governance, especially with respect to combating corruption and making services work for poor people.

The Public Sector Governance and Accountability Series advances our knowledge by providing tools and lessons from practices in improving efficiency and equity of public services provision and strengthening institutions of accountability in governance. The series highlights frameworks to create incentive environments and pressures for good governance from within and beyond governments. It outlines institutional mechanisms to empower citizens to demand accountability for results from their governments. It provides practical guidance on managing for results and prudent fiscal management. It outlines approaches to dealing with corruption and malfeasance. It provides conceptual and practical guidance on alternative service delivery frameworks for extending the reach and access of public services. The series also covers safeguards for the protection of the poor, women, minorities, and other disadvantaged groups; ways of strengthening institutional arrangements for voice and exit; methods of evaluating public sector programs; frameworks for responsive and accountable governance; and fiscal federalism and local governance.

This series will be of interest to public officials, development practitioners, students of development, and those interested in public governance in developing countries.

Frannie A. Léautier
Vice President
World Bank Institute

Preface

The practice of public financial management is now considered critical in combating corruption, alleviating poverty, and ensuring the effective use of internal and external resources. This volume aims to bring guidance on better practices in public financial management to the attention of policy makers and practitioners in developing countries with a view to reforming existing systems.

The volume provides an overview of local government financial accounting and reporting. Better practices in cash management are documented. The use of transparent procurement processes to mitigate corruption is elaborated. Practical guidance is imparted on how and when to use debt, how to assess debt affordability, what debt to use, how to issue debt, and how to manage debt. The use of internal controls and audits to ensure efficiency and integrity is highlighted. The role of external audit in combating corruption is also discussed, and audit methods to detect corruption are presented.

The volume represents a collaborative effort of the Swedish International Development Cooperation Agency and the World Bank Institute to support reform of the public expenditure management and financial accountability systems in developing countries, especially in Africa. We hope policy makers and practitioners will find this volume to be a useful tool in guiding their reform efforts.

Roumeen Islam
Manager, Poverty Reduction and Economic Management
World Bank Institute

Acknowledgments

This book brings together learning modules on local financial management prepared for the World Bank Institute learning programs over the past three years. These learning modules and their publication in the current volume were primarily financed by the government of Sweden through its Public Expenditure and Financial Accountability (PEFA) partnership program with the World Bank Institute, directed by the editor. The government of Japan provided additional financial support for the editing of this volume. The editor is grateful to Hallgerd Dryssen, Swedish International Development Cooperation Agency, Stockholm, for providing overall guidance and support to the PEFA program. In addition, Bengt Anderson, Goran Anderson, Gunilla Bruun, Alan Gustafsson, and other members of the PEFA external advisory group contributed to the design and development of the program.

The book has benefited from contributions to World Bank Institute learning events by senior policy makers and scholars from Africa and elsewhere. In particular, thanks are due to Tania Ajam, director, Applied Fiscal Research Center, South Africa; Paul Boothe, former associate deputy minister, Ministry of Finance, Canada; Neil Cole, director, South Africa National Treasury; Anders Haglund, PricewaterhouseCoopers, Stockholm; Roy Kelly, professor, Duke University; Florence Kuteesa, public finance consultant, Ministry of Finance, Uganda; John Mikesell, professor, Indiana University; Ismail Momoniat, director general, South Africa National Treasury; and Christina Nomdo, Institute for Democracy in South Africa, Cape Town.

The editor is grateful to the leading scholars who contributed chapters and to the distinguished reviewers who provided comments.

Anupam Das, Alta Fölscher, Adrian Shall, and Chunli Shen helped during various stages of preparation of this book and provided comments and editorial revisions of individual chapters. Kaitlin Tierney provided excellent administrative support for this project.

The editor is also grateful to Stephen McGroarty for ensuring a fast-track process for publication of this book and to Dina Towbin for excellent editing supervision. Denise Bergeron is to be thanked for the excellent print quality of this book.

Contributors

AAD BAC is full professor of accountancy, especially government accountancy, at Tilburg University in the Netherlands, where he is chair of the School of Accountancy. Since 1993, he has also been a visiting professor at the University of the Dutch Antilles at Curaçao. He combined his academic career with practice from 1974 until 2001 as a partner of Deloitte and its legal predecessors. In his practice as well as in his academic endeavors, he has specialized in financial reporting, financial management, administrative organization, and information systems (as an adviser), and auditing (as a practicing auditor) in the public sector. He has published papers, articles, and books, and lectured at a number of other universities and in other countries on these topics.

MUSTAFA BALTACI is deputy director of the Prime Minister's Inspection Board in Turkey. He was with the World Bank as a research analyst in 2005 working on public financial management, accountability, fiscal decentralization, internal control, and audit. He holds a master's degree in government administration and a diploma in public finance from the University of Pennsylvania.

W. BARTLEY HILDRETH is the Regents Distinguished Professor of Public Finance and director of the Kansas Public Finance Center in the Hugo Wall School of Urban and Public Affairs and the W. Frank Barton School of Business at Wichita State University. During fall 2005, he served as the Fulbright visiting research scholar in public policy at McGill University in Montreal.

DR. JESSE HUGHES has during the past 10 years, conducted research for the International Federation of Accountants and consulted on governmental financial management issues in many countries, including Armenia, Azerbaijan, Bosnia and Herzegovina, Macedonia, Malawi, Moldova, Nigeria, the Syrian Arab Republic, and Zambia. He taught accounting and financial management for 20 years at Hampton University, Hampton, Virginia, and Old Dominion University, Norfolk, Virginia, where he is professor emeritus of accounting. Before teaching, he worked for 20 years at the federal level as an auditor, management analyst, systems analyst, chief accountant, and comptroller. He is editor of the *Public Fund Digest* for the International Consortium of Government Financial Managers and is a member of its board.

ROWAN JONES is professor of public sector accounting, University of Birmingham, United Kingdom. He is coauthor (with M. W. Pendlebury) of *Public Sector Accounting* (5th edition, 2000) and coeditor (with K. Lüder) of *Reforming Governmental Accounting and Budgeting in Europe* (2003; Chinese translation, 2005).

M. CORINNE LARSON joined the MBIA Asset Management Group in July 1999. She is responsible for managing the marketing and client service functions for the firm's third-party accounts as well as for providing technical and educational services in cash management. She formerly served as assistant director in the research center of the Government Finance Officers Association (GFOA), where she was responsible for managing the association's cash management programs. She is a frequent speaker on cash management and investment topics and is the author of numerous publications, including *Investing Public Funds* (2nd edition). She served for seven years as the editor of *Public Investor*, GFOA's monthly investment newsletter, and sits on GFOA's Standing Committee on Retirement and Benefits Administration. In addition, She has more than 10 years' experience in corporate treasury management. She holds the designation of Certified Treasury Professional through the Association for Financial Professionals and sits on the association's Editorial Advisory Board for its professional journal, *AFP Exchange*. She received her bachelor of arts from Indiana University, South Bend, and her master of business administration from the University of Notre Dame, Indiana.

CLIFFORD P. MCCUE is an associate professor at the School of Public Administration, Florida Atlantic University, Boca Raton. His teaching and research interests are in public administration, public procurement, and public policy.

He is a senior research scholar in the Public Procurement Research Center at Florida Atlantic University.

GERALD J. MILLER, professor in the School of Public Policy and Administration at Rutgers University, the State University of New Jersey, Newark campus, teaches public budgeting and finance. During spring 2007, he is serving as the Fulbright visiting research scholar in public policy and administration at the University of Ottawa, Canada.

ERIC W. PRIER is an associate professor in the Department of Political Science, Florida Atlantic University. His teaching and research interests are in politics, public procurement, and public policy. He is a senior research scholar in the Public Procurement Research Center at Florida Atlantic University.

ANWAR SHAH is lead economist and program leader for public sector governance at the World Bank Institute, Washington, DC. He is also a member of the executive board of the International Institute of Public Finance, Munich, Germany, and a fellow of the Institute for Public Economics, Alberta, Canada. He has served the Canadian Ministry of Finance in Ottawa and the government of the province of Alberta, Canada, where he held responsibilities for federal-provincial and provincial-local fiscal relations, respectively. He has also advised the governments of Argentina, Australia, Brazil, Canada, China, Germany, India, Indonesia, Mexico, Pakistan, Poland, and Turkey on the reform of their fiscal systems. He is the lead author of a report evaluating World Bank assistance for governance reforms. He has published extensively on governance, anticorruption, fiscal management, fiscal federalism, local governance, and public and environmental economics issues.

SERDAR YILMAZ is a senior social development economist at the World Bank, working on decentralization, local governance, and accountability issues. Before joining the Social Development Department, he was with the World Bank Institute (WBI), where he coordinated curriculum development activities of the WBI's capacity-building programs on public finance, intergovernmental relations, and local financial management. His research interest areas are analysis of accountability in the public sector, analysis of intergovernmental policies in developing countries, and the role of infrastructure service provision in regional development patterns. His research has appeared in academic journals and books edited by leading academics in the field. He holds a PhD in public policy from George Mason University, Fairfax, Virginia.

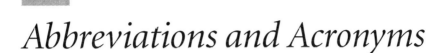

Abbreviations and Acronyms

ACH	Automated Clearing House
BCE	before the common era
CD	certificate of deposit
CEO	chief executive officer
CHU	Central Harmonization Unit
CMT	constant maturity Treasury
COSO	Committee of Sponsoring Organizations
EU	European Union
FDIC	Federal Deposit Insurance Corporation
FEE	European Federation of Accountants
FY	fiscal year
GAO	Government Accountability Office
GASB	Governmental Accounting Standards Board
GNP	gross national product
IAS	International Accounting Standards
IFAC	International Federation of Accountants
IFRS	International Financial Reporting Standards
IIA	Institute of Internal Auditors
INTOSAI	International Organization of Supreme Audit Institutions
IPSAS	International Public Sector Accounting Standards
IPSASB	International Public Sector Accounting Standards Board
ISA	International Standard on Auditing
IT	information technology
LOC	letter of credit
MOF	ministry of finance
NASBO	National Association of State Budget Officers
NSW	New South Wales

OECD	Organisation for Economic Co-operation and Development
PFM	public financial management
PIFC	public internal financial control
RFP	request for proposal
RRS	Representative Revenue System
SAI	supreme audit institution
SIGMA	Support for Improvement in Governance and Management
SOP	standard operating procedure
SOW	statement of work
TIC	true interest cost
ZBA	zero-balance account

Overview

ANWAR SHAH

Transparent and prudent local financial management has come to be recognized as critical to the integrity of the local public sector and for gaining and retaining the trust of local residents. Such integrity and trust are sometimes lacking in some local governments in developing countries, especially in the Africa region. This volume attempts to provide practical guidance to local governments interested in establishing sound financial management systems. Leading international experts have contributed to all relevant aspects of local public financial management—cash management, internal controls, accounts, audits, and debt management.

Rowan Jones (chapter 1) provides an overview of local government financial accounting and reporting. The chapter begins by identifying traditional functions of financial accounting and reporting, namely, the proper recording of transactions and accounting against the budget. It explains the contribution that cash-based accounting, commitment accounting, and fund accounting make to carrying out these functions. The chapter then discusses how the traditional functions of accounting can be expanded, most importantly, to include all relevant accruals and to provide financial statements for each local government as a whole. It also explains how budgets can usefully adopt an accrual basis. The chapter also addresses output measurement, which recently has been recognized as an important part of accounting theory and practice. An increasingly relevant connection between local government accounting and national accounting is discussed. Finally, given the

1

growing significance of financial reporting on an accrual basis, the chapter addresses International Public Sector Accounting Standards.

Chapter 2, by M. Corrine Larson, is concerned with the practice of cash management by local governments. Local government cash management is generally the responsibility of a finance director or a treasurer, depending on the size and structure of the governmental entity. The primary activities of the cash management function are to collect revenues owed to the government, pay the government's operating expenses, invest funds until they are needed for use, and safeguard the funds throughout the cash flow cycle. Technology and expanded investment authority have revolutionized cash management, which today is seen as an important finance function. The author stresses revenue collection as one of the main functions of local governments. Local governments collect funds from a variety of sources, including fines, fees, taxes, licenses, permits, and special assessments. Revenues should be received in a timely manner, credited to the proper fund, and deposited into the correct bank account as quickly as possible. Governments should also strive to collect all the monies owed by making the payment process simple and easy for their citizens and collecting on overdue accounts.

The author argues that the finance official in charge of the cash management function must also make sure the local government's obligations are paid on a timely basis and in a cost-effective manner. An equally important objective is to provide information on funding requirements to take the guesswork out of managing the government's liquidity. By knowing its disbursement requirements, the finance official can make effective investment decisions.

An important component of cash management is the investment function. Over the years, governments have been granted increased authority over how they can invest their excess funds. This expanded investment authority has allowed governments to increase their investment income. However, finance officials must protect their entities' funds and make prudent investment decisions. Integral to the investment function is cash flow forecasting to determine when the government will have funds to invest, how much money the government will have to invest, and for how long those funds can be invested.

In addition, the finance official must protect the funds during all phases of the cash management cycle by implementing effective internal controls and funds concentration procedures, collateralizing public deposits over the centrally insured limits (for example, in the United States, the Federal Deposit Insurance Corporation's limit of $100,000), and establishing and maintaining good working relationships with financial institutions and other business partners. A well-run cash management program protects a government's funds and makes the most efficient use of those funds.

Clifford P. McCue and Eric W. Prier (chapter 3) provide practical guidance in ensuring the integrity of local government procurement practices. The role that public procurement plays in good governance cannot be overstated, and the effective provision of public goods and services often requires efficient coordination by local government. This chapter identifies the opportunities for corruption in local government procurement while discussing the motivations and incentives of individual procurement officials to engage in such practices in developing countries. By examining the links between good governance and sound procurement policies and practices, the authors explain and defend how local procurement procedures can mitigate corruption in developing nations. Through the use of several examples, it is shown that adherence to a formal procurement planning process can provide needed safeguards against corruption. In addition, major concepts that underlie public procurement, such as transparency, equity, sustainability, and fairness, are discussed in terms of best practices.

The chapter concludes that for good governance to flourish within the public arena, procurement professionals must take a leading role in advocating for ethical practices by developing both the institutional and human capacity in procurement through the adoption of sound procurement practices in developing nations.

Gerald J. Miller and Bartley W. Hildreth in chapter 4 discuss debt management by localities and answer questions that will enable a governmental entity to be able to produce a set of fiscal policies tailored for its particular situation. The topics that the questions address are how to use debt, when to use debt, how to assess debt affordability, what debt to use, how to issue debt, and how to management debt. In the first area, the chapter discusses the purpose and sources for borrowed funds as well as the need for a capital improvement program, placing uses and sources of borrowed funds in a systematic analysis. The second area covers the specific projects for which debt is suited as well as the planning and legal framework that should accompany decisions to use debt. The third area concerns the amount of debt a locality can afford, using well-known measures to frame the analysis a locality should undertake. The fourth area outlines the types of debt and the important features of each. The fifth area outlines the process of issuing debt. The final area provides detailed information on managing the debt once borrowed, from investment of proceeds to refunding, and to the process for managing debt repayment in the face of a financial emergency.

Chapter 5 by Jesse Hughes is concerned with local government internal controls to ensure efficiency and integrity. The statutory and regulatory basis for internal controls varies from government to government. This chapter sets out the principles that underlie internal controls and the rules that must be followed to account for and to use the resources that are received and expended through the budget. Examples are given of internal controls that can assist managers in ensuring that internal control systems are comprehensive and effective.

Internal control can be defined as the whole system of controls, financial and otherwise, established to provide reasonable assurance of effective and efficient operations, reliable financial information and reporting, and compliance with laws and regulations. Internal control is necessary because organizations grow in size and complexity beyond the direct control of individuals and therefore require written control systems to manage operations; must demonstrate that they have identified, met, and monitored compliance with their statutory obligations; and face a wide range of financial and administrative risks. Internal controls are necessary to identify, evaluate, and control those risks.

Internal control systems provide reasonable assurance that the affairs of the budget institutions are managed properly, but those responsible for budgets must maintain vigilance because all system are susceptible to human error. The main risks to internal control procedures are those of management override, collusion, corruption, peaks and troughs of work or absences resulting in noncompliance with procedures, staff without the knowledge and skills to perform the procedure, misunderstanding about what the procedure should be, and not understanding the importance of the procedure.

The Committee of Sponsoring Organizations (COSO) of the Treadway Commission developed an Integrated Framework for Internal Control and this framework was later incorporated into an Integrated Framework for Risk Management. Basically, internal control can help an entity achieve its performance goals and prevent loss of resources. It can help ensure reliable financial reporting. It can also help an entity comply with laws and regulations, avoiding damage to its reputation and other consequences. In sum, it can help an entity get to where it wants to go and avoid pitfalls and surprises along the way. COSO indicated that an auditing function is established within an entity to assist in monitoring the effectiveness and efficiency of internal control systems.

All personnel within local government are responsible for assessing risk in their areas of responsibility and establishing those internal control procedures necessary to minimize risk. The basic rule is that management is responsible for establishing and enforcing internal controls. Auditors are responsible for checking the adequacy and effectiveness of those controls.

Mustafa Baltaci and Serdar Yilmaz in chapter 6 discuss the role of internal control and audit in the context of developing countries. They argue that fiscal decentralization in developing countries has been at the center of public sector reform in the last two decades. Yet, a closer look at the recent reforms in the developing world indicates that decentralization does not necessarily translate into better outcomes because of waste, corruption, and inefficiencies. The success of decentralization depends on the existence of a framework that keeps local or "subnational" governments on track and holds local government officials accountable for results—two missing components in most recent decentralization efforts. The authors make suggestions to close this implementation gap by developing a conceptual framework of internal control and audit at the local level. They analyze the role of internal control in public financial management practice and specify the necessary steps in establishing contemporary internal control and audit systems in a subnational government.

Chapter 7 by Aad Bac begins by explaining why auditing in government organizations is different from auditing in private business organizations. It draws from insights developed by academics in public administration and it elaborates on consequences of environmental factors and task-related factors specific to the public sector area. The author points out that an important denominator for the extent and content of government audits is the national discretionary power to legislate. Therefore, there is a wide variance in the extent and content of government audits among the jurisdictions of the world. As to the object of audit, the government auditor may encounter simple budget execution documents or full-fledged financial reports. Sometimes, audits will not cover financial documents, but will focus on the actions or conduct or performance of auditees; and sometimes, the systems will be judged.

Audit scope may range as wide as audits on compliance with laws and regulations regarding financial reporting, budget laws, and laws and regulations regarding the content of policy areas and programs. Of course, audits may cover the quality of financial reporting, depending on the kind of reporting, expressed as an opinion on the soundness of the accounts or the true and fair view of the financial reports. Examples of such audits are audits for orderly and verifiable financial management, and performance audits. Finally, audits may have a more forensic flavor when addressing abuse and improper use of laws and regulations or fraud and corruption. The chapter briefly reviews possible users of audits of government entities and deals with the way in which government audits can be instituted and organized. The chapter concludes with guidance on audit reporting.

1

Financial Accounting and Reporting

ROWAN JONES

Local government accounting, like all other accounting, focuses on the needs of specific organizations at particular times. It is an increasingly demanded part of the accounting discipline—a product of the accounting profession initially developed in the United Kingdom and the United States over 100 years ago.[1]

Its distinctive problem is how to account for local governments that provide services free at the point of delivery, financed primarily by taxation and grants. Ultimate responsibility is usually held by politicians endowed with finite, and short, time horizons—to the next election.

In the crucial but narrow sense of accounting as a control that ensures financial probity and guards against corruption, accounting in local governments has been as influential as in any other kind of organization. However, private sector accounting has, since the beginnings of the profession, become systematically associated with a much wider sense of accounting—the use of money to measure the performance of businesses. In a business, the value of services provided is given by the money the business collects from the sales it makes; because money is also used to measure the cost of services provided, money provides a universal measure of performance. The cost of services provided by local governments is also measured in terms of money, because governments have to buy in the same markets in which businesses buy. But the effect of financing governments by taxation is that the recipients of governmental services do not express their satisfaction in money terms. That universal measure of performance is not available.

The traditional response to this problem has been to limit the role of accounting in government to matters of financial probity: the proper recording of transactions, the control of spending against the budget, and the minimization of spending. Matters relating to the quantity and quality of services provided were left to service professionals and politicians. During the second half of the twentieth century, however, a stream of initiatives shared the same fundamental premise: that, given scarce resources, explicit measurement of the quantity, if not the quality, of services provided, linked to measurement of resources consumed, produces better services. These initiatives often did not emanate from accountants, although accountants were sometimes instrumental in the experimentation. One intention of these developments was to reduce the influence of politics by increasing the amount of economic calculation. From the point of view of accounting technique and practical implementation, the initiatives came in three forms chronologically: until the 1970s, they focused primarily on budgeting; subsequently, auditing was the medium; and from the 1990s onward, accrual accounting dominated.

Generally, local government accounting has been reformed before national government accounting, and reformed gradually. The most abrupt transformation came at the national level, in theory and increasingly in practice, during the 1990s. Previously, cash-based budgetary accounting systems developed for the purpose of control by the sovereign government were the norm and were largely unquestioned. Now, every such system is being questioned, and in significant cases radically changed toward accrual-based systems.

Probably the most visible change in Anglo-American business accounting in the second half of the twentieth century was the emergence of codified sets of accounting practices for external financial reporting. The United States took the lead in this, for companies listed on stock exchanges. The accounting codes have also usually been accompanied by conceptual frameworks, which are statements about the objectives of accounting and the constraints within which those objectives are to be achieved. The first major use of codes for government accounting followed the formation in the United States in 1984 of the Governmental Accounting Standards Board, which is responsible for state and local governments. During the 1990s, the accounting profession, through its worldwide organization (the International Federation of Accountants, based in New York City), began to develop International Public Sector

Accounting Standards (IPSAS) for accounting and reporting by governments, with explanatory material.

Thus far, the clearest triggers for change toward accrual-based accounting have been financial distress and fraud. Financial distress usually means that government spending has become too high to be borne by lenders or by taxpayers. Financial distress and fraud are not necessarily a function of accounting, although accounting is usually implicated either directly or indirectly. When accounting systems do change, it is often as a result of wider changes in management.

The case for accrual accounting is clear. Cash-based accounting, by its nature, ignores too many economic events; accrual accounting—necessarily in combination with cash accounting—is, in practice, the fullest method available for recording, measuring, and communicating such economic events. Whether for internal management of a government or for external accountability, cash accounting is too parsimonious with the truth. The benefits of accrual accounting are not, of course, free. Providing more, high-quality information involves increased processing expense; it also requires training to understand fully its benefits. Moreover, accrual accounting, while addressing the unacceptable ease with which cash flows can be manipulated, introduces significant reliability problems of its own, necessitating additional audit resources. Cash-based accounting is, by its nature, more reliable than accrual-based accounting, other things being equal, but is much less relevant.

Traditional Functions of Financial Accounting and Reporting

The traditional functions of financial accounting and reporting in government are the proper recording of transactions, and accounting against the budget.

Proper Recording of Transactions

In a context in which, in management theory and practice, change is judged to be good, accounting systems cannot be immune. However, of all the elements of management, accounting can be especially resistant to change. The traditional focus on the proper recording of transactions and on control of spending against the budget does not change. During exuberant periods of the economic cycle, this focus can be underemphasized but it can never be forgotten. Above all, it is a necessary precondition, though not a sufficient one, for guarding against corruption. Within government accounting, the traditional focus has been especially strong and is the main reason why accounting theory and practice in many organizations remained unchanged for so long. Sophisticated accounting systems are not necessarily required to maintain the traditional focus.

Records of transactions are the fundamentals of accounting systems. Whether these records should be expressed uniformly across a set of organizations[2] or whether their expression should be left to each organization to determine is a polarizing debate. Even in the latter case, some kind of uniform classification of the results of these transactions is required. The difference of opinion hinges on beliefs in the extent to which any accounting system can provide meaningfully uniform categories (of cost, for example). At one extreme is the view that uniform records produce uniform categories; the opposite view is that the economics of different organizations are different and no amount of uniformity in record keeping can change that. In practice, strong demand—especially from politicians and nonfinancial managers—for some degree of uniformity must be satisfied, regardless of whether the underlying records are expressed in a uniform way.

Some existing systems of recording transactions use single-entry bookkeeping; others double entry. In the Anglo-American context, single-entry systems are seen as archaic.[3] In the past, few systems were wholly comprehensive, integrated recording systems (the use of subsidiary systems being pervasive), but the prevalence of integrated information technology (IT) systems has changed this.

The enduring focus of accounting in government has been on internal financial control: the proper recording of transactions. Closely associated with this has been control of spending against the budget.

Budgetary Accounting

Budgets are requests for money, in local government for public money: taxation and grants. In their definitive form, budgets are requests by the executive of a sovereign government for authority from the legislature to impose taxes. In the context of local governments, budgets may be seen as requests by officers for the authority of the council of politicians.

Thus, budgets are not the product of accounting systems at all but, once they have been approved, it is the chief financial officer's role to monitor actual spending against the budget, to provide a crucial form of financial control, internal or external. The form and content of the budget can significantly influence the possible extent of the financial control; thus, finance officials would always want, even if they do not always have, a central role in forming the budget request. Moreover, the requirement usually imposed on local governments to balance their budgets (budgeted spending is to be financed by taxation), even if the measurement rules are often vague, adds to the influence of the budget on accounting.

The budget traditionally has been used to impose central financial control on all aspects of governments. Rules were developed, many of which are still in use, to provide control. Budgets that provide money for only a year, after which time they lapse (sometimes known as "annuality"), is one such rule. Another is the rule that budgets are provided gross, so that any income earned by a budget holder must be surrendered to the central coffers (the "gross budget principle"). This emphasis on central financial control has also been associated with the idea that public money had to be spent on the cheapest that money could buy, especially for routine, recurrent spending.

The form that budgets physically take varies across organizations and countries, and over time, as does the form of all financial statements. Traditionally common features of budgets emerge. Over the past five or six decades, these features have been challenged, particularly by techniques that shift the emphasis from what is to be spent under the budget (inputs) to what is to be achieved from the spending of the budget (outputs and outcomes). As comprehensive alternatives (program budgeting and zero-base budgeting are two major examples), these techniques failed to be accepted but elements of each continue to have relevance and be used.

Traditional budgets are based on the organizational structure, more specifically, identification of those officers within the government who are held accountable for spending money against budgets. This feature of budgets applies whether budgets are highly aggregated or whether there is significant devolution of budgets—the organizational structure locates the budgets.

Within each of the budgets thus identified, other common elements surface. Budgets are usually lists of what is to be bought with the money being requested—inputs. These may be very broadly specified and may, in an extreme example, be a single amount. They are more typically specified in much detail. The one amount for the whole of the costs of employees might be broken down into detailed items, such as overtime pay for wage earners. Again, however, whatever the level of specification, budgets are usually lists of inputs, often known as line items.

Budgets tend also to focus on one year, the coming fiscal year. This annual request embodies another common feature of budgets: the request for the coming year is justified in terms of marginal changes from the previous year's budget (commonly called incrementalism). The essence of this feature of budgeting is not that budgets must always increase but that budgets are justified by marginal changes from previous years, which may, in principle, be decrements.

In sum, budgets are traditionally line-item, incremental requests that reflect the organizational structure. Being expressed in money terms, they are natural ways of requesting money. They are also very good at providing a crucial sort of financial control that finance officials demand, in that budgets specifically identify who is spending money and what they are buying with it. This demand is not only in the interest of the finance officials themselves but is on behalf of the public, whose money is being spent. It is common for budgets to be enacted as law, in part to emphasize the importance of this kind of control. These traditional budgets are a natural part of the accountant's focus on financial probity.

Figure 1.1 is an example of a budget report expressed in line items. In practice, especially under accrual accounting, the basis of accounting against the budget can be different from the accounting in the financial statements. In such cases, a reconciliation of the basis of the budgetary accounting and the accrual accounting would usefully be provided.

An important part of budgetary control is the periodic, usually monthly, comparison of spending against the budget. This requires converting an annual budget into a profile of approximately how each budget is expected to be spent. Large parts of local government budgets can easily be profiled

In units of currency	Comparison of Budget to Actual Year ended [*date of financial statements*], 20xx			
	Original budget	Revised budget	Actual	Difference: under (over)
Revenues				
Taxes	xxx,xxx	xxx,xxx	xxx,xxx	x,xxx
Grants	xxx,xxx	xxx,xxx	xxx,xxx	(x,xxx)
Charges for services	xx,xxx	xx,xxx	xx,xxx	(xxx)
Total revenues	x,xxx,xxx	x,xxx,xxx	x,xxx,xxx	x,xxx
Spending				
General government	xxx,xxx	xxx,xxx	xxx,xxx	x,xxx
Department A	xxx,xxx	xxx,xxx	xxx,xxx	x,xxx
Department B	xxx,xxx	xxx,xxx	xxx,xxx	x,xxx
Department C	xxx,xxx	xxx,xxx	xxx,xxx	(x,xxx)
Total expenditure	x,xxx,xxx	x,xxx,xxx	x,xxx,xxx	(x,xxx)
Total net expenditure	x,xxx,xxx	x,xxx,xxx	x,xxx,xxx	x,xxx

Source: Author's illustration.

FIGURE 1.1 Year-End Budget Report

(salaries, financing charges, running expenses that are contracted to be paid for at specified dates), but for some items profiling can be difficult. Nevertheless, budget profiling is necessary to avoid what would otherwise be a continual questioning of budget holders about why their spending was not in a simple sense proportionate.

Accounting Bases

Cash accounting, or a basis of accounting that is close to cash, is traditional in government. In some parts of some governments, commitment accounting is also used. In addition, some form of fund accounting is commonly adopted.

Cash-Based Accounting

Cash-based accounting exclusively emphasizes accounting for transactions—what matters are the individual records of each transaction. Periodically, these records are summarized (weekly, monthly, and annual receipts and payments) and classified (monthly salary payments, monthly running expenses, monthly tax receipts), often to compare against budgets. These records are the foundation of all accounting systems, for all kinds of organizations (and individuals). They emphasize an accounting that is based on verification—fact-based verifiable transactions. An important part of this verification is reconciliation of the accounting with the local government's bank accounts. Cash accounting provides operating statements (payments minus receipts) and very simple balance sheets (cash balance).

Figures 1.2 and 1.3 provide examples of two financial statements under cash-based accounting. In both cases, the local government could also include the comparable figures for the immediately preceding financial year.

Pure cash-based accounting recognizes transactions only when cash flows out of, or into, the local government. However, in all but the very simplest of transactions, an accounting system could usefully recognize other events in the life of a transaction. Three events commonly used for purchases are goods or services ordered, goods or services received with invoice, and cash paid. Usually only two events for income earned are recognized: goods or services provided with invoice and cash received. Recognition of goods and services ordered is called commitment accounting and is discussed in the next section. Recognition of goods and services received or provided is usually judged necessary in any credit economy, in which all but the simplest transactions are based on credit given or received. A cash-based accounting of purchase transactions on credit might recognize that, along with cash

Statement of Cash Receipts and Payments Year ended [*date of financial statements*], 20xx	
	Unit of currency
Receipts	
Taxes	xxx,xxx
Grants	xxx,xxx
Borrowing	x,xxx,xxx
Receipts from trading activities	xx,xxx
Total receipts	x,xxx,xxx
Payments	
Salaries, wages, and other employee payments	x,xxx,xxx
Supplies and consumables	xxx,xxx
Grants	xx,xxx
Capital payments	xxx,xxx
Total payments	x,xxx,xxx
Increase (decrease) in cash	x,xxx
Cash balance at beginning of year	xx,xxx
Cash balance at end of year	xx,xxx

Source: Author's illustration.

FIGURE 1.2 Operating Statement under Cash Accounting Based on Line Items

payments, debts have been incurred by receiving goods and services with an invoice. In such an accounting, the operating statement records goods and services received (made up of cash payments plus or minus the change between opening and closing payables [creditors]), minus receipts; and the balance sheet records closing payables as well as cash balance.

Cash-based accounting might also recognize income transactions on credit, in which case the operating statement would also record income earned from goods and services provided (made up of cash receipts plus or minus the change between opening and closing receivables [debtors]) and the balance sheet would be extended to record closing receivables. In cases in which the local government "earns" income from goods and services, such an accounting would be useful.

However, significant proportions of a local government's income tend to consist of grants from other governments, including the national government, and taxation. Cash accounting for these kinds of income is useful and straightforward; recognition of receivables and payables might be useful but is also usually difficult. The general sense of the word "transaction" suggests

Statement of Payments Year ended [*date of financial statements*], 20xx	Unit of currency
Payments	
Operating	
Service A	xxx,xxx
Service B	xxx,xxx
Service C	x,xxx,xxx
Other	xx,xxx
Total operating payments	x,xxx,xxx
Capital	
Service A	x,xxx,xxx
Service B	xxx,xxx
Service C	xx,xxx
Other	xxx,xxx
Total capital payments	x,xxx,xxx
Total operating and cash payments	x,xxx,xxx

Source: Author's illustration.

FIGURE 1.3 Statement of Payments under Cash Accounting Detailing Operating and Capital Payments

the difficulties. A transaction implies at least two parties, each one having received something and given something up. When a local government receives grants or taxes, what is given up and when? And the corollary, when a government, other organization, or individual pays grants or taxes to a local government, what is received and when? There are three aspects to these difficulties. First, the point at which a grant or tax becomes due is much less verifiable, because it is much more a matter of opinion than with goods and services sold. One might argue that this point is totally verifiable because it is the point at which an invoice is issued, but the obvious response is that the point at which the invoice is issued is also a matter of opinion. Second, the accounting system has to confront the additional uncertainty involved in judging whether the grant or tax "due" will be received in cash. Even in cash accounting, uncertainty arises because the receipt of cash does not necessarily mean that the transaction is complete: there could be adjustments subsequent to, and sometimes distantly subsequent to, the receipt. Third, in settings in which politicians, service providers, and service recipients often have insatiable demands for more services, accounting systems typically have a bias toward prudence, so that expenses are overestimated and income underestimated.

For most elements of a typical local government accounting system, it would be prudent to recognize goods and services when received and before payments are made but to recognize income only when cash is received.

Discussion of cash-based accounting raises the question, even in large contemporary governments, of bookkeeping systems, and specifically whether double-entry bookkeeping systems are necessary. The increasing dominance of IT systems will render this question irrelevant, but in practice there are settings in which the question is important. In principle, pure cash accounting can be efficiently and effectively carried out with a single-entry system. However, recognition of invoices received necessitates double-entry bookkeeping, at a minimum to harness its undoubted benefits of self-balancing.

Commitment Accounting

An accounting system that recognizes goods and services ordered by the local government is called commitment accounting.[4] In principle, an accounting system could be devised that recognizes goods and services ordered from the local government but such a system would be unlikely to be useful. The main purpose of commitment accounting is in budgetary control; indeed, one of its main difficulties is its relationship to financial reporting.

Commitment accounting provides a more useful record of "spending" against a budget, for both the budget holder and those with higher responsibility for budgetary control, than either records of goods and services received (which are strictly unnecessary for commitment accounting), or of cash paid (which are necessary for all accounting systems). It records spending at the earlier point at which an official order is issued for the supply of goods or services, thereby recording a commitment by the budget holder and therefore by the local government to receive the goods or services in the stated quantity, at the stated price. Because commitment accounting depends on orders being issued, it applies only to parts of a local government budget, though it can relate to many small transactions: the parts to which it generally does not apply are employee expenses, financing expenses, and those running costs (such as gas, electricity, telephones) that are supplied without recurring orders.

The logic of commitment accounting is that the budget holder wants to spend the budget, neither underspending nor overspending. Although not always rational, typically more severe penalties apply to overspending than to underspending. Given that the practical imperative is not to overspend, an accounting system more prudent than cash-based accounting recognizes

51 91,229.

spending when orders are issued, rather than later when goods or services are received and paid for.

Three main problems trouble commitment accounting: under certain circumstances it can be costly and unreliable, and its usefulness can be questioned. It clearly adds to the complexity of accounting given that it must always be in addition to cash accounting; when it is also used in conjunction with a system that records goods and services received, the complexity is even greater. Not only must there be additional records for each transaction but also the record of goods issued would not necessarily be the same as the record of goods received, simply because the quantity of goods that arrive may not be what was ordered—and the price may be different. Any given transaction may begin at one cost when the goods are ordered, have to be adjusted to another when the goods are received, and end with yet another when the goods are paid for. Because commitment accounting tends to reflect numerous relatively small transactions, the additional entries and corrections can produce significant complexity.

Commitment accounting can be less reliable than cash-based accounting in budgetary control. If a budget holder sees that the budget for a period—especially for a year—is going to be underspent (measured by orders issued), commitment accounting provides easy opportunities to spend up to the budget merely by issuing orders. In principle, the term "merely" is inappropriate because issuing an official order is not a trivial matter; it would normally mean committing the local government to receiving the goods and paying for them. In practice, however, the uncertainty naturally occurring between the order and the payment can be exploited in different ways to spend a budget artificially. These ways range from the reasonably acceptable (ordering slightly before the goods are required) to the unacceptable (ordering goods that are not going to be received or paid for). This potential weakness of commitment accounting is overcome by increased monitoring by the controllers of the budget and by auditors, but at additional cost.

Commitment accounting becomes less useful from the perspective of financial reporting. A local government could not issue an annual external financial report for general use that defined its spending against its budget to include goods and services ordered but not received, simply because "spending" would be too easy to manipulate. The consequence is that internal financial reports monitoring spending against budgets would record goods and services ordered but not received, but the reports would have to be taken out of the definition of spending for an external financial report. As a result, the local government reports two measures of spending, one for internal and one for external use. Because the imperative of the one for internal use is to spend as nearly as possible to the budget, the one for external use (using the altered measure of spending) is likely to show underspending. Budget holders who want to increase their budgets might want to use this anomaly in negotiating subsequent budgets.

Fund Accounting

A central issue in accounting is the definition of the "reporting entity." This term is most commonly used in the context of external financial reporting and, while it has always been significant, has taken on greater importance as organizations have, legally and managerially, become more complex aggregations. The term does, however, have significance in the internal accounting for any organization. In business, the main issues relating to the reporting entity for external financial reporting contrast reporting for one company with reporting consolidated financial statements for a group of companies; within companies or groups of companies, debates would center on the adoption of cost centers, profit centers, and investment centers.

In government accounting, the more common issue relates to the use of funds and any subsequent consolidation of those funds, in either internal or external accounting. In this sense, a fund is a pool of resources assigned to a particular purpose and initially kept separate from other pools of resources; fund accounting then provides, in the pure case, a self-contained set of financial statements for each fund. Fund accounting is a consequence of the traditional focus on financial control and is a technical response to the instinct to designate money for specific purposes. It satisfies a demand for separate accounting for separate kinds of resources.

In local government, distinguishing between different kinds of income, with consequent distinctions between how each kind can be spent, is common—distinctions are made between income from a general property tax and a dedicated tax (the tax is assigned to be spent in a particular way before it is collected), between taxes and grants, between different kinds of grants, between loans and other income, between user charges and other income. It is common for the provider of a loan or grant to impose the distinction explicitly, or for the general law to impose the distinction on general or specific taxes. It is also common for local governments themselves to want to make distinctions, perhaps between resources that can be used only in the long term and those that can be used in the short term. In some contexts, those distinctions that are externally imposed are called restrictions; internally imposed are called designations. Both distinctions are natural but often introduce complexity. Although the source of income may be clear, many functions of a particular local government are carried out jointly, requiring difficult and arbitrary allocations of costs between funds, as well as other transfers between funds.

The main source of contention in fund accounting is not in the use of funds (although there has been debate about the number of funds one organization needs given that funds can proliferate), but rather in whether there should be, or to what extent there should be, consolidation of those funds, especially in external financial reports for general use. The main problem with fund accounting is that it can conflict with a view of the local government as a whole. While a provider of a specific grant may have understandable needs to see clearly how that grant is spent, the taxpayer (whether local or national) has an equally understandable need to see how the grant is spent in relation to the local government as whole, especially because the taxpayer is bearing the ultimate risk of that local government. In fact, given the complexities of fund accounting, the provider of the grant also ought to understand how the grant is spent in the context of the other funds. The same is true of a lender, even when the loan has a specific charge on particular assets. A lender whose loans are secured by the taxable capacity of the local government obviously needs to see the local government as a whole.

However, consolidation of funds in financial statements, by its nature, obscures the individual funds and can mislead. Resources that the consolidated financial statements appear to suggest are available to be spent on any purpose (perhaps to the general benefit of the community) may be legally restricted to narrow purposes; or resources only available in the long term may appear to be available to be spent now. If there were no constraint on the length and complexity of financial statements, the solution would always be to provide both individual fund and consolidated financial statements. There is a constraint, however, and the increasing tendency is for the external financial statements to be consolidated, if not wholly then in part, with the fund statements being provided separately for specific needs.

Expanding Traditional Functions

The traditional functions of accounting and reporting have been challenged in recent decades by accrual accounting, accrual budgeting, and output measurement.

Accrual Accounting

The meaning of the term "accrual accounting" (sometimes called accruals accounting) can vary considerably, in theory and practice. In its fullest sense, accrual accounting is the comprehensive and continuous recording of all revenues, expenses, assets, liabilities, and cash flows of the local government. Accrual accounting affects the recording of transactions, the periodic internal financial statements, and the published financial statements. A prerequisite of accrual accounting systems is a comprehensive record of assets owned (which usually does not exist in extant local government accounting systems) and of liabilities incurred (which probably does, except that contingent liabilities are usually not recorded).

The meaning of "comprehensive" is still controversial. The traditional basis of all accounting was historical cost. In business accounting practice, historical costs are changed to some form of current value (increasingly referred to as "fair value") in many ways; however, a comprehensive system of current-value accounting, while it has been experimented with in the past, is not part of extant practice. In some of the new government accounting systems that have adopted accrual accounting, a wider use of current-value accounting is in use, even if stopping short of being wholly comprehensive.

The chapter has discussed that cash accounting can be extended to recognize payables and receivables, increasing the number of items in the balance sheet with consequent effects on the operating statement. Accrual-based accounting recognizes more items. Recognition of payables means that, in addition to the measurement of cash outflows, the accounting system provides a measure of goods and services *received*. The most obvious next step for accrual accounting is to recognize inventories, so that the accounting system provides a measure of goods and services *used* (by adjusting cost of goods and services received for changes in the opening and closing inventories); in this, the accounting system also provides a measure of inventories held. In many parts of a local government's budget, such adjustments might not produce material change in the measure of costs, in which case they would not be made. Inventory valuation is often not without measurement difficulties, but there have long been routine methods of dealing with them.

In the assets section of the balance sheet, another major item that a full accrual accounting would recognize is depreciation on depreciable assets. This, as with inventories, is concerned with including in the cost of service provided a relevant measure of goods and services used. Clear examples of depreciable assets are equipment and vehicles. Accrual accounting provides a valuation of the depreciable assets for the balance sheet and a charge to the operating statement for the period's depreciation.

However, other classes of assets are less clearly defined as depreciable. One such is often referred to as heritage assets (a site of historical importance, for example), meaning assets that are not normally going to be sold, cannot be replaced, and, while they may require conservation, do not depreciate in the normal sense; some would insist that such assets cannot and should not have a financial value assigned to them. Another is infrastructure assets (water pipes, for example) for which it has been argued that a systematic engineering plan to maintain the assets, with consequent maintenance costs at planned points in the future, provides a more relevant measure of cost than a depreciation charge would. In fact, this argument has more generally been applied to buildings: as long as the useful economic life of a building is maintained indefinitely, a depreciation charge is obviated.

Also in the assets section are assets that are not depreciable and, therefore, that do not have a direct effect on operating costs, but that should be recorded in the balance sheet to provide a comprehensive account of assets owned. The clearest example is land, which under normal circumstances is not depreciated. Other examples would include those assets that in some circumstances might be depreciated, but that have been judged not to be depreciable.

In the liabilities section, all explicit liabilities would be recorded, in addition to the short-term payables that a cash-based system might recognize. The most significant effect on the operating statement would usually be any consequent charge for interest, on an accrual basis. Rather than recording the interest payments made, as the operating statement under cash-based accounting would, a full accrual accounting would record the interest due on all liabilities.

Figures 1.4, 1.5, and 1.6 give examples of the three main accrual-based financial statements. If these statements were presented in accordance with IPSAS, they would have comparative figures for the immediately preceding financial year. The accrual-based operating statement in figure 1.5 could also be presented giving expenses classified by what was purchased (salaries, wages, supplies, and so forth).

Because of the importance of cash in any organization, accrual-based financial statements are accompanied by a statement of cash flows. The ideal form of this statement draws the figures directly from the cash accounts (hence known as the direct method). Figure 1.7 is an example.

Although a literal interpretation of the term "accrual accounting" does not necessarily require each organization to produce one set of consolidated financial statements, that production is the usual expectation. Because all but the smallest local governments are complex, this consolidation has to be based on a determination of which entities should be included in it and which should not. The typical dilemma is between adopting the criterion of "ownership," which might produce a legal determination, or the criterion of "control," which might produce a political or economic one.

Statement of Financial Position at [*date of financial statements*], 20xx	*Unit of currency*
ASSETS	
Current assets	
Cash and cash equivalents	xxx,xxx
Receivables (debtors)	xxx,xxx
Inventories (stock)	xxx,xxx
Prepayments	xx,xxx
Investments	xx,xxx
Total current assets	x,xxx,xxx
Noncurrent assets	
Receivables (debtors)	x,xxx,xxx
Investments	xxx,xxx
Other financial assets	xx,xxx
Infrastructure, plant, and equipment	xx,xxx
Land and buildings	xxx,xxx
Total noncurrent assets	x,xxx,xxx
Total assets	x,xxx,xxx
LIABILITIES	
Current liabilities	
Payables (creditors)	xxx,xxx
Short-term borrowing	xx,xxx
Current portion of long-term borrowing	xx,xxx
Provisions	x,xxx
Total current liabilities	xxx,xxx
Noncurrent liabilities	
Payables (creditors)	xxx,xxx
Long-term borrowing	xxx,xxx
Provisions	xx,xxx
Total noncurrent liabilities	xxx,xxx
Total liabilities	x,xxx,xxx
Total net assets	x,xxx,xxx
NET ASSETS	
Capital contributed by the government	xxx,xxx
Reserves	xxx,xxx
Accumulated surpluses (deficits)	xx,xxx
Total net assets	x,xxx,xxx

Source: Author's illustration.

FIGURE 1.4   Accrual-Based Statement of Financial Position

Statement of Financial Performance	
Year ended [*date of financial statements*], 20xx	
	Unit of currency
Operating revenue	
Taxes	xxx,xxx
Fees	xxx,xxx
Grants	x,xxx,xxx
Other	xx,xxx
Total operating revenue	x,xxx,xxx
Operating expenses	
General	x,xxx,xxx
Service A	xxx,xxx
Service B	xx,xxx
Service C	xx,xxx
Total operating expenses	x,xxx,xxx
Surplus (deficit) from operating activities	xxx,xxx
Finance costs	xx,xxx
Gains on sale of equipment	xx,xxx
Total nonoperating revenue (expense)	xxx,xxx
Net surplus (deficit) before extraordinary items	xxx,xxx
Extraordinary Items	(xx,xxx)
Net surplus (deficit) for the year	x,xxx,xxx

Source: Author's illustration.

FIGURE 1.5 Accrual-Based Operating Statement

Accrual accounting is often discussed in the context of the financial accounting and reporting system, which is where accrual adjustments would be made in the first instance. But the need for comprehensive measures of revenues, expenses, assets, liabilities, and cash flows is as important for the internal management accounts, so that managers have a complete accounting of their actions.

Accrual accounting in government is not without controversy but its benefits are obvious. Cash-based accounting systems provide a limited view even of the economic events affecting a government. Most important, they cannot provide measures of the cost of services provided in any meaningful economic sense—only accrual accounting can. In practice, accrual accounting may fall short of the ideal, especially when the accrual accounting is historic cost accounting. Notable examples of government accounting now adopt forms of current-value accounting.

Statement of Changes in Net Assets

Year ended [*date of financial statements*], 20xx

In units of currency	Contributed capital	Revaluation reserve	Accumulated surpluses (deficits)	Total
Opening balance	x,xxx,xxx	xx,xxx	x,xxx,xxx	x,xxx,xxx
Changes in accounting policy	(xxx)	n.a.	(xxx)	(xxx)
Restated opening balance	x,xxx,xxx	xx,xxx	x,xxx,xxx	x,xxx,xxx
Surplus on revaluation of property	n.a.	x,xxx	n.a.	x,xxx
Deficit on revaluation of investments	n.a.	(x,xxx)	n.a.	(x,xxx)
Net gains and losses recognized in the statement of financial performance	n.a.	xxx	n.a.	xxx
Net surplus (deficit) for the year	n.a.	n.a.	x,xxx,xxx	x,xxx,xxx
Closing balance	x,xxx,xxx	x,xxx,xxx	x,xxx,xxx	x,xxx,xxx

Source: Author's illustration.
Note: n.a. = Not applicable.

FIGURE 1.6 Accrual-Based Statement of Changes in Net Assets

Accrual accounting has an additional benefit over cash accounting: the latter is too easy to manipulate, in particular by postponing cash payments from one fiscal year to another. Furthermore, because any comprehensive system of accounting necessarily includes records of cash flows, in principle a full accrual-accounting system only enhances any existing cash-based accounting system and takes nothing away.

Clear benefits always impose costs. Accrual accounting requires greater accounting sophistication, necessitating increased education and training, as well as more sophisticated hardware and software. Moreover, whether the accrual accounting is based on historic costs or current costs, it is by its nature replete with arbitrary judgments. Finally, although accounting standards and auditing limit the scope for producing diverse measures from the same data, they by no means eradicate it.

Accrual Budgeting

The case for accrual budgeting follows from an accrual-accounting system. Because budget-to-actual comparisons, whether formal or informal, are fundamental, if the actuals are accrual based then so must the budget be. However, accrual budgeting as a term and as a practice is neither well known

Cash Flow Statement	
Year ended [*date of financial statements*], 20xx	
	Unit of currency
CASH FLOWS FROM OPERATING ACTIVITIES	
Receipts	
Taxes	xxx,xxx
Sales of goods and services	xxx,xxx
Grants	x,xxx,xxx
Other	xx,xxx
Payments	
Employee costs	(x,xxx,xxx)
Suppliers	(xxx,xxx)
Interest paid	(xx,xxx)
Other payments	(xx,xxx)
Net cash flows from operating activities	x,xxx,xxx
CASH FLOWS FROM INVESTING ACTIVITIES	
Purchase of equipment	(xx,xxx)
Proceeds from sale of equipment	xx,xxx
Net cash flows from investing activities	xxx,xxx
CASH FLOWS FROM FINANCING ACTIVITIES	
Proceeds from loans	xxx,xxx
Repayment of loans	(xxx,xxx)
Net cash flows from financing activities	xx,xxx
Net increase (decrease) in cash and cash equivalents	xx,xxx
Cash and cash equivalents at beginning of year	xx,xxx
Cash and cash equivalents at end of year	xx,xxx

Source: Author's illustration.

FIGURE 1.7 Cash Flow Statement under the Direct Method

nor well understood. In business accounting, although the term is not used, the practice is familiar: it is that part of budgeting that produces estimated income statements and balance sheets. Transferring this practice to government budgeting, in which the budgets have traditionally been cash based, requires a significant change in the way that budget holders think about "spending." To take one example, under a full accrual basis, spending would include a charge for depreciation of depreciable assets; many budget holders would need persuading that this was part of their spending.

In practice, accrual accounting has often been introduced as a separate accounting system from budgetary accounting, which remains on a commitment basis and a cash basis.[5] The pragmatic attraction is the wealth of additional data provided in the accrual accounts. These data do not necessarily change the way that a government functions, not least because the budgets still occupy most people's attention when concerned with financial matters.

Output Measurement

In recent decades, measurement in government has increased inexorably. More financial measures have been produced and published, as have more nonfinancial measures. Producing the measures has posed little difficulty and, given the availability of computing, their storage and reproduction have become easy. This increase in measurement has a fundamental premise: given scarce resources, explicit measurement of the quantity, if not the quality, of services provided, linked to measurement of resources consumed, produces better services.

The emphasis of public sector auditing is on probity (also referred to as regularity), more specifically on whether spending has been proper and whether the spending has conformed to the budget. Often explicit, though sometimes implicit, in this kind of audit is a certification of financial statements.

To audit the propriety of spending, one must make judgments about the quality and quantity of services provided but, because these elements were not always measured, their role in auditing was tacit. This role changed in the early 1970s with the formalization of the idea that, in addition to the regularity of spending and the certification of financial statements, govern-ment auditors must take a stance on the quality and quantity of services provided in light of resources consumed. Subsequently, the phrases "value for money auditing" and "performance auditing" became commonplace. However, auditors were often not required to offer opinions on the perform-ance of governments, but rather were required to offer opinions on whether governments had installed suitable systems for allowing the governments to judge their own performance. In this way, audit stimulated an explosion of performance measurement, soon followed by explicit treatment of quality issues—although the governments themselves often developed the measures.

Output measures emphasizing "economy," "efficiency," and "effectiveness" are useful in the absence of natural measures of performance, such as profit, in a local government. Economy refers to least cost; efficiency compares, in different ways, inputs and low-level (or intermediate) outputs; effectiveness refers to higher-level outputs. The three ideas have to be used in conjunction with one another. Low-level and high-level outputs describe the hierarchical nature of outputs from any service: all outputs are relevant but the low-level outputs have limited relevance (but are easier to measure) and the higher-level outputs have wider relevance (but are harder to measure). The same trade-off observed in traditional accounting systems—greater relevance at the sacrifice of some reliability—can be observed in output measurement. In the extreme case, no set of measures, however sophisticated, can capture everything about a service provided; in this case, "outcome" is used to refer to the extremely important but unmeasurable results of service provision.

Applying these terms to a refuse collection service financed not by user fees but by general taxation, effectiveness asks one to consider whether the service provided is appropriate for the local community, incorporating measures of higher-level outputs perhaps by surveying users. Efficiency judges whether the ratio between the lower-level outputs, such as the number of collections made per week, and the cost of those collections (unit cost per collection) was optimal. Economy ought not, in principle, be a relevant idea, because if the service is judged to be efficient and effective that should be enough. However, public money is usually in short supply. Given that judgments about outputs are always uncertain and that shortages can be severe, economy can dominate the other ideas in asking one to judge whether the service was provided as cheaply as it could have been, with only minor emphasis on whether the service was efficient and effective.

Output measurement is, therefore, necessary to provide as full a view as possible about performance. Generating and publishing unit cost statistics, in which the outputs are at such a low level that they are properly considered measures of input (costs per pupil in a school, for example), are relatively easy, as are low-level measures of output on their own (pupil-to-teacher ratios, for example). However, making judgments about overall performance is difficult. Formal, auditable records of the measures are required; but even when the reliability of the measures is satisfactory, the more difficult question concerns their relevance to overall performance. One tendency has been to produce too many low-level measures, in trying to capture as many of the complexities as possible; this can produce confusion, given that the relationship of each of the low-level measures to performance as a whole is made more complicated. Generally speaking, erring on the side of producing a few key measures of output but using great caution in interpreting them is the better route.

Cash-based accounting cannot contribute to measures of efficiency in any meaningful sense. Accrual accounting can, by providing measures of costs of service provided, which can then be compared with measures of quantity and quality of output to produce measures of performance. As the adoption of accrual accounting has increased, so have requirements to publish such measures and, at least by implication, to use these measures in the management of organizations. The associated audit requirements may have been the stimulus, and may continue to be; yet, there are settings in which higher-level governments have required lower-level governments to use specific performance measures using specific bases.

Data for National Accounting

Local government accounting, as with all other accounting, is concerned with accounting for one organization, at one point. At the same time, each country has a system of statistics about its economy, ultimately collected, measured, and communicated by the government. All economic activity is included and one classification is economic activity by each sector of the economy. One of those sectors is the government itself, which includes local governments. This statistical system is known as "national accounting" (somewhat confusingly because it is not accounting in the accounting profession's sense). National accounting is now a harmonized and standardized system, deriving its theoretical framework from economics, while being carried out by government statisticians; many of the statistics are derived from accounting data.

The global system is called the System of National Accounts and is promulgated by all the major international bodies concerned (including the United Nations, the International Monetary Fund, and the World Bank). This national and regional accounting is used to monitor the national economies of the world; the International Monetary Fund also uses its own system of government finance statistics (whose central focus is on imports and exports).

National accounting is distinctly different from accounting, even though both systems are in part addressing the same economic activities of local government. National accounting, by its nature, demands comparable information across all local governments in each economy. Local government accrual accounting—also by its nature—cannot provide such information. This contradiction is essentially avoided by using statistical processes. However, the needs of national accounting suggest that local government accounting systems with uniform classifications would, at least for those purposes, be preferred.

National accounting is accrual based, although it uses different accrual bases from those used in any government accounting. However, the use of accrual accounting in local government accounting systems would significantly improve the reliability of national accounting. One obvious example is that a government that adopted accrual accounting would, probably for the first time, generate reliable measures of depreciation of depreciable assets. In its absence, under cash-based accounting systems, national accounting has to make inferences about depreciation. Hence, given the increasing profile of national accounting, improvements in its methods might stimulate accrual-based government accounting.

Financial Reporting Standards

Accrual accounting requires financial reporting standards. A set of international public sector accounting standards has been developed in recent years.

International Public Sector Accounting Standards

IPSAS are a set of measurement and disclosure policies (that is not exhaustive and that explicitly allows choices) for financial reporting on an accrual basis, for use by the governmental organizations of the world. They are based on historical cost but allow use of current values. IPSAS will potentially lead to two kinds of change—the first toward accrual accounting in each government, the second toward standardized accrual accounting across governments.

IPSAS are a product of the accounting profession, more specifically, of what was a committee and is now a board (the International Public Sector Accounting Standards Board, IPSASB) of the International Federation of Accountants (IFAC). Because IFAC's member bodies come from more than 100 different countries, it represents many different social, political, economic, and legal contexts. However, in its own words it is "the global organization for the accountancy profession," with a mission in the public interest "to strengthen the worldwide accountancy profession and contribute to the development of strong international standards by establishing and promoting adherence to high-quality professional standards, furthering the international convergence of such standards" (IFAC 2006). A similar body represents the accounting profession in Europe, with overlapping membership with IFAC, called the European Federation of Accountants (known, from the French, as FEE), which has a public sector committee, and which supports IPSAS. The same is to be expected of the individual professional accounting bodies that are members of IFAC and FEE.

IPSASB issues standards (required to be followed), guidelines (recommended), studies (providing advice and including study of best practices), and occasional papers. It has issued 21 standards on accrual accounting and a standard on the cash basis of accounting, which includes requirements under the cash basis, as well as illustrative financial statements and requirements relating to consolidated financial statements. The cash-basis IPSAS also includes additional disclosures in financial reports that are encouraged rather than required.

IPSAS are explicitly based on International Accounting Standards (IAS). (Since 2001, newly issued standards have been known as International Financial Reporting Standards [IFRS]). IAS were a product of the accounting profession, specifically of the International Accounting Standards Committee, which had the same membership as IFAC but which had administrative headquarters in London. IFRS are now produced by the International Accounting Standards Board, which is a body independent of the accounting profession, legally incorporated in the United States but still with its administrative headquarters in London. IAS were originally written for businesses. Their primary focus is on reporting by companies to investors and creditors; indeed, some standards are even more narrowly concerned with the reporting of companies listed on stock exchanges. IPSAS are now being produced that relate to specific governmental issues not addressed by IAS or IFRS.

Currently, IPSASB's first priority is to develop standards on issues that specifically relate to the public sector (for example, heritage assets, nonexchange transactions including taxes and transfers, and social policies of governments). Its second priority is to continue the convergence of IPSAS with IAS and IFRS when appropriate for the public sector. Its third priority is convergence of its standards with the statistical bases of national accounting.

IPSAS, notwithstanding their name, are narrower than accounting standards: they are standards of financial reporting. They are recognizably part of the Anglo-American tradition in which a codified set of accrual-based measurement and disclosure policies is published widely, after due process, by a nonprofit, nongovernmental, and nonpolitical body with the self-proclaimed responsibility to make the rules but without the direct power to enforce them. In a local government context, such power tends to come from a higher-level government or from a lender or donor.

Although IPSAS are rules about financial reporting, implicit in them is the requirement to have accounting systems that are capable of producing reliable, accrual-based financial statements. Probably because of the provenance of IPSAS, they do not address accrual budgeting. IPSASB has not yet produced a conceptual framework for its standards.

Summary

Management of other people's money is a heavy burden; managing public money even heavier. The traditional focus of local government accounting— on the proper recording of transactions and on control of spending against a budget—should not change. However, much more information can now be provided in a government accounting system without reducing its traditional focus, including economically relevant measures of cost of service provided, with clear segregation of capital and current costs, and comprehensive measures of indebtedness and of assets employed. Thus, substantially widened measures of government performance are facilitated. All of these can be provided in budgets as well as in financial statements.

Accrual budgeting and accounting, in their fullest sense, are the comprehensive and continuous recording of all revenues, expenses, assets, liabilities, and cash flows of the organization: they affect the recording of transactions, the internal financial statements, and the published financial statements. Moreover, while the traditional basis of all accounting is historical cost, current value is gaining ever-wider use.

The costs of this additional information are not trivial. The necessary IT systems are becoming much more freely available but storing and retrieving data are only one part of the process. Understanding the subsequent information is also required, and this requires investment in education and training. The availability of IPSAS helps reduce the costs and provides a unique opportunity to further the cause of convergence in the government accounting systems of the world. Comprehensive, standardized accrual-based accounting systems in local governments will emerge only in the distant future, but many of their additional elements are being developed by individual, and groups of, organizations.

One dominant theme in the sometimes bewildering changes in governmental accounting and budgeting over the past 50 years, as the size and complexity of the public sector have continued to grow, is the increasing reluctance of those at the center of each government to bear the financial risks of that government. This reluctance has led to increasing recognition of those risks, as well as to formal devolution of some of them from one level of government down to another, and from one level of government down to other entities. IT and accounting have made this recognition possible and will be central to its understanding.

Notes

1. A comprehensive treatment, in English, of the theory and practice of government accounting in continental Europe has only very recently become available. Lüder and Jones (2003) describe, for the core government services, government accounting and budgeting in each of nine countries, at national and local levels (and state or regional levels, when applicable), in their current and prospective forms. The nine countries addressed are Finland, France, Germany, Italy, the Netherlands, Spain, Sweden,

Switzerland, and the United Kingdom. The book explains that much of continental European practice is diverse, between countries and within them, but that continental Europe's heavy reliance on the law is fundamentally different from much of Anglo-American local government accounting. The book also shows in all of the nine countries under study that local government accounting is now accrual based. However, because there is no imperative for these accrual accounting reforms to be standardized, they are at different stages of implementation and are being implemented in different ways.

2. Continental European practice typically imposes this as part of a uniform "chart of accounts."
3. This view is not to deny that some existing single-entry systems may be sound in providing the traditional focus of government accounting or that in specific cases the costs of converting them to double entry may not yet be worth bearing.
4. In the United States, the equivalent term for commitment is encumbrance.
5. This system is especially true of some continental European systems.

References and Other Resources

International Public Sector Accounting Standards Board (IPSASB) of the International Federation of Accountants (IFAC). 2006. *2006 Handbook of International Public Sector Accounting Standards.* http://www.ifac.org.

Jones, R. 2002. "Public Sector Accounting." In *The International Encyclopedia of Business and Management*, 2nd ed., ed. M. Warner, 5454–62. London: Thomson Learning.

Jones, R., and J. Craner. 1990. "Accrual Accounting for National Governments: The Case of Developing Countries." *Research in Third World Accounting* 1: 103–13.

Jones, R., and M. Pendlebury. 2000. *Public Sector Accounting*, 5th ed. London: Financial Times/Prentice Hall.

Lüder, K., and R. Jones, eds. 2003. *Reforming Governmental Accounting and Budgeting in Europe.* Frankfurt: Fachverlag Moderne Wirtschaft.

Tanzi, V., and T. Prakash. 2003. "The Cost of Government and the Misuse of Public Assets." In *Public Finance in Developing and Transitional Countries*, ed. J. Martinez-Vazquez and J. Alm, 129–45. Cheltenham, UK: Elgar.

United Nations Statistics Division. 1993. *System of National Accounts.* New York: United Nations.

2

Local Government Cash Management

M. CORINNE LARSON

Cash management as a public finance discipline has changed significantly over the years. Before the 1970s, most cash man agement activities involved paying bills and collecting fees, fines, and other revenues. Excess funds sat idle in bank checking accounts or were invested in local bank certificates of deposit. Beginning in the 1970s, citizens began demanding more services from local governments while concurrently rebelling against increased taxes. The demand for more services and shrinking revenues caused finance officials to develop ways to maximize the use of their funds. At the same time, interest rates began to rise and eventually reached a peak on March 30, 1980, when the federal funds rate (the rate banks charge one another for overnight loans) rose to 20 percent. Higher interest rates made more effective cash management practices worthwhile because the extra effort that went into actively managing cash balances was offset by increased investment income. Conversely, the new millennium saw interest rates fall to historic lows. The federal funds rate fell to 1 percent on June 30, 2003. The need to manage funds effectively was once again highlighted because many governments depend on investment income as an important revenue source, and lower interest rates significantly reduced investment earnings, causing many governments to suffer severe budgetary constraints.

The evolution of technology also has played an important role in changing cash management practices over the past two decades. The banking industry has created new products that allow depositors access to real-time account balance information and the ability to move funds electronically. The U.S. Federal Reserve System has improved check processing and expedited the availability of funds. Wall Street firms have designed new financial products that allow investors to earn higher yields on idle cash. All these factors have combined to make cash management an important part of the finance function.

The cash management function is generally housed in the finance office and can be the responsibility of a finance director or a treasurer, depending on the size and structure of the local government. One employee may handle the entire treasury function or several employees may be assigned to portions of this function. Larger governments, for example, may have treasury staff devoted to collecting revenues and other staff focused on investing funds, and assign disbursements and accounting and record-keeping functions to other staff members in the finance department.

The objectives of cash management involve bringing funds into the government's treasury as quickly as possible, paying the funds out as efficiently as possible, and making effective use of those funds until they are needed for operating expenses. On occasion, a government may find that it has a revenue shortfall during the fiscal year and may need to borrow funds to bridge this gap. The amount and timing of the borrowing may be the responsibility of the finance official in charge of cash management or may fall to another staff member such as the budget officer. Another related objective of cash management is to provide accurate and timely records to document the government's cash management activities. An example of the cash management cycle is shown in figure 2.1. The objectives of cash management are further explained in this chapter.

Collections

Revenue collection is one of the main functions of local governments. Local governments collect funds from a variety of revenue sources, including fines, fees, taxes, licenses, permits, and special assessments. Revenues should be received in a timely manner, credited to the proper fund, and deposited into the correct bank account as quickly as possible. In addition, governments should strive for high collection rates for all revenues owed and keep the payment-making process simple and easy for citizens.

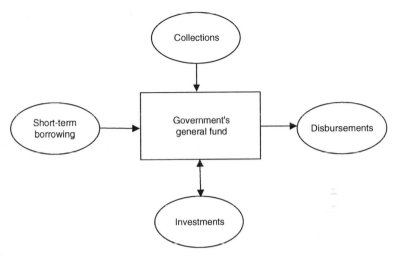

Source: Author.

FIGURE 2.1 Cash Management Cycle

Collection Methods

Local governments collect monies owed in a variety of forms, such as coin and currency, paper checks, credit card charges, Fedwire (an electronic payment system operated by the U.S. Federal Reserve System), or Automated Clearing House (ACH) credits (an electronic payment system that operates through a network of automated clearinghouses). Each form of collection has its own merits.

Coin and Currency

Over-the-counter collections of coin and currency allow a government to receive "good" funds, funds that are available for immediate use. The receipt of coin and currency, however, requires staff to count, wrap, and deposit cash into a local bank and may require the use of an armored car service, which is an additional expense to the government.

Paper Checks

Paper checks are the most common means of paying obligations. Local governments typically accept checks over the counter and by mail. Checks should be deposited in the bank the same day they are received. Depositing checks the day they are received helps expedite the availability of funds by getting the checks into the Federal Reserve payment system as quickly as possible. A drawback to accepting paper checks is the risk of "bad" checks—checks written on accounts with insufficient funds to cover the amount of the check. Collecting on bad checks can be a costly and time-consuming activity for a local government's staff.

Credit Card Payments

Credit card payments allow a government to receive funds in one day and are becoming more commonly used for fees and taxes. To accept credit card payments, a local government contracts with a credit card service provider and pays a discount fee on each transaction. A drawback to accepting credit cards is that a taxpayer can challenge a charge and the government could lose its funds through a charge-back by the credit card company. In addition, many governments cannot reduce the amount of taxes paid to cover the discount fee charged by the credit card companies, and credit card companies do not allow vendors to pass on the discount fee to the credit card holder. However, governments can impose a convenience fee for paying by credit card. This is a particularly common practice for Internet transactions. In addition to Internet transactions, credit card payments are commonly used for over-the-counter collections, telephone transactions, and mail-in payments.

Fedwires

Fedwires are electronic transfers operated by the Federal Reserve System. Funds sent by Fedwire are available for use immediately. Fedwires generally are used for large dollar payments because of the cost associated with them. Receiving a wire transfer can cost $9–$15 and sending a wire can cost $8–$20, depending on the sending method (telephone or personal computer) and if it is repetitive or nonrepetitive. A nonrepetitive wire is a one-time transaction and is more costly than a repetitive wire, which is a wire that is routinely sent and is set up with a code at the sender's bank to expedite the transaction.

ACH Transactions

ACH transactions take one day to become available funds and are a cost-effective means of collection. An ACH transaction is an electronic funds transfer that moves through a network of automated clearinghouses that operate similarly to the Federal Reserve's Fedwire system but at a fraction of the cost. For example, a Fedwire may cost $15 and an ACH transaction may cost $0.20. ACH transactions are typically used for online payments and allow citizens an alternative payment method. Online payments benefit a local government in several ways, including reduced staff time needed to provide face-to-face services, reduced incidences of bad checks, and faster availability of funds.

Objectives of a Collection System

The objectives of a collection system are to accelerate the receipt of available funds, safeguard the government's cash while it is in the government's possession, and keep banking costs to a minimum by having an appropriate account structure and restricting the number of bank accounts managed by outlying locations. To set up an effective collection system, governments should understand the concept of float and how float affects the availability of funds, and should produce timely and accurate reports.

Float

Float is the time it takes for a payee (the government) to receive funds available for use from a payer (the taxpayer). There are many types of float:

- Mail float is the time it takes for a check mailed by the payer to be received by the payee.
- Processing float is the time between receiving a check and depositing that check in the bank.
- Check-clearing float is the time between depositing a check and the check clearing the payer's bank account.
- Availability float is the time it takes for a deposited check to become usable funds.

How does float affect the collection process? Float can cost the government money because the government cannot benefit from funds received until those funds clear the payment-processing system and become usable funds. The benefit of reducing float can be seen in the following example: Assume a government collects $10 million in property tax from a corporation and the government's investment rate is 5.25 percent. By reducing float by two days, the government benefits by $2,917 on an annual basis:

$$(\$10 \text{ million} \times 2 \text{ days} \times 0.0525/360) = \$2,917$$

A government depositing a check from a taxpayer drawn on the same bank will receive same-day credit for the check, assuming that it is deposited before the bank's cutoff time. For example, if the check is deposited by noon and the bank's cutoff time is 2:00 p.m., the government will receive same-day credit. If that check is deposited at 3:00 p.m., the government will receive next-day credit. Checks drawn on the same bank where they are being deposited are referred to as "on-us" checks.

Assume a taxpayer uses a different bank in the same city. Typically, the government's bank will receive one-day availability on this check because it must go through a local clearinghouse before it becomes available funds.

Now assume a taxpayer is a corporation that uses an out-of-state bank. The corporation's check may take one or two days to become available funds, depending on what bank it uses and that bank's relationship to the government's bank. For example, if the two banks have a correspondent relationship, they will provide one-day credit on the funds. If the two banks do not have a relationship, then the out-of-town check will have to clear through the Federal Reserve System and be presented at the drawee's bank to become available funds. When this happens, the check may have one- or two-day availability depending on the Federal Reserve district in which the banks are located and on the government's bank's *availability schedule*. An availability schedule is a listing of how soon a bank will give credit for checks drawn in certain Federal Reserve districts.

In the past, check-clearing float and availability float could take up to seven days. Today, it generally takes less than three days for a check to become available funds. The Federal Reserve System has worked to eliminate risk in the payment system and the passage of the Check Clearing for the 21st Century Act (Check 21) in 2003 changed the way paper-based checks are processed.

Check 21 allows banks to convert a paper-based check into an electronic image, known as a substitute check, to expedite the movement of checks through the U.S. payment system by eliminating the physical transport of paper-based checks. When a local government receives a paper check, it is converted into an electronic image that is moved through the payment system. The electronic image carries the same information as the original paper check, which is destroyed when it is converted into an electronic image. Any future requests for a copy of a check are made from the electronic image. Check 21 makes the check-clearing process faster, and has helped reduce check-clearing float.

Availability of Funds

An important goal for any finance official is to improve the availability of funds. The more quickly funds can become available funds, the sooner the government can make use of those funds. Improved technology has allowed finance officials to maximize the availability of funds by electronic funds transfers. For example, governments that collect property taxes through an escrow agent can receive funds electronically and thus speed up the availability of funds. Many states have implemented electronic programs and pay local governments via the ACH system with next-day availability. This payment method is cost-effective for both the sender and receiver of funds.

Accuracy and Timeliness of Reporting

One of the most important components of any collection system is accurate and timely reporting. Local governments need financial management software that allows collection staff to update records frequently. Accurate, up-to-date information allows governments to pursue delinquent collections and avoid alienating citizens by eliminating outdated or inaccurate account information.

Collection System Design

Collection systems vary among governments depending on the type and size of the entity, the nature of revenues received, and the payment methods allowed. Some collection systems are centralized, which means that one department is responsible for all collections. Other systems are decentralized and each department collects its own revenues. The finance official should limit the number of offices that collect revenue and implement procedures that protect the government's funds and allow for efficient cash management practices.

Revenue Sources and Cost-Effective Collection Methods

Some governments make arrangements with local financial institutions to accept over-the-counter collection of taxes and other payments. This type of collection can speed up the availability of funds, help reduce the workload of the government, and tighten internal controls for the government by keeping paper checks out of the government's office.

Many governments with recreation centers, civic centers, golf courses, and other public services find accepting credit card payments to be cost beneficial even though they must pay a discount fee to credit card companies. A growing number of governments allow their citizens to pay for services online either directly or through vendors who accept secure Internet payments. Offering online services to citizens benefits governments in a number of ways, including reduced staff time providing face-to-face service, fewer problems with bad checks, and faster availability of funds. Credit card payments also benefit citizens by making payments more convenient and saving citizens time. For example, citizens can handle a number of transactions online such as license and permit renewals and enrollment in recreation programs.

An ACH credit for tax payments by corporations is an effective payment mechanism providing a service to both the government and the corporation. The corporation can keep its funds longer and know for certain when the tax payment will clear. The government will know that it is receiving funds on the due date and that those funds will be available funds in one day. By conducting a cost-benefit analysis, a government can determine which payment methods would be most effective for the types of revenue it collects.

Bank Balance Reporting

Finance officials need daily information on bank balances, cash receipts, and other transactions that affect their cash positions. Online reporting systems from banks are cost-effective ways to make sure the finance official knows exactly how much cash is collected and how much of that cash is available for immediate use or has one- or two-day float, for example. When bank account balances are reported through an electronic connection, finance staff can update the daily cash position worksheet, track check clearings, monitor automated payments such as debt-service payments, and record any electronic deposits. This type of information greatly improves the accuracy of record keeping and allows the government to manage its cash more effectively.

Lockboxes

One method used to collect checks is a lockbox. Lockboxes are common in the private sector but not so in the public sector, for a variety of reasons. One reason governments use lockboxes less frequently is that most taxpayers are located in the same or a nearby geographic area. Another reason is that many governments are restricted to using in-state banks and may be required by statute to physically receive a tax payment.

A lockbox is simply a post office box used to collect checks that are retrieved by a bank and processed around the clock to reduce float. Most lockboxes are situated in major cities to reduce mail float. Ideally, a lockbox would be established in a city or cities closest to customers remitting the greatest number of checks or the greatest amount of dollars. Citizens mail payments to a post office box that is emptied daily by the bank. Receipts are immediately deposited and a record is sent to the government electronically, by mail, or by courier. Some lockbox users prefer to receive a fax that lists the dollar amounts of deposits and have copies of checks sent by regular mail. Others prefer to pay extra for courier service and receive the information the next day. More sophisticated users have the bank electronically update their accounts receivable records. A lockbox can speed up collections because checks are collected 24 hours per day and on weekends and are sent through the check-clearing process more quickly.

Depending on the nature of the government's collections, it may use a retail lockbox, a wholesale lockbox, or both. A retail lockbox is used for collecting a large number of small dollar checks. For example, a public utility may contract with a bank or third-party provider to collect its checks and process the payments electronically using scannable documents that are mailed to the customers with their invoices. A wholesale lockbox processes a smaller number of larger dollar payments. A government might use a wholesale lockbox for property tax payments or other large payments. Some governments may need both types of lockboxes.

By using a lockbox, the government keeps the checks out of its physical office and reduces staff processing time. For example, a lockbox would eliminate the need for employees to open envelopes with checks, copy checks, make out deposit slips, and take those deposits to the bank on a daily basis.

Zero-Balance Accounts

Many governments use zero-balance accounts (ZBAs) to collect funds. The balances on these accounts are brought to zero at the end of the day and transferred to a concentration account. These accounts are especially useful for governments that need to segregate funds in different bank accounts. Also, government agencies at outlying locations, such as community recreation centers, parks departments, and civic centers, find ZBAs useful because they can deposit their funds into a branch of the government's bank. At the end of the day, the bank will automatically transfer those funds into the government's master ZBA or concentration account. Using a ZBA account structure reduces the government's bank costs and allows for the automated transfer of funds into one account for investment.

Funds Concentration

The number of bank accounts maintained by a government should be kept to a minimum. Sometimes, however, a government must maintain separate bank accounts for a variety of reasons, such as segregating monies designated for specific funds or to make accounting for different fund types easier. When separate bank accounts are used, a government often will move funds in those accounts into a concentration account, commonly referred to as a general account. Concentrating funds into one account allows the government to make the most effective use of its cash by pooling funds for investment purposes, thereby reducing transaction costs related to investments.

Cost-Effective Methods of Moving Funds

Concentrating funds effectively is an important cash management function. How funds are concentrated depends on the number and types of accounts and the number of banks used by a government. Funds must be moved as inexpensively as possible. Once funds are concentrated, they should be invested. Funds left in a concentration account as idle balances are not productive and incur an opportunity cost of lost earnings.

Generally, the concentration account is maintained with the government entity's primary bank. Depending on how a government has its accounts structured, any disbursement accounts are funded by the concentration account and any deposits made are moved at the end of the day to the concentration account. Governments can use a number of the available bank products to concentrate funds. Bank products are becoming increasingly sophisticated as technology improves and are becoming more affordable for smaller governments.

Zero-Balance Accounts

As mentioned in the previous section, ZBAs are cost-effective ways to concentrate funds. A drawback to ZBAs is that the finance official will not know how much activity occurred in the account until the next business day. Governments must set up an internal reporting system for outlying locations to notify the main office of any deposits or the main office may need to get deposit information the next day through a bank balance reporting system.

ACH Transactions

Governments can also move funds by ACH. This concentration method is particularly useful and cost-effective for governments that use more than one bank. For example, banks charge on average $0.12 to initiate an ACH debit using bank software and a nominal fee (typically $0.21) to credit an account where the funds are deposited (Phoenix-Hecht Company 2006). Funds moved by ACH will have one-day availability unless the accounts are in the same bank. Then the funds will have same-day availability.

Fedwire

Some governments use Fedwires to move funds. This method assures the government of receiving same-day use of the funds but can be very expensive. Concentrating funds by wire can cost on average $8–$10 if the wire is set up as a repetitive wire and sent via personal computer and $9–$15 to receive an incoming wire. This concentration method is generally used only for large dollar amounts; for example, Fedwire is used for transferring funds to and from investment accounts.

To calculate the minimum transfer amount at which it makes economic sense to use Fedwire, divide the cost of the wire (both as an outgoing wire from one bank and as an incoming wire to another bank) by a daily investment rate (the overnight investment rate divided by 360). In the example below, assume the total cost of the wire is $15 and the government receives 5.25 percent on overnight investments. The minimum amount of the wire is $102,857.

$$\text{Cost of wire}/(\text{annual interest rate}/360) = \text{Minimum amount of a wire}$$
$$\$15/(0.0525/360) = \$102,857$$

Automatic Sweep Accounts

Another useful tool to concentrate funds is an automatic sweep account. A sweep account is a ZBA account from which the government's available funds are swept into an investment vehicle, such as an overnight repurchase agreement or a money market mutual fund, at the end of the business day. At the beginning of the next day, the funds are returned to a concentration account. Sweep accounts often have a balance threshold and will sweep funds over the amount of the threshold into the investment vehicle. Governments that have large bank balances may find sweep accounts cost-effective. Governments that have liquidity problems may find that sweep accounts cost more than the interest earned on the account. Figure 2.2 shows a sample account structure and flow of funds.

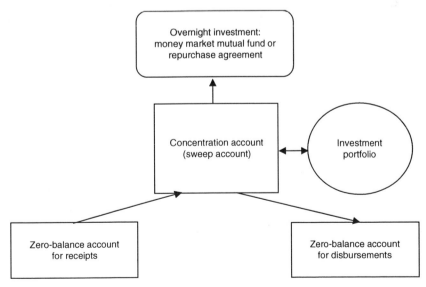

Source: Author.

FIGURE 2.2 Account Structure and Flow of Funds

Safety of Deposited Funds—Collateralization Methods and Practices

The safety of funds deposited with banks and other depository institutions is a primary concern for the finance official entrusted with the care of public funds. The only way to fully guarantee the safety of public funds on deposit with financial institutions is through the pledging of securities above the U.S. Federal Deposit Insurance Corporation (FDIC) limit of $100,000. Hundreds of depository institutions failed in the late 1980s and early 1990s across the country. These bank failures highlighted the need to pay careful attention to protecting government deposits and prompted many state legislatures to draft laws requiring the collateralization of public deposits. These laws specify the types of collateral that banks may pledge to protect public deposits and the levels of protection required.

Since that time, the health of the country's financial institutions has greatly improved. Today, consolidation of commercial banks into fewer nationwide institutions has changed the face of the banking industry. Although banks are more diversified and less exposed to regional economic downturns, risk of bank failure remains. Governments can take concrete steps to protect their deposits.

Most states have enacted statutes that either require or permit depositories to pledge collateral securities to secure public deposits. Typically, high-quality government securities (such as U.S. Treasury obligations, federal agency securities, and municipal bonds) are pledged to protect funds. In those states where no laws govern public deposits, governments may be able to have their deposits collateralized according to local ordinances and practices. Some states have collateral pools and other states allow governments to set their own rules and make their own agreements with local banks. Many governments that are not required by law to collateralize their deposits do so voluntarily to ensure the safety of their funds from any potential default by financial institutions. Governments should implement risk control measures such as (a) the development of a formal risk management policy, (b) routine credit analysis of financial institutions, and (c) the use of fully secured investments.[1]

It is also important to identify the government's exposure to depository risk. Finance officials find that demand deposits can be difficult to collateralize because of fluctuations in cash flow. Some governments use sweep accounts or other similar vehicles to ensure that funds are automatically invested in repurchase agreements or money market mutual funds on an overnight basis to eliminate excess balances on deposit and thus reduce the government's exposure. If a block of collateral securities is used to protect demand deposits, the finance official should study the maximum risk exposure that occurs during cash flow peaks. Governments whose peak cash balances significantly exceed their collateral levels should enact policies that acknowledge this problem and require their banks to adjust the collateral accordingly.

Some states permit financial institutions to pledge securities at face value rather than market value. If the market value of the security is less than par, the deposits may be undercollateralized and thus exposed to some risk. Finance officials should recognize this risk and require that deposits be secured by short-term, high-quality securities such as U.S. Treasury bills, or that deposits be secured by securities over the amount of exposure (for example, 102 percent). Some states have specific laws regarding the percentage of coverage required and the types of securities that can be pledged.

Public deposits are best protected by collateral that is held in safekeeping by an independent third-party bank. To accomplish this, the securities can be held at a Federal Reserve Bank or its branch office or another commercial bank.

Disbursements

State statutes and local ordinances outline general disbursement procedures, including methods of approval and responsibilities of government officials. Disbursement procedures are designed to safeguard the government from incorrect claims and to keep spending within budgetary guidelines. Cash management is concerned with the most effective and efficient way to pay approved disbursements.

Objectives of a Disbursement System

The main objective of a disbursement system is to pay the government's obligations in a timely and cost-effective manner. An equally important objective is to provide the finance official with information on funding requirements and to take the guesswork out of managing the government's liquidity. By knowing the disbursement requirements, the finance official can make effective investment decisions or know with certainty if any funding shortfalls will occur and make the necessary arrangements to cover those shortfalls cost-effectively. Another objective is to reduce or eliminate opportunities for fraud and theft.

Disbursement Float

Disbursement float is the time between a payment (a check, for example) being prepared and its being presented for payment at the government's bank. Like collection float, many factors can affect disbursement float, such as (a) mail time for a check to reach the payee, (b) the time it takes a payee to deposit a check, (c) the Fed district where the check is initially deposited and the Fed district where the check is drawn, (d) the receiving and paying banks' relationship, and (e) the payment method. If a government pays by ACH credit, a one-day disbursement float results. That means the government would have use of those funds for one additional day. Wire transfers are immediately available funds so there would be no disbursement float.

Timing of Disbursements

The finance official must work with other departments to determine the timing and amount of payments that need to be made. The finance official makes decisions such as whether to take advantage of vendor discounts when offered. Effective cash management practices involve setting up a disbursement schedule that allows a government to pay bills timely but eliminates frequent check runs. Many governments issue checks once a week or even twice a month. By issuing checks in batches, governments can manage their cash flows more effectively and save on banking transaction costs, check supplies, and postage.

Disbursement System Design

Some governments have a centralized disbursement system while others have a decentralized system. A main advantage of a centralized disbursement system is that bill paying can be matched to cash inflows. This payment is particularly important if governments have large expenditures and seasonal cash flows. A centralized disbursement system also allows a government to streamline the number of checking accounts that must be maintained, reduces the number of transactions and checks issued, and limits the amount of oversight needed to monitor account activity.

   In some cases, a decentralized process may be necessary for satellite locations and for emergency purposes. If some decentralization is needed, finance officials should require frequent reporting to the main office where the staff should monitor the outlying location's cash requirements and reconcile its bank accounts.

Disbursement Methods

The standard disbursement process usually requires the receipt of an invoice that must be matched to a purchase order (if required) and receipt of goods and services. Depending on the type of payment, a government may choose to pay by check, ACH credit, or wire transfer. Wire transfers are rarely used for vendor payments. Because wires are expensive to send, governments generally use them only when required to by contractual obligations or if the dollar amounts are very large. Paying by wire allows the government to hold on to its cash until the payment due date.

ACH credits are increasingly being used, especially for federal tax payments, corporate trade payments, and employee and benefit-related pay. In fact, many employees are discovering the benefits of receiving their pay by direct deposit. Most governments offer direct deposit and encourage employee participation. The many advantages to direct deposit include

- reduced check-processing charges;
- reduced staff time preparing checks, replacing damaged checks, and making special arrangements for absent employees;
- reduced employee time for cashing checks;
- reduced account reconciliation time;
- reduced storage costs for canceled checks; and
- reduced lost or stolen checks.

Precautions for Checks

A major problem with using checks for disbursements is that they can be stolen or altered. The revised Uniform Commercial Code places the burden on employers to keep their check stock secure. Because check fraud has become a billion-dollar business, banks have come up with a service to help reduce check fraud called positive pay.

Banks typically offer two types of positive pay services. Standard positive pay requires the government to transmit to the bank a file of legitimate checks issued. When a check is presented for payment, the bank's software matches the presented check to the issue file. Checks that match the issue file are paid and those that do not are returned to the issuer unpaid. Some banks will notify the government of rejected checks and allow them time (usually 24 hours) to research the item and advise the bank on whether to accept the check. With this service, the bank retains the responsibility for handling exceptions.

The other type of positive pay service is reverse positive pay. With this service, the bank sends the designated contact at the government entity a transmission of the check's magnetic ink character recognition line or images of the check being presented for payment. The government then has to notify the bank within a specified time which checks to pay and which to return. With this service, the issuer has the responsibility for handling exceptions.

Internal Controls

Internal controls ensure the integrity of the disbursement system. Segregation of duties can help protect a government's funds and can be achieved by separating various functions of the disbursement process. Duties such as authorization of payments and disbursement processing should be segregated. The employee who enters disbursement requests into the accounts payable system should not distribute checks. This level of segregation may be difficult to achieve for smaller entities with one person overseeing the finance function. However, any level of segregation that can be achieved will provide added protection to the organization.

Banking Relationships

Because banks are an integral part of a government's cash management program, it is essential that the government establish and maintain a good working relationship with its banks. The key to a good banking relationship is to find a bank that can provide the services a government needs at a competitive price and that can provide those services with minimal errors.

Financial Institution Selection

Many local governments use a competitive bidding process for selecting financial institutions and banking services. Some governments issue requests for proposals (RFPs) for banking services on a routine basis to determine if they are receiving competitive pricing from their banks. How often the RFP is issued depends on issues such as the following:

- *The type of service the government is currently receiving.* Governments might consider issuing an RFP sooner if its bank begins making errors, if the availability of deposits seems to be less favorable than what other banks offer, or if the bank's financial condition deteriorates.
- *Mergers and acquisitions.* Banks that have merged or been acquired by another bank may not offer the same level of service or types of products. In these cases, the government may consider bidding out its banking to find a more compatible business partner.
- *Competition in the area.* Because of the numerous mergers and acquisitions in the banking industry, a government may find that there are few banks

that qualify to respond to its RFP, particularly if the government is required to do business with banks only in its geographical area. In these instances, governments might enter into longer contracts with the winning banks and issue RFPs less often—perhaps every four to five years. An RFP is a labor- and time-intensive project that can tie up staff time for several months.

To help with developing an RFP, many professional associations have created sample documents that describe the key components.[2] A well-developed RFP will include minimum qualifications to bid, a description of the current system, a description of any services desired, and a standardized response form or specific guidelines for responding to the request. The RFP should include size requirements for eligible banks, particularly if the government has significant amounts of cash. A government with $10 million may need only one local bank to handle all of its needs, whereas a government with $100 million may need a bank for custodial safekeeping, a bank for depository services, and a bank or brokerage firm for investment services. Qualifications to bid also may include geographic restrictions, ability to handle special conditions, collateral requirements, or a Community Reinvestment Act rating.[3]

To compare individual bank responses more easily, a government can develop a matrix of evaluation criteria. The evaluation criteria should be weighted to reflect the government's ranking of most important to least important attributes and ratings should be assigned to each bank. The weighting and rating criteria should be kept simple to avoid complicating the evaluation process. Once a winning proposal is accepted, a written banking services contract formalizes the relationship.

Ongoing Relationship Management

Many factors may lead a government to change banks. However, changing banks is costly and time consuming. New checks must be ordered, old check stock must be destroyed, banking instructions for Fedwires and ACH transactions must be updated, and staff must be trained on new bank systems. Nevertheless, the finance official should conduct a periodic evaluation of the government's banking relationship.

Questions to consider in evaluating a bank's performance include the following (Lockhart 2004):

- Does the bank provide all the needed services?
- Are the bank's rates on deposits competitive?

■ Does the bank have an aggressive availability schedule?
■ Does the bank have state-of-the-art technology?
■ Do bank personnel communicate with the government's staff effectively?
■ Is the bank responsive to questions from the government's staff?
■ Are problems resolved quickly and to the satisfaction of all parties?

In many cases, the finance official and the banking relationship officer have a long-term affiliation. The bank may be familiar with the government's treasury operations and may have addressed those needs over the years. While the relationship may be beneficial from an operating standpoint, it may not be from a cost standpoint. The finance official should weigh the advantages of an established relationship against the potential cost savings and improved services resulting from a new bank relationship.

Account Analysis Summary

An account analysis is a monthly statement that banks supply to their institutional customers to show the cost of services provided. The information shown on an account analysis includes actual services provided, the number of occurrences of service (for example, number of checks presented and cleared), the unit cost per item, and the total charge per service. Finance officials should request an account analysis for each bank account along with a summary statement for all accounts. Compensation to the bank should be based on the consolidated statement, not individual account statements, because some accounts will have less activity and the balances from those accounts will help offset services from other accounts.

Cash Flow Forecasting

Although accurately predicting the peaks and valleys of cash flows is one of the most difficult aspects of cash management, a timely and accurate cash flow forecast is the basis for a sound investment program. An accurate forecast can strengthen an investment program by allowing the finance official to determine how much money will be available for investment, when this money will become available, and how long it will be available. These considerations are important because yields are often linked to the size and maturity of an investment. Accurate cash flow forecasts can also aid government officials in making prudent decisions about the timing of major purchases and in estimating if and when short-term borrowing in the form of revenue anticipation or tax anticipation notes may be necessary.

Types of Cash Flow Forecasts

A cash flow forecast is a schedule of expected receipts and disbursements for a given period. The types and frequency of forecasts prepared will depend on several factors. Governments with predictable cash flows and sufficient cash reserves can usually get by with an annual forecast. An annual forecast provides an overview of the expected cash position by month. Most governments prepare an annual forecast and use it to make longer-term investment decisions. Governments with volatile cash positions, erratic cash flows, or changing demographics may need more frequent and detailed forecasts. A monthly forecast estimates weekly cash positions and helps monitor the accuracy of the annual forecast. It is more operational than an annual forecast. This type of forecast is used by governments with fluctuating cash flows or liquidity problems. A weekly forecast estimates daily cash positions and can help monitor the accuracy of the monthly forecast. This forecast can be useful for governments that need to monitor their cash positions closely. A daily forecast is a cash position worksheet. It tries to predict available fund balances for the next day and is based on actual bank balances. It can help with overnight investment decisions.

Some finance officials prepare project-based forecasts. A project-based forecast is useful for long-term construction projects and capital projects. It provides monthly data on project status and should be accompanied by a schedule of payments. This forecast requires cooperation from contractors or in-house project managers to keep the finance official informed on the status of a project because projects often fall behind schedule or go over budget.

Forecasting Cash Flows

Preparation of a cash flow forecast can benefit from identification of major routine transactions, such as accounts receivable collections, accounts payable disbursements, payroll and related expenses, and debt-service payments, and from a schedule for these payments throughout the fiscal year by month. The current annual budget document can provide an estimate of anticipated revenues and expenditures while historical data from the general ledger will help identify infrequent receipts and disbursements.

Using Historical Data

Typically, the finance official estimates monthly receipts and disbursements based on data from prior years. These data can be gathered by analyzing the prior year's cashbook or bank statements and developing a month-by-month summary of recurring receipts and disbursements. Once those data are gathered, the finance official adjusts them to reflect any anticipated changes to the historical receipts and disbursements for the current forecast.

Adjusting Historical Data

A comparative analysis of two to three years can help pinpoint any patterns or trends in cash flows. A review of historical receipts and disbursements, and identification of any transactions that may be affected by collection rates or changes in economic or demographic conditions and their impact on the area, by federal or state aid funding, by purchases of capital items, by changes or revisions in local tax levies or tax laws, by effects of unseasonable weather, and by labor negotiations will help improve the accuracy of the forecast.

For example, if a government typically collects 95 percent of revenues owed, the forecasted receipts should be 95 percent of the projected revenues, not 100 percent. A collection rate can be determined by dividing the amount of cash received by the amount of revenues billed. Suppose a local government budgets property tax collections of $29.4 million for a given year. Historical analysis shows that the government averages a 95 percent collection. The estimate for tax receipts for the coming year should be 95 percent of $29.4 million, or $27.9 million.

When examining receipts, governments should also consider payment patterns for their areas. For tax payments, finance officials can conduct a study of payment patterns by analyzing the percentage of tax payments made based on mailings of the tax bills. Some citizens will pay as soon as they receive the bill, while others will wait until the due date to pay. Most citizens fall somewhere in between. By determining the percentage of bills paid within the first month of mailing, 30–45 days after mailing, and so forth, finance officials can get a more accurate idea of when to expect the tax receipts.

Disbursements can be adjusted similarly. For example, if the expected inflation rate is 3 percent for the coming year, estimates for disbursements such as payroll, utilities, and supplies will need to be adjusted upward by simply multiplying the historical data by 3 percent. Thus, if a government spends a yearly average of $26 million on payroll and payables, the forecasted amount should be $26.78 million for the new year. If these purchases are spread evenly throughout the year, the forecast would show a monthly expense of $2.25 million.

Monitoring Forecast for Accuracy

Throughout the year, the finance official should adjust the cash flow forecast as needed and keep the data as current as possible, revising the forecast with any new information that may become available. Tracking the actual cash flows also helps the finance official recognize cash flow patterns and aids in producing a more accurate forecast in the future. Ongoing monitoring of the cash flow forecast helps officials identify problems in the annual budget estimates early on, helps identify record-keeping inaccuracies by tracking the variance from forecasted to actual, and aids in internal control by isolating collection problems or missed deposits.

Governments may find that they do not need sophisticated software to project their cash flows. A good understanding of the entity's cash flow patterns and a simple spreadsheet software program are all that is needed to create a usable cash flow forecast. Table 2.1 presents a sample cash flow forecast that was prepared using an electronic spreadsheet. This forecast demonstrates cash flows for a local government that receives property tax revenue and sales tax revenue. Property taxes come in twice a year, in January and July. Sales tax revenues and other revenues come in steadily throughout the year. This forecast shows the government's actual cash flows for the first quarter of the year and its projected cash flows for the remainder of the year. The government would prepare a forecast for the current fiscal year and the next one to two years, depending on its investment horizon.

This type of forecast is useful for determining the net change in cash position by month. If the projected net change is positive, the government can expect to receive more cash than it pays out, and if it is negative, it can plan for those shortfalls and schedule investment maturities to cover them.

Using the Forecast for Investment Purposes

The government in Table 2.1 expects to collect $4.14 million more than it plans to pay out in April. It has investment maturities of $5.25 million coming due. Because the net cash position is positive in April, this government will not need those funds, so the finance official would look at upcoming months to determine when those funds will be needed. In looking at the projected net change in May, the government has a slight shortfall of $218,000. but has an investment maturity of $1.525 million coming due that will cover the shortfall. In June, there is a negative net cash position, so the finance official can schedule some of the funds in April to mature in June to cover those cash needs and invest the balance of the funds longer term to take advantage of higher interest rates in the future.

The purpose of preparing a cash flow forecast is twofold. Governments need to have enough liquidity on hand to cover anticipated and unanticipated cash needs, and governments need to invest idle funds to generate interest income. When using a cash flow forecast for investment purposes,

TABLE 2.1 Cash Flow Forecast
U.S. dollars

	Beginning balance	Jan. 2006	Feb. 2006	March 2006	April 2006	May 2006	June 2006	Total
Beginning balance	54,525,000							
Property tax revenues		5,855,000	1,500,000	0	5,855,000	1,500,000	0	14,710,000
Sales tax revenues		320,000	295,000	205,000	320,000	295,000	205,000	1,640,000
Water		250,000	250,000	250,000	250,000	250,000	250,000	1,500,000
Other revenues		57,000	57,000	57,000	57,000	57,000	57,000	342,000
Payroll and payables		−2,230,000	−2,230,000	−2,230,000	−2,230,000	−2,230,000	−2,230,000	−13,380,000
Capital projects		−500,000	−400,000	−375,000	−37,000	−40,000	−35,000	−1,387,000
Other expenditures		−550,000	−375,000	−250,000	−50,000	−50,000	−50,000	−1,325,000
Projected net change		3,202,000	−903,000	−2,343,000	4,165,000	−218,000	−1,803,000	
Portfolio income and maturities		0	0	0	5,250,000	1,525,000	100,000	
Projected portfolio balance		57,727,000	56,824,000	54,481,000	58,646,000	58,428,000	56,625,000	
Actual portfolio balance	54,525,000	55,053,000	58,236,000	58,899,000				
Variance from forecast		2,674,000	−1,412,000	−4,418,000				
Actual net change		528,000	3,183,000	663,000				

Source: Author.

a government's idle funds may be broken down into two categories—*liquid funds*, those funds needed for liquidity purposes, and *core funds*, those funds that will not be needed to cover immediate cash needs. Liquid funds are invested in local government investment pools, money market mutual funds, or other short-term instruments, such as commercial paper, certificates of deposit, or U.S. Treasury securities with maturities under one year. Core funds are invested in securities with maturities greater than one year.

A government can use its cash flow forecast to determine how much of its portfolio is core funds and how much is liquid funds. As shown in Table 2.1, this government has a core fund balance of $54 million. This balance can be determined by analyzing the projected portfolio balance. The projected portfolio balance in this example never falls below $54 million. This government knows that it can invest up to $54 million of its portfolio and still maintain adequate liquidity to meet its operating needs. Any funds above $54 million would be needed for liquidity purposes and would be invested in liquid instruments, such as a local government investment pool.

Each month, the finance official would enter the portfolio's actual balance and calculate the net change. This information will help gauge the accuracy of the forecast and will alert the government to any budgetary problems or concerns.

Investing

Another important component of cash management is the investment function. Over the years, governments have been granted increased authority and latitude in how they can invest their funds. Expanded investment laws have allowed many governments to increase their investment income and help ease their fiscal constraints. However, with this expanded authority has come some catastrophic losses of funds. An investment official must balance the desire to earn additional investment income with the need to protect the entity's funds.

Investing can be thought of as a three-step process. In step one, the investor must become familiar with and understand the various risks of investing before making any purchases. Step two involves the purchase of an investment instrument that complies with the government's written policies and procedures and results in a market rate of return on the government's funds. Step three recognizes the trade-off between risk and reward by producing investment reports that summarize the government's investment program, publishing the performance results, and recapping economic activity for the period.

Investment Objectives

Interest earnings are often an important revenue source. Finance officials must try to earn the best return possible without sacrificing the safety of the funds. Finance officials must also perform this function within the constraints of state statutes, local laws, ordinances and charters, and internal policies and procedures. In addition, finance officials must make their decisions based on the principles of safety, liquidity, and yield.[4]

Risks of Investing

Certain risks are inherent in any investment instrument. Even the safest, most conservative investment has some risk associated with it. The investment of public funds requires that the finance official understand the risks of a particular investment option.

Credit Risk

Credit risk is the risk that the issuer will be unable to redeem the investment at maturity. Credit risk can be controlled by carefully screening and monitoring the credit quality of the issuers, limiting investments to those of the highest credit quality, and holding collateral with a third-party custodian against certain investments, such as certificates of deposit and repurchase agreements.

Liquidity Risk

When making investment decisions, finance officials must also look at a security's liquidity risk. Liquidity risk involves the ability to sell an investment before maturity. Closely related to liquidity risk is marketability risk, or the ability to sell an investment before maturity without incurring a significant loss in price. Exposure to liquidity risk can be reduced by restricting maturities for operating funds, purchasing investments that have an active secondary market so the security can be sold before maturity if the government needs the funds to meet operating expenses, and preparing a cash flow forecast so that investment maturities can be scheduled to coincide with operating needs. By scheduling investments, the finance official can avoid selling an investment early to meet unexpected cash flow needs and possibly incurring a loss on a security.

Market and Interest Rate Risk

Market risk is the risk that the value of an investment will decrease because of movement in the financial markets. With fixed-income securities, market risk—changes in the market price—is confined to interest rate risk. If the going market interest rate falls during the holding period, the market price of the security will increase. (The price of the security at maturity is always the same.) However, if the market interest rate rises, the security price will fall, and an investor might incur a loss if the security is sold before maturity. Because of the effects of the discount rate over time, the prices of longer-term securities vary more than those of shorter-term securities when there are changes in the market rate. Therefore, longer-term securities generally carry a higher yield than short-term issues to compensate the investor for committing funds into the future.

Reinvestment Risk

Reinvestment risk occurs when interest from an investment cannot be reinvested to earn the same rate of return as the original funds invested. For example, falling interest rates may prevent bond coupon payments from earning the same rate of return as the original bond. This is a risk when investors buy callable securities, that is, securities that give the issuer the right to redeem a security on a given date or dates (known as the call dates) before maturity. Essentially, an option to call the security is sold by the investor to the issuer, and the investor is compensated with a higher yield. Issuers typically exercise call options in periods of declining interest rates, thereby creating reinvestment risk for the investor.

Reputational Risk

In the public sector, another risk associated with investing is reputational risk, or the risk that government officials will lose stature by making investment mistakes. Reputational risk harms the governmental entity as well as the investment official. The best protection against this risk is a well-managed investment program.

The effects of various risks are illustrated by the highly publicized investment losses of 1994. Public entities from California to Maine lost millions of dollars when the market values of their investments fell because of rising interest rates. How did this happen? The early 1990s brought low interest rates, prompting investors to purchase securities with high market volatility to increase their investment earnings. With higher returns, however, comes higher risk. Investors learned this lesson when they needed to sell investments before maturity and found that they either could not find a buyer for their securities or had to sell the securities below the principal amount invested. Investors who held their investments to maturity discovered the market value of their portfolios was significantly less than the historical cost. Many finance officials associated with these losses lost their jobs and some faced prosecution.

Evaluation of Investment Alternatives

Because of the investment losses of the mid-1990s, most local governments are required to have a formal investment policy. Although a formal investment policy identifies investment objectives, defines risk tolerance, assigns responsibility for the investment function, and establishes control over the investment process, it does not tell the finance official what investment instruments to purchase, how much to invest, or how long to invest funds. Finance officials typically make investment decisions based on cash flow needs. In many cases, idle funds are deposited in interest-bearing accounts or invested in short-term liquid investments such as a local government investment pool or overnight repurchase agreements until the funds are needed for liquidity purposes. When large amounts of cash will be available for a substantial period, the finance official may choose to invest in longer-term instruments, such as U.S. Treasury securities or other fixed-income investments allowed by state statute and the entity's investment policy.

The following criteria will help finance officials achieve their investment goals.

Legality

Is this investment an allowable investment option? Most state statutes contain specific language that outlines what types of securities are allowable investment options for local governments. Some state statutes are less clear and leave room for interpretation. Finance officials must understand their states' statutes and their local investment policy restrictions and make sure their investment decisions comply with these guidelines.

Safety

How safe is the investment? What is the credit risk? Is there any possibility the government can lose its principal? Generally, the higher the yield, the greater the risk an investment instrument carries. Therefore, high-yield investments with a great degree of credit risk are unsuitable investments for local governments.

Liquidity

How easily can invested funds be converted to cash without a significant loss in value? The more liquid an investment, the easier it will be to obtain funds if unanticipated cash needs arise. Some investments, such as nonnegotiable certificates of deposit, are highly illiquid. If a government does not have good cash flow projections, illiquid investments should be avoided. Also, many governments keep a portion of their portfolios in readily available assets, such as investment pools, to ensure that they have cash on hand to meet unexpected needs and invest a portion of their portfolio in longer-term securities, such as two-year Treasury notes, to take advantage of higher yields in a normal yield curve environment.

Yield

What is the return on the investment? Finance officials should seek to earn the highest return possible after balancing concerns for legality, safety, and liquidity. By establishing a benchmark for performance, finance officials can evaluate the effectiveness of their investment programs. Benchmarks are discussed later in this chapter.

Suitability

Is an investment a suitable choice? Simply because an investment may be allowed by statute does not mean that it is suitable for a government's portfolio. Some investments, such as mortgage-backed securities, can experience great price volatility in changing interest rate environments and have other risks such as prepayment risk (the risk that homeowners will prepay their mortgages during falling interest rates and leave the investor to reinvest the funds in a lower interest rate environment). Similarly, zero coupon bonds and securities with maturities greater than five years are unsuitable investment options for operating funds.

Competitive Quotes

One way to ensure that finance officials receive the best price and yield on securities is to seek competitive quotes for all investment purchases and sales. Many governments establish a minimum number of competitive bids that must be obtained before making an investment purchase. Smaller governments often do not use the services of broker-dealers, limiting their investment purchases to financial institutions. However, these investors can still benefit from obtaining competitive bids for certificates of deposit if they use more than one bank. For governments that may have only one or two sources for investments, quotes can be verified against published sources in the financial press or from online services.

Analysis of Allowable Investment Instruments

When looking at investment options, all aspects of the investment transaction must be considered. Some investments are more liquid than others, some investments are subject to more price volatility, and some investments are more expensive relative to other options. In addition, the attitudes of the citizens, the governing body, and the elected officials should be taken into account before making an investment purchase. If the entity has a low risk tolerance, only relatively stable investments should be made.

The following investment instruments are typical allowable investments for local governments.

Local Government Investment Pools

Local government investment pools can be state-sponsored or can be organized as joint-powers pools where local governments pool their cash for investment. A state investment pool consolidates excess cash from local governments often with its own excess cash to create one large sum of money. The advantage of a local government investment pool is that the pool of funds can be invested at a higher yield than if each participant of the fund invested individually. Each pool participant receives a share of the interest earned on a periodic basis. Most pools allow participants to make deposits or withdrawals on a daily basis.

Investing in a pool often makes the most economical sense (a) for governments with less than $10 million to invest, (b) when funds are invested for a short time, (c) if the investment function lacks the staff to administer a more aggressive investment program, or (d) if interest rates are expected to be volatile. Because pools generally maintain a weighted average maturity of 90 days or less, the rate paid on a pool will lag market rates. When interest rates are falling, the rate on a pool will be higher than overnight money investments until the existing investments in the pool mature and are replaced with investments at the new lower rate. Conversely, when interest rates rise, the rate paid on a pool will be less than rates paid for overnight investments.

Mutual Funds

A mutual fund is an open-ended fund operated by an investment company that raises money from shareholders and invests in a group of assets, in accordance with a stated set of objectives. Mutual funds purchase various investment vehicles, such as stocks, bonds, and money market instruments. A money market mutual fund is an open-ended mutual fund that invests only in money markets.

These funds invest in short-term (one day to one year) debt obligations such as Treasury bills, certificates of deposit, and commercial paper. The main goal of a money market mutual fund is the preservation of principal, accompanied by dividend payments. The fund strives to maintain a net asset value of $1 per share, but the interest rate does fluctuate. Money market mutual funds are required to be registered with the U.S. Securities and Exchange Commission and must follow the SEC's Rule 2a 7, which governs the credit quality of the investments purchased, sets diversification guidelines for funds, limits the maturities of the investments, and requires funds to strive for a net asset value of $1 per share. The portfolios of these funds are controlled by a prospectus and investment policies established by boards of directors. Money market mutual funds are often tied to bank sweep accounts.

Some public entities invest in bond mutual funds. A bond mutual fund invests in bonds, typically with the objective of providing stable income with minimal capital risk. Bond funds are more volatile and do not necessarily strive to maintain a net asset value of $1 per share. Many bond funds are limited to investing in U.S. Treasury and agency securities and have low credit risk; however, bond funds do have significant market risk and liquidity risk. When interest rates rise, the value of a bond fund can decline below a net asset value of $1 per share. When this happens, investors often try to liquidate their holdings, thus causing the bond fund to experience principal loss and liquidity issues.

Certificates of Deposit

Nonnegotiable certificates of deposit (CDs) are time deposits that pay a fixed rate of interest and have a set maturity date that can range from a week to several years. Early redemption of a nonnegotiable CD can result in significant penalties so investors should view these investments as highly illiquid. Also, because CDs are only insured up to the FDIC limit of $100,000, governments need to conduct a credit analysis of the bank offering the CD and buy only collateralized CDs. Collateralized CDs typically pay a lower interest rate than other investment options because banks factor in the cost of tying up collateral for these investments.

CDs make sense if investors can lock in a favorable interest rate and are confident they will not need their funds for the term of the deposit. Smaller governments with a limited number of investment options may wish to diversify their portfolios and find that CDs can be a good complement to investment pools in certain interest rate environments.

Governments that invest in negotiable CDs should be aware that these deposits cannot be collateralized because there is no way for the bank to determine that the CD is owned by a public entity. In fact, many states do not allow local governments to invest in negotiable CDs for this reason. If a local government wishes to invest in a negotiable CD, it should evaluate the financial strength of the bank and obtain short-term and long-term debt ratings from a nationally recognized statistical rating organization such as Standard & Poor's, Moody's Investors Service, or Fitch. A government will have exposure to a bank's credit risk when it purchases a negotiable CD.

Repurchase Agreements

A repurchase agreement (repo) is a simultaneous transaction between a buyer of securities (the investor) and a bank or securities dealer. In a repo transaction, the investor exchanges cash for temporary ownership of securities, with the agreement that the securities will be "repurchased" on a certain date and at a specified interest rate. There are three types of repos. An *overnight repo* matures on the next business day and is a commonly used cash management tool that allows the finance official to make effective use of excess funds. Often sweep accounts will have an overnight repo as its investment mechanism. *Term repos* have a defined maturity date with a fixed interest rate. This type of repo is advantageous in a falling interest rate environment because the investor can lock in a rate. *Flex repos* are often used for bond proceeds. They allow the investor to withdraw funds from the repo to make payments on a project.

Treasury Securities

Treasury securities are commonly used investment instruments in the public sector. Treasury securities are highly liquid, marketable securities and are fully guaranteed in principal and interest by the U.S. government. Treasury securities used by public sector investors are bills and notes. Bills are short-term, marketable securities issued on a discount basis. Bills come in maturities of three and six months. Notes are coupon-bearing securities with maturities over 1 year and up to 10 years. The Treasury also issues bonds with original maturities of more than 10 years and STRIPS (Separate Trading of Registered Interest and Principal of Securities), which are zero coupon bonds with maturities of one month to 30 years.

Because Treasury securities have an active secondary market, investors can often sell them before maturity without suffering a significant price loss and may sometimes make a gain on the sale. Another advantage of Treasury securities is that investors can purchase securities on the secondary market to meet almost any maturity requirement. Because the market for these securities is so active, bid-offer spreads are generally narrow so investors can easily determine if they are receiving a fair price for the investment.

Government Agency Securities

Government agency securities receive a lot of attention because investors do not understand the difference between a true government agency security and a security issued by a government sponsored enterprise. The only government agency that issues money market securities is the Government National Mortgage Association (Ginnie Mae). Other government agencies issue long-term securities in smaller quantities that are unsuitable for operating funds.

Government-Sponsored Enterprise Securities

Government-sponsored enterprises, including the Federal National Mortgage Association, Federal Home Loan Mortgage Corporation, Federal Home Loan Bank, and Federal Farm Credit Bank, are rated by nationally recognized statistical rating organizations and do not carry the full faith and credit guarantee of the U.S. government although they do carry an implied guarantee of assistance if they should run into financial problems. These agencies issue large blocks of securities on a frequent basis and in a variety of structures and maturities. Securities issued by government-sponsored enterprises tend to enjoy an active secondary market and are appropriate for operating funds, in most cases.

Corporate Debt

Many local governments, particularly larger ones, invest in corporate securities such as commercial paper and corporate notes. These securities often offer higher returns than the investment alternatives discussed above. Commercial paper is a short-term investment with maturities under 270 days, issued on a discount basis. Corporate notes are coupon-bearing securities with various maturities. Investors considering corporate securities should analyze the short-term and long-term debt ratings of the issuers. Most state statutes have specific guidance on the use of corporate securities.

Delivery versus Payment

When investing public funds, financial officials should insist that all transactions take place on a delivery versus payment basis. In a delivery versus payment transaction, the buyer's funds are released when delivery of the seller's securities (or collateral) is received. Both parties send their respective cash and securities to a third-party custodian who will send a written confirmation of the transaction when it is successfully completed. This payment arrangement protects the buyer from any fraudulent activities on the part of the seller and from any credit risk on the seller's part. If the seller were to default or go bankrupt, the buyer would have ownership of the securities.

Investment Performance Evaluation and Reporting

Timely and accurate reporting is an important part of the investment program. Governments need timely reports to see how their investments are performing. Benchmarks must be established and performance must be measured against the benchmarks. Regular investment reports must be prepared for review by the governing body.

Performance Benchmarks

A benchmark is a measure that allows investors to compare their portfolios' performance with that of a similar standard portfolio or security type. Setting a performance benchmark can be a frustrating experience for finance officials who must place a higher priority on safety of principal than on yield for portfolios made up of operating funds. Performance goals must be carefully set to reflect market conditions and levels of risk tolerance as specified by the government's investment policy. The finance officials must be able to achieve the benchmark goal by following the guidelines of the investment policy. The challenge for investment policy makers is to choose a benchmark that sets a realistic performance goal without placing an undue burden on the investment staff.

Monitoring Investment Performance

Performance benchmarks will vary based on the investment management style of the portfolio. Some governments that have many portfolio holdings in a variety of securities will use an index of similar securities as a performance gauge. For example, governments with portfolios that have an average weighted maturity of more than one year and less than three years might use the Merrill Lynch 1–3 Year Treasury Index as the benchmark. For most governments using a standard buy-and-hold investment strategy, an appropriate benchmark is a constant maturity Treasury (CMT). Yields for CMTs are posted on the U.S. Treasury's Web site and can serve as a good proxy for a conservatively managed investment portfolio. Finance officials can create spreadsheets to capture the monthly average yields for CMTs in a variety of maturities and for various time frames. For example, a government with a portfolio that has a weighted average maturity of 90 days could compare its performance against the average yield for a 90-day Treasury bill for the month, trailing six months, trailing one year, and trailing five years. This comparison allows the finance official to evaluate the entity's performance against an objective market measure during various interest rate cycles.

Portfolio Reporting

Because reporting is such an important part of the investment process, reports should be sent on a regular basis to the governing body, the investment oversight committee (if one exists), and others as deemed appropriate. The following information typically is included in the report:

- A listing of investments by type and as a percentage of the portfolio
- A listing of investments by maturity date
- The cost of each investment, its yield, and accrued interest
- The market value of each investment
- Weighted average yield-to-maturity of the portfolio

A sample portfolio holdings report is presented in Table 2.2.

Reports should also comply with requirements set by the Governmental Accounting Standards Board (GASB).[5] GASB pronouncements that affect the investment program include GASB Statement 31, Accounting and Financial Reporting for Certain Investments and for External Investment Pools, which requires governments to report their investments with maturities of more than one year at market value at least annually. The other pronouncement is GASB Statement 40, Deposit and Investment Risk Disclosures, which requires governments to report their exposure to credit risk, concentration of credit risk, interest rate risk, and foreign currency risk associated with deposits and investments.

Conclusion

A well-run investment management program protects a government's funds and makes effective use of those funds through the efficient investment of public monies. Similarly, by using cost-effective methods for processing receipts and disbursements and implementing an efficient collections program, a local government can reduce cash management costs and collect all monies owed. Trends toward electronic commerce are increasing each year, bank products are becoming more sophisticated allowing governments to dedicate fewer resources to the cash management function, and investing public funds has gained importance in the finance office. This chapter has discussed tools and techniques for effectively managing cash and investments.

TABLE 2.2 Sample Portfolio Holdings Report

Government ABC Portfolio Holdings Report 2/28/2006

Description	Purchase date	Rate/ coupon	Maturity/ call date	Par value/ shares	Historical cost/accrued int. purch.	Amortized cost/accretion (amortization)	Fair value/ change in fair value	Unrealized gain (loss)	Int. rec'd/ int. earned	Total accrued interest	% of portfolio (at cost)	Yield	Moody's rating
U.S. Treasury													
91282BCQ1 T-note	8/1/2005	2.750	7/31/2006	1,000,000.00	989,140.63 / 0.00	995,465.32 / 835.34	991,900.00 / 800.00	−3,565.32	0.00 / 2,127.07	0.00	14.01	3.87	Aaa
91282EK2 T-note	12/23/2005	4.250	10/31/2007	1,000,000.00	997,031.25 / 6,222.38	997,329.44 / 122.78	992,700.00 / −2,400.00	−4,629.44	0.00 / 3,287.29	14,205.80	14.12	4.42	Aaa
TOTAL				2,000,000.00	1,986,171.88 / 6,222.38	1,992,794.76 / 958.12	1,984,600.00 / −1,600.00	−8,194.76 / 0.00	0.00 / 5,414.36	14,205.80 / 0.00	28.13		
Government-sponsored enterprises													
3133X3DG5 FHLB	1/28/2004	2.500	4/28/2006 4/28/2006	1,100,000.00	1,102,156.00 / 0.00	1,100,000.00 / 0.00	1,095,930.00 / 1,540.00	−4,070.00	0.00 / 2,291.66	2,520.83	15.61	2.51	Aaa
3136F3NX0 FNMA	7/2/2003	2.625	4/28/2006 4/28/2006	2,000,000.00	2,017,880.00 / 0.00	2,000,000.00 / 0.00	1,993,000.00 / 2,800.00	−7,000.00	0.00 / 0.00	4,375.00	28.58	2.63	Aaa
TOTAL				3,100,000.00	3,120,036.00 / 0.00	3,100,000.00 / 0.00	3,090,470.00 / 4,340.00	−11,070.00 / 0.00	2,291.66 / 2,291.66	6,895.83 / 0.00	44.19		

Corporate													
90331HJN4	2.400	10/22/2004	3/12/2007	1,000,000.00	986,520.00	994,180.85	970,300.00	−23,880.85	0.00	11,266.67	13.97	2.99	Aa1
U.S. Bank					0.00	433.34	−400.00		2,000.00				
36962GB78	3.500	2/16/2006	5/1/2008	1,000,000.00	967,900.00	963,418.39	968,600.00	181.61	0.00	11,666.67	13.71	5.05	Aaa
GE Capital									1,458.34				
Total				2,000,000.00	1,954,420.00	1,963,032.58	1,938,500.00	−23,699.24	2,000.00	22,933.34	27.68		
					0.00	433.34	−400.00	0.00	3,458.34	0.00			
Grand total				7,100,000.00	7,060,627.88	7,055,827.34	7,013,570.00	−42,964.00	4,291.66	44,034.97	100.00	3.42	
					6,222.38	1,391.46	2,340.00	0.00	11,164.36	0.00			

Source: Author.
Note: Values in the shaded areas are in U.S. dollars.

Notes

1. Larson (2005) provides a detailed discussion of collateralization practices and safeguards.
2. The Association for Financial Professionals maintains a library of articles on issuing RFPs and on banking relationships and has a number of RFPs available electronically. See Association for Financial Professionals (2003).
3. A Community Reinvestment Act rating is a federal measure of how well banks meet the credit needs of the communities they serve.
4. For an in-depth discussion of public sector investing, see Miller, Larson, and Zorn (1998).
5. The purpose of the Governmental Accounting Standards Board is to establish standards of state and local governmental accounting and financial reporting. Further information can be found on the board's Web site, http://www.gasb.org.

References and Other Resources

Association for Financial Professionals. 2003. *Standardized RFPs: Effective Tools for Selecting Cash Management Banks*, 2nd ed. Bethesda, MD: Association for Financial Professionals.

Larson, M. Corinne. 2005. *An Introduction to Collateralizing Public Deposits*. Chicago: Government Finance Officers Association.

Lockhart, Kevin. 2004. "Core Banking Services." In *Banking Services: A Guide for Governments*, 62. Chicago: Government Finance Officers Association.

Miller, Girard, M. C. Larson, and W. P. Zorn. 1998. *Investing Public Funds,* 2nd ed. Chicago: Government Finance Officers Association.

Phoenix-Hecht Company. 2006. *The Blue Book of Bank Prices, 2005–2006*. Research Triangle Park, NC: Phoenix-Hecht.

3

Local Government Procurement and Safeguards against Corruption

CLIFFORD P. MCCUE AND ERIC W. PRIER

Purchasing records dating as far back as 300 BCE in Athens reveal government engagement in procurement (Coe 1976: 87). Today, public procurement officials around the globe control spending equivalent to approximately 30 percent of a nation's gross national product in any given year (Callender and Mathews 2000). Such enormous influence within the world economy probably comes as little surprise to most people who receive benefits and services from their governments.

Although corruption is ancient, much of the current literature on corruption is devoted to the institutional and individual analysis of its causes and consequences in numerous areas, such as procurement auctions, taxation, economic growth, bureaucratic red tape, economic integration, and decentralization (Banerjee 1997; Bibhas 2003; Compte, Lambert-Mogiliansky, and Verdier 2005; Ganuza and Hauk 2004; Gurgur and Shah 2005; Marjit, Mukherjee, and Mukherjee 2000, 2003; Shleifer and Vishny 1993; Wallace and Haerpfer 2000). Although a mild debate continues about whether the causes of corruption are context specific and culturally bound (institutional) or the product of individual desires, recent scholarship typically concludes that one-size-fits-all anticorruption strategies are less effective than targeting a specific country's corruption problems within its own sociopolitical and supplier-competitive context (Celentani and Ganuza 2002; Kaufman 1998; also see Robinson 1998).

From a development perspective, establishing sound procurement policies and practices is necessary to reduce corruption and increase transparency. Local policy goals to provide adequate health care and education while promoting economic development require getting the most out of the limited resources available at the local level for the purchase of goods, services, and infrastructure. Furthermore, effective local government procurement policies and practices contribute to sound financial management of public resources (Hunja 2003). Effective provision of public goods and services often requires coordinated delivery of materials and services, which the local government purchasing apparatus must accomplish in an efficient manner. It is difficult to imagine how a local government can deliver substantial improvements in a particular policy objective without a financial management system that includes effective public procurement policies and practices. This recognition accounts in part for the growing interest in public procurement planning and in global attempts to mitigate procurement corruption.

This chapter identifies the opportunities for corruption in local government procurement while discussing the motivations and incentives of individual procurement officials to engage in such practices in developing countries. It does not attempt to outline how corruption can be eliminated, because it may never be completely eradicated (Klitgaard 1988; Pope 1996). Rather, the goal is to identify the contours of public procurement issues at the local level in developing countries and then to identify a set of process issues that can be implemented at the local level to minimize the potential for corruption.

Overview of Public Procurement

This section reviews procurement at the local level, its evolution and goals, and the opportunities for corruption.

The Nature of the Purchasing Profession at the Local Level

For various reasons, most public officials at the local level want control of procurement decisions, often because they may feel that they know best what supplies and services are needed to do their jobs most effectively. However, because of the specialized nature of public procurement, these line personnel are often not adequately trained to perform the most fundamental purchasing and contract administration processes. Thus, competence is a must in today's complex decision-making environment. Moreover, effective regulations and training on evaluation criteria, purchasing procedures, and proper inventory controls are also important. Whether in developing countries or developed countries, local procurement officials typically play supporting roles within public organizations. However, because the environments in which they operate can differ markedly across agencies, jurisdictions, and even governments, procedures and the problems they are devised to address vary as well.

Numerous political issues also fall outside the regulatory environment, such as political tussles over determining the administrative locus for procurement decisions, and the complementary potential for political capture at the local level. Consider that local procurement officials in developing countries are likely to be appointed in patronage or client systems, and thus have few skills beyond those of a clerk; yet, at higher levels, regional or national government procurement officials are likely to think more strategically and be less concerned with parochial local issues. This can make the alignment of incentives difficult. When a close network of friends and colleagues biases information dissemination and retrieval toward local interests, and when a strong group of elites has captured the local community, the professional capacity in procurement is impaired. Close-knit social networks at the local level potentially discourage arm's-length transactions.

Importance of Public Procurement in Good Governance

The term "corruption" is used to describe a large range of illegal activities, but a common definition is "the abuse of public or private office for private or personal gain." Adopting a more comprehensive definition, the Asian Development Bank (2003: 3) says that corruption "involves behavior on the part of officials in the public and private sectors, in which they improperly and unlawfully enrich themselves and/or those close to them, or induce others to do so, by misusing the position in which they are placed." This is consistent with the procurement guidelines issued by the World Bank (2004: 8) when it defines a corrupt practice as "the offering, giving, receiving, or soliciting, directly or indirectly, of anything of value to influence the action of a public official in the procurement process or in contract execution." In all of these cases, politically corrupt practices involve officials misusing public power in the pursuit of illegitimate private advantage. Moreover, because it is usually hidden from public view, corruption can be conceptualized as the covert privatization of government functions (Passas 1997), and it usually prevails against the public interest.

Because corruption is often an everyday occurrence in many less-developed countries, understanding the process by which procurement decisions are made or avoided is crucial, and this necessitates understanding good governance more fully. Whether in reference to the public or private sector, in general, governance describes the process of making decisions and implementing them. Governance includes both formal and informal actors and the structures by which decision making and implementation occur. It also might include the exercise of political, economic, and administrative authority to manage a nation's affairs because it should account for the complex mechanisms, processes, relationships, and institutions through which citizens and groups articulate their interests, exercise their rights and obligations, and mediate their differences (UNDP 1997b). Moreover, good governance promotes efficient public management by relying on public participation, accountability, and transparency to ensure that activities and process outputs meet intended goals and standards (UNDP 1997a).

In general, good procurement practices coupled with good governance share many of the assumptions found in contemporary democracies, namely, that unenumerated and unspecified rights are believed to exist independently and before the creation of government (for a critique of the assumptions, see Prier [2003: 25–36]). This is suggested by World Bank initiatives that are "pro-people, pro-jobs, and pro-nature" and that pursue sustainable human development through increases in institutional capacity that give priority to the poor, advance women, sustain the environment, and create needed opportunities for employment and other livelihoods for the present and future needs of society.

Many of these principles of good governance are pursued in developing countries. For example, the nongovernmental organization Campaign for Good Governance, located in Sierra Leone, equates good governance with freedom, democracy, and gender equality in the hope that it will increase citizen participation in governance through advocacy, capacity building, and civic education to build a more informed civil populace and a democratic state. This is unsurprising because in an increasingly globalized environment, corruption tends to undermine public trust in politicians and in political institutions and processes no matter where they are located.

Good governance is often considered an ideal that is difficult to achieve in its totality; yet, there appears to be common agreement that more political activity in civil society and genuinely competitive elections should be promoted (USAID n.d.), because corruption is the antithesis of good governance. Consequently, the belief is widely shared that public institutions advance human rights by conducting public affairs and managing public resources openly, impartially, and honestly. This can be done by creating and strengthening checks and balances in the political and procurement systems, and by giving oversight to proper authorities and civil society. It also entails creating a meritocratic, sufficiently paid civil service that operates in an environment promoting accountability in public expenditures.

Evolution and Goals of Public Procurement

Much of the literature dealing with public procurement reveals an unstated expectation that individuals often have incompatible beliefs about what actions define the "public good"; thus, prevailing norms about appropriate behavior may, in fact, provide superficial guidelines for how and what to buy at the local level. Saying that the "public interest" should make clear the proper course of action for government officials is no longer sufficient. To cope with this situation, managerialism and the public choice movement have taken hold within scholarly circles; as a result, there is, more generally, a global movement toward market-oriented efficiency in public procurement and public sector management.

In developing countries, though, many local-level procurement systems are characterized by inordinate control in an effort to prevent corruption and other abuses. Problems remain, however, because contemporary rational decision making assumes that the motivations for selection and use of decision rules in public procurement are widely shared and understood. At the same time, the procurement official must increasingly make risk assessments of goods and contracts in an inherently uncertain environment. However, as many developing nations continue to liberalize, procurement officials find that there are disagreements about procurement objectives and values held by the citizenry. This disconnect creates heterogeneous evaluative criteria for determining the proper buy decision in any given circumstance. Therefore, local governments and their officials must be made aware of these frictions. Perhaps this underpins the movement in developed countries toward benchmarking and performance measurement in local procurement that encourages planning and sound contract administration (Coe 1999).

Opportunities for Corruption in Public Procurement

The literature examines two kinds of corruption. The first is called grand corruption and is practiced by elites; it tends to erode the very system in which it is practiced. The second is referred to as petty corruption, and it is engaged in by bureaucrats who thereby threaten the efficacy of governing institutions. The two are generally thought to be interlinked because petty corruption can lead to grand corruption and vice versa.

In less-developed countries, one of the main avenues of corruption for local procurement officials is the "speed-money" exchange (Bose 2004; Guerrero and Rodríguez-Oreggi 2005; Marjit, Mukherjee, and Mukherjee 2000). This exchange can take many forms, but all involve the capacity to harass, delay, or withhold the decisions handed down by procurement officials unless a bribe is given. Whether it involves the ability to slow down existing registration and prequalification procedures for public works contractors, or the actual decision to buy a particular commodity or service from a specific vendor, the potential threat of procurement process distortion unless a bribe is paid creates numerous opportunities for corruption in local procurement.

Consider the case of supplier prequalification procedures required in an invitation to bid on a construction project. Because prequalification applications may be either complete or incomplete, incomplete applications must be delayed while complete applications can be processed. Thus, the discretion given to the procurement official and the procedures used can affect processing times; yet, as Bose (2004) points out, there is no transparent way to ascertain whether a supplier application has been returned as incomplete with good reason. However, failure to stop an incomplete application will be exposed subsequently by another official, especially under a decentralized procurement system. Decentralization implies that clearances are needed from a number of people, depending upon the type of buy or the agency for which the service is contracted. Experience and the institutional memory of the procurement official will indicate which clearances will ultimately be required and by whom up or down the procurement chain. Thus, spending time on an unnecessary clearance (delaying) may never come to light, but failing to obtain a necessary clearance will show up later in the purchasing process. Therefore, all procurement procedures should balance the need for controlling such abuses against the need for efficient decision making.

There may be times when a potential contractor or supplier must pay even if the government contract was obtained legally. For example, short open-contracting periods during which the official is waiting for all bid proposals may create incentives for contractors to "grease the wheels" for their own firms by offering kickbacks to officials who can block submission of bids by citing some "irregularity" in the paperwork or procedures. In this case, it may not matter that an outright refusal will not be forthcoming because processing can be delayed, and the potential supplier may be in no position to wait out the postponement. This process suggests that, in general, because suppliers do not value their time equally, some contractors and vendors are more willing to pay the speed-money than others who can wait out the delays. This willingness may have the long-term effect of reducing supplier competition, but more important, it also distorts good governance in public procurement.

There are also opportunities for collusion among bidders for a government contract. Types of collusion include bid rigging, bid manipulation or fraud, and bid orchestration. On the government side, because the procurement official is entrusted to verify the delivered quality of goods and services, there may be incentives to either distort the rankings of the quality of submitted bids or allow the awarded firm to produce at a lower quality level than required by the specifications in the statement of work. In addition, procurement officials might demand kickbacks, or knowingly allow product substitution or substandard parts or materials.

Numerous opportunities to engage in procurement corruption at the local level can surface. They include out-and-out theft through either embezzlement or stealing money or supplies, fraudulently inflated costs or labor mischarges, bribes to procurement officials or extortion of vendors by the official, or simply administrative conflicts of interest. In some circumstances, insider trading might be possible, as well as illegal commissions or personal favors, and favoritism and nepotism. In some developing countries, elections can be influenced by local politics, so there may be pressure for illegal political contributions to officials or political parties. Finally, money laundering can occur through public procurement offices.

Public organizations around the globe are increasingly using a wider variety of service delivery mechanisms in the belief that competition will spark efficiencies, leading inevitably to greater reliance on contracting out for services previously provided by a career civil service. Thus, procurement authority and decisions are increasingly delegated to lower levels of government or to private firms, and when coupled with preferential policies in public procurement such as mandates to buy locally or from small or minority-owned businesses, the opportunities for corruption expand.

As a general rule, the larger and more complex the organization or level of government, the longer it usually takes to make purchases because numerous rules and procedures typically lead to delays. However, agency response can lead to a strategy of overstocking to ensure supply. Thus, local governments confront an inherent trade-off in determining how rigidly to follow the procurement rules. Follow the rules too strictly and inflexibly and inefficiencies may result. Open up discretion to the local procurement official and the potential for corruption increases.

Government Systems and the Potential for Corruption at the Local Level

The type of government system appears to matter in the propensity to engage in corruption. The literature makes clear that the causes of corruption tend to be complex, but corruption thrives in the developing world because of the prevalence of weak public institutions, low levels of education attained by the majority of citizens, and the presence of an underdeveloped civil society. Moreover, the way power is distributed and exercised within a country has been shown to have an effect on corruption at the local level, so that procurement issues in one country may be less important in another. Common sense suggests that because a professional civil service tends to lead to a well-performing public sector, professionalization of procurement officials must be a target of any reform.

Although some claim that the way to permanently curb corruption is to reduce the government's role in the economy (Becker 1994, 1997), Galtung correctly points out that Denmark, Finland, the Netherlands, Norway, Sweden, and Switzerland consistently score the highest on Transparency International's Corruption Perception Index; yet they "do not read like a who's who of capitalist laissez-faire. And those who have liberalized and deregulated their economies in the past few years already had low levels of corruption before" (Galtung 1998: 123). Because of this situation, the distribution of power within a country may be more important than the amount of government activity.

Federal and Unitary Government Systems

From its laws to its procedures and rules, the system of government can profoundly affect a nation's procurement system. Three fundamental types of governments are found around the globe. In a *unitary system*, power resides at the national level; subnational governments are merely administrative arms of the central government. A second type of government is a *confederation*—the regional or state governments are the locus of sovereignty and they band together to create the national government. The central government is subservient to the wishes and dictates of the regional governments. A third system of government is *federalism*, in which the central government and regional or state governments exercise power with autonomous authority in the same political system.

The latter system tends to produce a diverse array of protections while encouraging innovation, but problems arise in coordinating multiple autonomous governments that may duplicate activities. Moreover, some federal systems give each government supremacy in its constitutionally assigned area, while in other systems the lines of authority are blurred. Because federal systems tend to have concurrent powers exercised by both national and subnational governments, interjurisdictional rivalries can end up undermining anticorruption strategies.

The main reason the institutional structure of the procurement system is important concerns the overlap between levels of governmental functions, which leads to coordination and regulatory problems in purchasing. As a consequence of blurred lines of authority, interpretations of what is appropriate in procurement can be frustratingly muddled in a federal system. In such an environment, local capture can lead to corruption opportunities in one area of the country while not in others. Thus, at the very least, an integrated system of procurement standards and operating procedures is needed for fighting corruption; this can be aided through increased cooperative procurement among regional and local governments.

Central Procurement Structure

Because institutional arrangements are important to curbing corruption in developing countries, locating the overall responsibility for procurement policy in one government entity, such as a national ministry, proves beneficial. Although the links between decentralization and corruption are not entirely clear (Fjeldstad 2003: 4), recent research suggests that devolution and decentralization are desirable (Bardhan and Mookherjee 2000; Gurgur and Shah 2005). However, decentralizing procurement in developing countries must be approached with caution—the lack of technical expertise at the local level can prevent positive outcomes because decentralization makes bribes more accessible (Bardhan and Mookerjee 2003; Carbonera 2000).

Where corruption is widespread, attempting to deal with it as a series of isolated problems is generally ineffective. Sustainable anticorruption efforts depend on a number of stakeholders all performing their parts in a holistic manner (Pope 2000). Because enforcement alone is often uncertain and inadequate, and high penalties almost always fail to deter crime (Marjit and Shi 1998), some strategies should focus on prevention even when conceived and planned at the national level, while some elements must be planned and implemented entirely at the local level—participation by all levels of government, including local, is needed to achieve success (United Nations Office on Drugs and Crime 2004). Government procurement and contract management systems are especially vulnerable to corruption in times of tight budgets or high inflation, because payments to vendors can be delayed, and civil servants' pay may be inadequate to resist corruption. Indeed, Van Rijckeghem and Weder (1997) provide evidence that corruption is slightly lower in developing countries where civil servants are paid better.

The proper level of decentralization is difficult to assess because one procurement process that effectively reduces the opportunity for corruption in one government may be ineffective in another local government. Because of the nature of grand corruption, especially in developing countries where it is endemic and nationwide, the central government must have some role in monitoring the performance of local procurement officials. By serving as a procurement watchdog, the national government can guarantee a floor for the provision of services and reserve the prerogative to intervene when required.

Centralization versus Decentralization

Developing countries must consider the repercussions of the way in which power is distributed and exercised along the public procurement pipeline. For many reasons, corruption is minimized when transparency of the procurement system is maximized, yet when decisions are not made locally, local beneficiaries have difficulty understanding how and why the actual procurement decisions were reached. Thus, these countries must weigh the efficiencies that can come from a centralized national procurement system against the loss of accountability and legitimacy that may result from opaque decision-making structures at the local level.

The most decentralized procurement architecture shifts power to the lowest levels of government and their line staff. By fragmenting authority, decentralization is often seen as one of the best ways to increase intergovernmental competition, strengthen checks and balances, increase accountability by responding to local needs, and possibly reduce the role of the state in general. The problem remains that decentralization may also increase the potential for corruption at the local level if officials in these positions have the opportunities outlined earlier to engage in corrupt practices. Because of lower capacity in financial management and auditing systems and greater constraints on fiscal resources at the local level (which often lead to lower pay for these officials), strong incentives to engage in corrosive practices may exist. Thus, developing countries must consider the trade-offs and differing capacities of their governments when choosing their procurement systems.

Conflicts Arising from Different Political Systems

The trend in developing countries has been toward greater procurement decentralization. However, relying solely upon decentralization to mitigate corruption may be a fool's errand, because local capture of communities could lead to more corruption. The possibility still remains, too, that decentralization exacerbates inequity in the quality of governance between better-off and less-well-off regions (Bardhan and Mookherjee 2006; but see Shankar and Shah 2003).

Vagstad (2000) analyzes the connection between the degree of information dispersion and the optimal decision structure in procurement. Vagstad points out that centralization may be too costly because of agency costs associated with distortions and bureaucracy costs such as those associated with the costs of establishing a central regulatory body. Whether this cost component is large enough to favor decentralizing procurement processes and procedures remains an open question because the relevant circumstances in developing countries are often context specific. Indeed, an argument for centralization is evident when one remembers that there is typically biased favoritism toward local information, thus corrupt local decisions can be masked even when following procedures consistent with national directives.

Regardless of the political system, corruption at the local level can be combated in other ways. For instance, a procurement manual that outlines standardized procedures might be used by each jurisdiction. Another way to combat corruption in some developing countries is to use procurement planning as a tool to prioritize an array of strategic reform options that are then tied to mainstream anticorruption measures. Adhering to good governance principles, the procurement plan uses rigorous data analysis and is participatory and homegrown, and backed by that country's political leadership. Indeed, adoption of procurement planning in Ghana helps to explain the movement on corruption in that nation (African Development Bank 2003).

The Procurement Process as a Safeguard against Corruption

Identifying the appropriate procurement process policies and practices can substantially reduce corruption. The model discussed here not only establishes a framework that reduces the opportunity for procurement process distortion (Monczka and Trent 1998), but may also increase transparency. When decision-making authority is open, fair, and competitive, and when there are multiple stakeholders involved in the decision process, the potential for procurement process distortion is greatly reduced.

According to Hinson and McCue (2004), the procurement planning process model is relatively straightforward: (a) establish a procurement strategic plan, (b) formalize the plan through normal legislative processes,

(c) implement the plan through good contract administration processes, and (d) evaluate the plan upon completion of the procurement process. Each step will be discussed below.[1]

Phases of the Public Procurement Planning Process

Limiting the opportunity for process corruption and transforming the overall goals and objectives of a particular procurement into measurable activities that can be used to plan, budget, and manage the procurement function require formal procurement planning. Appropriate procurement plans provide a means of preparing and documenting the various activities of a particular procurement activity. When properly formulated, a procurement plan minimizes the various risks associated with a particular purchase, aids project management and contract administration, helps identify roles and accountability structures, and addresses many ethical or probity concerns that may arise in the process of acquiring goods and services.

Procurement planning can also help in developing supplier relationships to enhance the acquisition and production of goods and services in the local community. By identifying specific functional demand attributes, planning links procurement expenditures to specific goals and objectives within the organization. Ultimately, linking resource allocation decisions in a priority-setting model, informing managers they must either confirm or change current procurement policy or program directions to meet those goals, and sharing the results of procurement process outcomes with both internal and external procurement stakeholders greatly reduce the probability for corruption and can result in positive change in organizational culture, systems, and operational processes.

The complexity of any procurement planning process is directly related to the amount to be expended, the difficulty in securing the needed goods or services, and the risks associated with the project. This complexity often involves assessing the degree of difficulty of securing supply, knowing the purchasing objectives, and gathering information on requirements and market characteristics. In addition, a purchasing strategy (otherwise known as a procurement plan) that is monitored and updated periodically should specify performance indicators and measures that determine when the purchasing objectives have been met.

Table 3.1 provides a nonexhaustive list of considerations that have been shown to help in developing a procurement plan for local governments. The collection and synthesis of this information should be used to generate a procurement profile with baseline information that will provide stakeholders the opportunity to evaluate where the local government is expending its

TABLE 3.1 Components of Procurement Planning

Procurement Profile Generation. A procurement profile will contain, at minimum, the following:

- What goods and services are purchased annually?
- Which department is buying specific goods and services?
- How much is spent on each good and service?
- How are goods and services purchased?
- From whom are the goods and services purchased?
- What is the geographical location of suppliers?

Supply Risk Analysis. The tool commonly used for evaluating the risks associated with specific commodities to be provided by suppliers is supply positioning.

- How critical are the goods and services to the local government?
- What are the risks associated with each good or service to be purchased?
  - product-related risk
  - organization-related risk
  - supplier-related risk
  - market-related risk
- What are the results of an evaluation of the key supply markets from which the local government acquires goods and services?
  - How many suppliers are there, and what are their market shares?
  - What is the availability of alternative or substitute products?
  - What is the degree and type of competition between suppliers?
  - What is the nature and quality of the supply chain?
  - What environmental factors affect the supply market?

Market Evaluation. Examine the impact of the local government's purchasing activities on its key supply markets.

- What is the local government's value as a customer to specific suppliers?
- How are suppliers likely to view the local government's business?

Procurement Integration. Assess each department's procurement function, including its structure, role, systems processes, and capability.

Procurement Forecast. Determine both the intermediate and long-term purchasing needs of the organization and develop strategies to facilitate the goals and objectives of the procurement plan and the organizational strategic plan.

Source: Adapted from Queensland State Government (2001).

resources. The next phase is to evaluate levels of risk for each supply market and each expenditure category. Following these two phases, each supply market from which the government has purchased specific goods and services should be evaluated. The procurement profile can be used to determine the impact of the expenditure patterns on various local supply markets that provide goods and services to the government, and it can help in the evaluation of institutional processes and capabilities (labeled procurement integration in the table). Finally, historical and current supply patterns can be forecast to estimate both the intermediate and long-term procurement needs of the organization. These estimates provide useful benchmarks for establishing and evaluating the effectiveness of the procurement plan, the nature of any risk associated with various supply categories, and the nature and timing of resource demands. For the purpose of this chapter, only the development of the procurement profile and analysis of procurement risk will be discussed. Those interested in learning more about market evaluation, procurement integration, and procurement forecasting should refer to the citation provided at the bottom of table 3.1.

The first step in accumulating the information necessary to generate a procurement profile is to identify the horizontal and vertical functions within the local government. In most cases, simply creating or reviewing an organizational chart will suffice. Typically, an organizational chart will provide enough detail to identify the various agencies involved in the procurement function. Once all the agencies are known, the next step is to identify all the programs and activities associated with each department and to locate the individuals actively involved in the purchasing process. This process may require further discussion with the various departments about what is being accomplished, how, and by whom. This promotes transparency by fixing responsibility and accountability at the individual level and, in turn, reduces the incentives for individuals to distort the procurement process.

Next, the local government general ledger and accounts payable ledger should be examined. These documents provide a rich source of information regarding the amount or quantity purchased, by whom and from whom, and when, as well as other general vendor information. Using the data on the general and accounts payable ledgers (as well as all supporting documentation) requires working with finance or accounting personnel to obtain expenditure reports for all the goods and services the organization consumed. A breakdown by the general ledger account code usually provides sufficient detail to commence this process; however, unless the procurement department has maintained this information, the general ledger codes are not a good descriptor of the goods and services charged to a particular activity. Thus, it may be necessary to "drill down" into the general ledger codes and categorize the transactions into meaningful groups for generating the procurement profile.

A suggested criterion for grouping purchases is that categories should represent related goods and services that might logically be purchased together in the same purchasing action and from the same market sector.

For example, in some organizations, requests for proposal (RFPs) may be invited for construction activities as one product group rather than a number of separate items such as architectural services, engineering services, air-conditioning items, and so forth.

In addition to reviewing the accounts payable and general ledgers, information can be gathered from vendor listing files, departmental staff who deal with suppliers, vendors' references, the Internet, and the suppliers themselves, to more fully understand the markets in which the suppliers are operating. In some instances, the same supplier may appear under different categories. For example, an office supply company may appear under office supplies, computer equipment, and furniture. Therefore, subcategorization that cross-lists vendors with their product and service types may be useful in the long run.

Some of the preliminary factors to consider when categorizing expenditures include the differences and similarities in risk involved with procuring the various goods or services, supplier capability, application of the product or service in the department, and similar or related market analysis. Nails, hammers, nuts, and bolts may be categorized into "building hardware" for a department undertaking building maintenance. For each item, the purchase risk may be similar—low risk with easily obtainable supply for those items that are put to the same general use. However, consultancy services for engineering and architectural services would be separated because the purposes of the services are sufficiently different to warrant a division of profiles, especially given that supplier capability required for building engineering and design is quite different, and the levels of risk in each instance may also vary.

All procurement expenditures should be placed in an electronic database for easy reference and analysis. Expenditures can then be rank ordered from highest to lowest, ensuring that high expenditure areas are categorized first—typically, the top 20 percent of entries account for approximately 80 percent of total procurement spending. Focusing specific planning activities on the largest expenditure categories in the procurement profile increases the likelihood that the procurement process can be transformed into an intelligence-gathering device for efficient and effective procurement resource allocation decisions that mitigate corruption.

Once the procurement profile is generated, the next step is to discuss the outcomes of the categorization with the key local stakeholders involved in purchasing and supplier management to ensure that the goods and services are logically grouped in relation to the use of the products. All goods and services should be included in the profile regardless of who purchases the goods or services or what amount is spent on them. As discussed previously, local governments may delegate purchasing authority to various functional areas, leading to an inclination to exclude such expenditures. This is particularly true in service areas such as public safety, public works, or education. Also, unless internal transfers and interdepartmental transfers are properly identified, information extracted from accounts payable can be distorted to hide corruption.

Once a procurement profile is generated by department and by activity, past expenditures can be extrapolated and analyzed using vendor-related information. The vendor profile should include, at a minimum, the following:

- Vendor name and unique identification number
- Vendor address and location identifier (to be used in a regional analysis)
- Total amount spent with the vendor for each fiscal year
- Number of invoices processed for the vendor and their amounts and transaction method (RFPs, procurement cards, emergency purchase orders, and so forth)
- The general ledger codes to which the expenditure was posted for the vendor
- Which department or agency used the vendor (with amount if possible)

Vendor identification numbers indicate the amount spent on each item for each supplier or group of suppliers within a particular time frame, while location identifiers help identify and analyze local and regional spending patterns. Identifying the procurement technique used for each purchase aids in determining if the government is overly reliant on one particular solicitation technique, and shows whether consolidating invoices to a particular vendor can decrease transaction costs.

Formalizing Procurement Safeguards

Whenever possible, local governments should use a formal sourcing strategy. This can be accomplished by appropriate bidding procedures soliciting competitive quotations, or by negotiated pricing arrangements. The process through which formal solicitations are issued, offers are made, contracts awarded, and goods or services received tends to vary according to the vendor or contractor's compliance with specifications, price, delivery, service, terms and conditions, location, or other relevant factors identified in the procurement plan.

Types of Specifications and Standards

The link between procurement planning and identification of specifications and standards becomes readily apparent when the way in which goods and services are to be acquired is documented. For most goods and services, a statement of work (SOW) should be developed before the beginning of the contract administration phase. The SOW spells out in detail all the specifications and standards that must be achieved to fulfill the contract requirements. It will also contain specific, detailed responsibilities for both the vendor or contractor and the local government. Although the contract itself may explain a payment plan, further detail may be included in the SOW. According to Wikipedia, SOWs should contain, at a minimum, the following:

- *Scope of work.* Describes the work to be done in detail and specifies the exact nature of the work or the product to be delivered.
- *Location of work.* Describes where the work is to be performed or the product is to be delivered.
- *Period of performance.* Specifies the allowable time for projects or deliverables, such as start and finish times, number of hours that can be billed per week or month, time when work is to be performed (evenings, weekends), and anything else that relates to scheduling.
- *Deliverables schedule.* Lists the specific deliverables, describing what is due and when.
- *Applicable standards.* Describes any industry-specific standards that need to be adhered to in fulfilling the contract.
- *Acceptance criteria.* Identifies how the local government will determine if the product or service is acceptable and what criteria will be used to state the work is acceptable.
- *Special requirements.* Specifies any special hardware or software, specialized workforce requirements (such as degrees or certifications for personnel), travel requirements, and anything else not covered in the contract specifications.

Once the SOW is completed, a contract administration plan must be drafted. The plan, along with each action expected of the contractor and the local government, must be stated along with time lines and standard benchmarks. The plan should include a communication strategy, a responsibility matrix (for both the vendor or contractor and the local government), a work breakdown structure, and a schedule of key tasks. A checklist of all contractual issues, based on the contract itself and tasks identified throughout the contracting term, should be generated. Some items to include in this checklist are

- contract start and end dates;
- all relevant costs;
- invoice and payment due dates;
- due dates for benchmarks and deliveries;
- installations, implementations, and training details (if applicable); and
- the explicit responsibilities and promises listed in the contract or identified in the SOW for all contractors and for the local government.

Determining the Method of Source Selection

The nature of the goods and services to be consumed by the local government will determine the best strategy for selecting the supplier. Generally, selection methods can be categorized as either formal or informal. The different solicitation methods as identified in the Federal Acquisition Regulation (FAR 2005) are described in the following:

- *Formal bids and contracts.* Formal bids use legal advertising, detailed specifications or statements of work, and a formal bid opening at a prescribed date and time. Formal bids are typically solicited through an invitation to bid or through an RFP, and they are awarded by the governing board. Contracts resulting from the formal bid process may be of several types:
  - — Firm or fixed-price contracts are awarded for a specified quantity of goods or level of services for a specific time. Based on the terms of the contract, delivery may be in one or several shipments.
  - — Price agreements are awarded for anticipated amounts during a certain period. These contracts are binding for the full period regardless of quantity.
  - — Construction contracts are typically awarded for a specific public works project. These contracts have additional requirements, such as bid, performance, and payment bonds; and insurance requirements, and must be performed by a licensed contractor.
  - — Service contracts are typically awarded for services such as maintenance of equipment or professional services. These contracts are awarded based upon the criteria set forth in the RFP.
- *Informal quotations and contracts.* The informal quotation and bid process is used for purchases under a predefined formal bid limit or when formal bidding processes are unrealistic or inefficient. Purchase orders and

contracts resulting from the informal bid process can cover a wide variety of goods and services. Generally, there are two types of informal quotations:
— Written quotations are solicited by mail, e-mail, or fax without the formalities of an open and advertised public bid.
— In many situations, telephone quotations are used to purchase goods and services.

▩ *Open purchase orders.* Occasionally, open or blanket purchase orders are set up to allow authorized individuals or departments to purchase low-cost or emergency items on an as-needed basis. Open purchase orders are typically for a designated period and based upon annual fixed pricing or discount schedules offered to the local government.

The use of informal source selection should be minimized to reduce opportunities and the temptation for corruption, and to ensure that the local government is receiving the best price and highest quality and that the vendor or contractor is capable of delivering as promised. The two primary methods for informal source selection are sole-source procurement and emergency procurement.

In some situations, a contract may be awarded for a good, service, or construction item without competition if the procurement plan identifies that only one source can provide the required material, service, or construction item. Sole-source procurement must be avoided except when no reasonable alternative source exists. A written determination of the basis for the sole-source procurement should be included in the procurement plan. Typically, construction services are not procured under sole source, but in some cases professional services may be procured (University of Minnesota 2004) by this method.

If a threat to public health, welfare, or safety exists, or if a situation arises that makes other bidding procedures impracticable, unnecessary, or contrary to the public interest, allowance should be made for emergency procurements. A written determination of the basis for the emergency and for the selection of the particular contractor should be documented and shared with key stakeholders.

According to the University of Minnesota (2004) purchasing practices, factors to be considered in determining whether competitive sealed bidding is not practicable include the following:

▩ Whether the contract needs to be other than fixed price.
▩ Whether oral or written discussions may need to be conducted with suppliers concerning technical and price aspects of their proposals.

▪ Whether vendors or contractors may need to be afforded the opportunity to revise their proposals, including price.
▪ Whether an award based upon a comparative evaluation as stated in the RFP will differ so markedly in price, quality, and contractual factors that another bid process will be more advantageous to the local government. Quality factors include technical and performance capability and the content of the technical proposal.
▪ Whether the primary consideration in determining award may not be price.

For both sole-source and emergency purchasing, the local government must be assured that the selection process is not intended to circumvent the responsibilities associated with formal bid procedures.

Contract Administration

Contract administration is the management of a contract for goods or services after the vendor or contractor has been selected, and involves all the actions necessary to execute the contract, including precontract review, contract execution, and postcontract evaluation. The specific nature and extent of contract administration will vary from contract to contract and by goods and services procured. Depending on the nature of the contract, a contract can be administered by one person (project manager) or by a team (project management team), and can range from the mere acceptance of delivery from and payment to the vendor or contractor (normally for small purchase orders such as office supplies) to extensive involvement by project managers, finance and budgeting staff, procurement officials, and all individuals who have a substantive stake in the contract (such as construction projects).

Some of the major determinants affecting the level of sophistication demanded during the administration of the contract include the nature of the work, the type of contract, the value of the contract, and the experience and commitment of the personnel assigned. In many cases, procurement officials do not directly administer contracts but instead advise and assist the contract officer or project manager.

Assessing Contract Risks Concerning Corruption

Although assessing contract risk is a continual process throughout the contractual stream, contract administration is the phase where one is likely to more easily observe the manifestations of risks associated with corruption. Consider that risk management generally refers to the process of assessing and measuring risks associated with a specific contract, and then developing action plans to manage the potential risk. However, because there are so many potential risks in any contracting environment, this chapter focuses on managing risks associated with corruption. Thus, the procurement plan is a tool that can help manage and evaluate the trade-offs associated with transferring the risk of bearing the costs of corruption to another party, attempting to avoid the risk, reducing the negative effects of the potential risk, and accepting some or all of the consequences of a particular risk. Again, it should be clear that although identifying and evaluating numerous risks typically occur early in the contracting process, the contract administration phase is where most of these risks are borne.

Ideally, risk management ranks the risks and first addresses those with the greatest potential loss and the greatest probability of occurring. Balancing risks with a high probability of occurrence but lower loss against risks with high loss but lower probability of occurrence can be a difficult task in local government contract administration.

An articulated risk management process consists of five basic steps—establishing the risk context, identifying potential risks, analyzing risks, evaluating risks, and addressing risks. Because a fundamental component of risk management is open and honest communication, consultation is required to ensure adequate information is provided and risk mitigation strategies are disseminated to all interested parties. Monitoring and review are also intrinsic parts of risk management.[2]

The first step is to establish the contractual *risk context*, including planning the remainder of the process and mapping out the scope of the contract. It also includes the identity and objectives of stakeholders, the basis upon which risks will be evaluated, specification of a framework for the process, and an agenda for identification and analysis.

After establishing the contract context, the next step in the risk management process is to *identify potential risks*. Risks are events that, when triggered, will cause unanticipated problems. Hence, risk identification can start with the source of potential problems, or with the potential problem itself.

- *Source analysis.* Sources of risk may be internal or external to the procurement system that is the target of risk management. Examples of risk sources are varied and could include the potential for corruption from stakeholders of a project, to the behavior of a supplier's employees, to threatening weather over an airport.
- *Problem analysis.* Risks are related to certain identifiable threats. Examples include the threat of a supplier losing money on a particular contract and thus reducing the level or quality of goods and services, the threat of abuse of privacy information, or the threat of accidents and casualties. Threats may come from stakeholders, customers, or even legislative bodies.

When either source or problem risk is known, the events that a source may trigger or the events that can lead to a problem can be investigated. For example, stakeholders withdrawing during a project may endanger funding of the project; privacy information may be stolen by employees even within a closed network; or lightning striking a radio tower may shut off communication for some time.

The method of identifying risks may depend on culture, industry practice, or compliance (as defined by past performance). Common risk identification methods include the following:

- *Objectives-based risk identification.* Any event that could negatively affect achieving a stated objective partly or completely is identified as a risk.
- *Scenario-based risk identification.* In scenario analysis, different scenarios are created. The scenarios may be the alternative ways to achieve a stated objective, or an analysis of the interaction of forces in, for example, a market or a political battle with a local community pressure group. Any event that triggers an undesired scenario alternative is identified as a risk.
- *Taxonomy-based risk identification.* Taxonomy-based risk identification is a breakdown of possible risk sources. Based on the taxonomy and knowledge of best practices, a questionnaire can be compiled from key sources that can identify possible risk factors by source.
- *Common-risk checking.* Across many industries, various lists that identify specific risks are available. Each risk in the list can be checked for application to the particular procurement. For example, the Common Vulnerability and Exposures list identifies known risks in the software industry.

Once potential risks have been identified, they must then be *analyzed* for their potential severity of loss and the probability of occurrence. These quantities can be simple to measure, in the case of the value of a lost building, or impossible to know for sure in the case of the probability of an unlikely event occurring. Therefore, in the assessment process, it is critical to make the best possible educated guesses to properly prioritize the implementation of the risk management plan.

The fundamental difficulty in risk *evaluation* is determining the rate of occurrence, because statistical information is not available on all types of past incidents. Furthermore, evaluating the severity of the consequences (the impact) is often difficult for nonmaterial assets. Asset valuation is another concern. Thus, "best guesstimates" along with available statistics are the primary sources of information. Nevertheless, risk evaluation should produce information for the organization's management so that the primary risks are easy to understand and risk management decisions can be prioritized. While numerous risk formulas exist, perhaps the most widely accepted is the following:

$$\text{Risk} = \text{probable rate of occurrence} \times \text{impact of the event}$$

Proper risk management typically involves frequently performed risk assessments that use simple methodologies. In procurement, the findings of risk assessments are typically presented in financial terms. For example, Robert H. Courtney Jr. (1970; 1977) proposed a formula that calculates the annualized loss expectancy to compare the expected loss value with the security control implementation costs (a cost-benefit analysis). Although it is but one way of thinking about risk management, the Courtney formula has been adopted as a standard assessment by the U.S. government (NBS 1981). Moreover, because there are potentially infinite possibilities in determining the correct matrix of responsive behaviors to risks, there is no strict formula that can be offered on how to properly *address risks.*

Mirroring what have come to be known as Courtney's Laws of Security, clearly, perfect mitigation has infinite cost, and there is no such thing as zero risk. Hence, one must determine the acceptable levels of corruption that result from contracting out government services. Moreover, one should account for the fact that there will be differential costs associated with mitigating corruption up and down the contractual stream. This awareness means that if contractual risks are transferred to the contractor, there will be determinable costs associated with monitoring the corruption potential that can occur between contractor and subcontractors. As a result, different strategies may have to be employed at various stages of contract administration.

Key Responsibilities for Contract Administrators

Good contract administration requires that procurement officials become familiar with the specifics identified in the contract, regardless of whether they were involved in negotiating it. The contract not only identifies what is required of the vendor but also spells out the responsibilities of the local government in facilitating the transaction.

According to the University of Minnesota's (2004) purchasing practices, good administration of contracts also requires that precontract conferences be held before commencement of the contracts. Internal conferences should be held to familiarize the project manager or project team with the contract, the SOW, and the contract administration plan. In most cases at the local level, the team may be brought in earlier to help with preparing the SOW and the contract administration plan. External conferences must be held to bring together the internal team and the vendor's or contractor's team to ensure that everyone understands the responsibilities, the contract, the SOW, and general expectations, as well as contractual prohibitions for both parties. Notes or formal minutes of these meetings should be taken and sent to all participants with an invitation for additions or corrections. This transparency ensures that all parties are familiar with all expectations, and if changes need to be made before implementation of the contract, all parties have agreed to the changes.

While the contract is in force, the following activities must be performed and tracked:

- Execute changes to the contract by a formal amendment.
- Determine the authorized signer of amendments.
- Monitor and document progress, and conduct regular progress reviews with the vendor or contractor and with the local government contract administration team.
- Identify issues or problems with contract deliverables, discuss solutions with the vendor or contractor, and work to resolve the problems with the vendor or contractor.
- Accept or reject services performed.
- Review checklist to ensure that all deliverables are being or have been completed.
- Review and accept or reject invoices based on benchmarks.
- Pay according to the payment schedule.
- Document lessons learned for the next round of contract administration.
- If an award was based on specific résumés or specific personnel being assigned to the project, confirm that those people are the ones actually working on the project (University of Minnesota 2004).

Contract Termination

Contract closeout begins when the contract has been physically completed, that is, all services have been performed and products delivered. According to the Federal Acquisition Institute (2004), closeout is complete when all administrative actions have concluded, all disputes have been settled, and final payment has been made. The process can be simple or complex, depending on the contract type; it requires close coordination among the contracting office, the finance office, the program office, and the contractor. Contract closeout is an important aspect of contract administration.

The contract audit process also affects contract closeout. Contract audits are required to determine the reasonableness of fulfilling the original contract, what is allowed to be amended or allowed in change orders, and how costs can be properly allocated under the terms of the contract. A closeout audit will reconcile all final claims of the contractor under the contract. If completion of the closeout audits is delayed, contracting officials often cannot complete the closeout process for many cost-reimbursement contracts. It is important that contracting officials have a good working relationship with the auditors to accomplish contract closeout (FAI 2004).

Payment Process

Voucher processing is just as important as any other aspect of contract administration. Payment to the contractor for the supplies and services delivered is the government's obligation under the contract. The government expects the contractor to meet all contract requirements for quality, quantity, and timeliness (FAI 2004). The contractor expects no less of the government in meeting its obligation for timely, accurate payment for goods and services received, so a process for quickly and efficiently meeting this obligation is essential. Therefore, it is incumbent upon local program, procurement, and finance officials to understand clearly their roles and responsibilities related to reviewing and processing vouchers. This will ensure that payment is only made to contractors who perform in accordance with contract terms and conditions, and will help establish an ethical environment of fairness in which to conduct business (FAI 2004).

Ethical Procurement Evaluation

The importance of standardized ethical practices cannot be overestimated, and such practices should be laid out in a manual. In an era of outsourcing and contracting, creating a transparent environment requires attention to detail, standardizing best practices, and clearly outlining extensive instructions to bidders. Ensuring fairness also requires documents that establish the eligibility of the bidder and the goods and services that will be provided, as well as the institutionalized documentation establishing the conformity of those goods and services. Moreover, immovable deadlines for submission and the period of validity of bids should be clearly outlined; once bids are obtained, they should be sealed and marked. Failing this, opportunities for corruption increase; yet, procedures should be created for those rare circumstances when late bids might be acceptable, and under what conditions withdrawal, substitution, and modification of bids might be appropriate.

There should also be a transparent process for the evaluation and comparison of bids that minimizes ad hoc procurement decisions. Of course, to get the most competitive price, confidentiality of bids should be required, but once the preliminary examination of bids and their terms and conditions is completed, the technical evaluation should lead to a ranking of submissions. At this point, it becomes clear that issues of domestic or local preference must be addressed within the manual, because preferences are notorious for circumventing procedures designed to mitigate corruption.

To minimize the possibility of collusion among vendors, local procurement officials should maintain the right not only to accept or reject any or all bids, but also to vary quantities of purchase at the time of award. Finally, the criteria for awarding the contract should be clearly specified, and a performance security on large contracts should be obtained.

To address corruption in the field of public contracting, Transparency International has developed templates for agreements between the government and all bidders that provide for several different sanctions when violations occur. Labeled "Integrity Pacts," they contain the mutual rights and obligations of all parties to the pact, and specify that neither side will engage in bribery or collude with competitors. Moreover, the pacts tend to have disclosure agreements whereby bidders report all commissions and similar expenses paid to anybody connected with the contract. Integrity Pacts are similar to "no bribery pledges" used by the World Bank (1997).

Performance Measures

In the face of tight budgets, many line personnel in developing countries have realized that a transparent public procurement system contributes to good governance and fighting corruption. Consistent with a clear legal framework and the mechanisms for enforcing procurement rules, measuring the performance of procurement officials is key to obtaining good outcomes. Unfortunately, many developing countries often lack clear, concise, and consistent directives on how to conduct procurement. Even where a procurement code might exist, the procedures and legal covenants governing public procurement are often contradictory. The World Bank regularly carries out assessments of the strengths and weaknesses of procurement systems in the countries where it lends, and recent scholarship has noted the importance of developing appropriate performance measures as a potent anticorruption tool and as a vehicle for improving service delivery (Klitgaard, Maclean-Abaroa, and Parris 2000).

Assessment of contractors' performance should include provisions for measuring outputs reflecting specific target conditions of the service levels mandated by the contract. Although beyond the scope of this chapter, it is important that service levels be defined in the contract, and the exact specifications be spelled out because the contractor becomes fully responsible for the design, durability, and performance of the works necessary to reach the required service level. Common examples of this type of contract at the local level are road-building and maintenance contracts. However, there are potential conflict of interest considerations, especially if the locality is contemplating the establishment of long-term commitments like public-private partnerships between the contractor and the government, or highway franchising (Engel, Fischer, and Galetovic 2005).

Other opportunities for conflicts of interest arise if the developing country exhibits the "revolving door" between public office and the private sector. Many nations allow public officials to enter the private sector very shortly, or even immediately, after leaving government service and to join companies with which they were transacting business (Passas 1997). This situation can often create costly scandals, such as the 1991 Goldenberg scheme within the Kenyan government.

Transparency International—Kenya (2004) estimates the total costs of corruption in the Goldenberg scam at fully 10 percent of Kenyan gross domestic product or US$600 million. The usual suspects were identified in facilitating corruption, including weak and unaccountable enforcement institutions, poorly designed oversight and monitoring institutions, gaps in procurement integrity, the need to service patronage networks in politics, and weak political commitment to fight corruption. However, the scandal resulted in the creation of a Public Complaints Office and the potential for creating future local ombudsmen. Moreover, Kenya passed the Public Officer Ethics Act in addition to the Public Procurement and Disposal of Assets Bill. These reforms have resulted in a significant decrease in the Kenya Bribery Index since 2002.[3] In local governments, there has been a substantial reduction in petty bribery since 2001 when local authorities occupied 6 of the 10 most corrupt institutions in the nation.

Nonetheless, designing an appropriate anticorruption regime is fraught with hazard, because additional oversight can potentially lead to larger social welfare loss than the loss in the presence of corruption (Bose 2004; Mookherjee and Png 1995).

Evaluation Techniques

Informed procurement decisions are key to effective and efficient government, and properly evaluating when and how to purchase goods and contract out for services can result in substantial savings to the public. Although numerous evaluation criteria can be used, three ways to help ensure efficiency are briefly described below: optimum replacement cycle, life-cycle costing, and the options to lease or purchase equipment.[4]

Procurement officials should determine the optimal time to replace equipment by comparing the cost of repairing it with the cost of replacing it. By factoring in the replacement value, the discount rate, and the time value of money, one can calculate which alternative is more cost-effective. Often used in replacement of motorized equipment, accurate maintenance and repair records must be kept to utilize this technique. However, for energy-consuming goods, equipment, or buildings, life-cycle costing is the superior method, because it accounts for maintenance, repair, and energy costs while controlling for the salvage value of the item. These two purchasing options should be compared with the alternative of leasing equipment or facilities. Leasing may be justified if the discounted cost of the lease is less than the total cost of outright purchase. Although an in-depth discussion is beyond the focus of this chapter, these alternatives present corruption hazards, because they require a sophistication that may not be present at the local level in many developing countries.

Consider the case where there are few if any department heads or consultants. Because small local units typically lack such expertise, they often must rely upon the cues of larger governments. They may adopt specifications created by the national government or by the vendors themselves.[5] As discussed earlier, specifications are a clear and complete description of the essential qualities that products and services should have, and if a vendor's specifications are chosen, the incentives of vendors to bribe the procurement official to adopt their specifications can lead to diminished competition. Thus, regulations and procedures should suggest (if not mandate) the use of agencies that specialize in preparing and maintaining specifications, either at the state or national level, and they should require that chosen vendors meet or exceed the adopted specification requirements.[6] Regardless of the technique used, the procurement official should use only those factors, methodologies, and criteria that were defined in the RFP and the bid data sheet.

Feedback and Monitoring

To create and maintain a transparent and competitive environment in public procurement, the public should have mechanisms for feedback and monitoring. Because bidding vendors are particularly interested in a transparent process, a few simple steps can help solidify accountability over procurement decisions. The first involves wide advertising of procurement opportunities with guarantees that the bids will be accepted according to strictly objective criteria. In addition, the bid evaluation and contract award procedures should be transparent and clear to all stakeholders. Finally, enforceable rights of review should be established if procurement officials breach the rules. This latter mechanism provides the legal basis for stakeholders (most commonly those bidders who were excluded or were denied the contract) to challenge the actions of procurement officials when they act contrary to the rules.

There are numerous ways to obtain information. For example, Hakobyan and Wolkers (2004) outline numerous diagnostic tools used in 25 African countries to assess the extent of bribery in urban areas: budget transparency, "social" audits, government procedure reviews, and audits of local administrations. This information is typically obtained from interviews and focus groups of households, government officials' perceptions, experts, and document analyses. These studies help raise awareness through media coverage and advocacy, and they tend to develop ownership within the localities. For example, a 2001 survey of government officials' perceptions of corruption in Bisho, Eastern Cape, South Africa, tracked officials' perceptions and experiences of corruption to acquire benchmark information on the exposure to corruption in the Eastern Cape's capital and to measure the effectiveness of various anticorruption measures.

There are other ways to gain feedback and assess the costs of corruption to stakeholders, but all tools should be designed to reduce the costs of services to the public and to create an ethos of accountability. The United Nations (2001) has also created a systematic measurement system that attempts to bring service providers and citizens closer together. Called service delivery surveys, they are community-based, fact-finding instruments intended to measure the "leakage" of resources from institutions that are supposed to be using those resources for social objectives but that have diverted them to private gain. Widely used in developing countries around the globe, the surveys are a good indicator of corruption and help produce a baseline of service coverage that is then used to benchmark progress. The process brings the local community into the strategic planning phase of service provision, and the information can be used to help procurement officials respond better to stakeholders by focusing more on results than on inputs. However, successful feedback takes a great amount of time and commitment from political officials.

Ethics and Professionalism

Although punishment, prevention, and public education are the three main principles at the core of many national anticorruption strategies (Matscheza and Kunaka 2000), ethics and professionalism must be front and center in public procurement in all developing countries. There are at least two reasons why corruption is so difficult to overcome in developing countries. The first is low pay, especially at the local level. The second involves the combination of local and state capture represented by interests within society deeply vested in maintaining the status quo, coupled with the lack of political will to implement and enforce needed procurement changes. Indeed, endemic corruption in the form of nepotism and bribery in Africa was determined to be the result of "avarice," not of something inherently wrong with the system (Wraith and Simpkins 1978), and this is a problem of ethics.

Because social development is a complex phenomenon, it may be that the initial phases of fighting corruption actually create more problems in the short term (Johnston 1993). Moreover, case studies of Botswana, Ecuador, Hong Kong (China), Mali, Senegal, and Tanzania all reveal that universal approaches to designing and implementing effective anticorruption strategies do not succeed. This suggests that individually tailored strategies requiring exceptional political will are probably the norm (Doig and Riley 1998), as evidenced by the cases in China, Pakistan, and the Republic of Korea (Asian Development Bank 2001). The large amounts of public funds expended in public procurement provide multiple incentives for both public officials and potential suppliers in the private sector to maintain the status quo of corrupt practices. Indeed, in many developing countries, public contracts are often the reward for political supporters, and this practice can only be stopped by public officials holding themselves to standards of conduct that preclude this behavior.

Professional Codes of Ethics

Public procurement officials often face an array of options in any decision because of the lack of universal criteria for determining all purchases in the public arena. Working with often contradictory public goals, a procurement official's values and ethics can play a large part in serving the public interest. Thus, political commitment is important, because the tone from the top helps create an ethical culture, and codes of ethics are one important mechanism to convey behavioral norms to local officials. More than a list of goals and objectives, the code sets forth what is to be valued in the organization and helps to define the integrity of the individual.

Although the agents for transmitting prescribed values can be parents, religion, school, peers, media, professional and legal training, and life experiences, the role of ethics, culture, and social norms should not be discounted. Because there is a mutual reinforcement of values and the purchasing decisions that flow from them, values can get updated and redefined based on experience, learning, and training. Thus, the contextual history and the anticorruption environment of the procurement organization are important in any ethics training program.

Values and ethical principles should guide procurement actions by offering an answer to the question of what one should do in a specific situation, but a problem remains in that situational ethics are learned and remain flexible and adaptable to a particular state of affairs. Thus, anticorruption strategies should incorporate values that are prized and that help define moral boundaries of individual behavior.

Efforts have been made to nationalize ethics and integrity in local governance in the developing world. One recent example is Uganda, where not only was a Directorate of Ethics and Integrity established in the Office of the President, but the Parliament instituted a Parliamentary Local Governments Public Accounts Committee to handle oversight of the use of public funds in local governments (African Development Bank 2003). These actions are intended to alert local communities to the dangers of corruption while strengthening the capacity of local governments to be transparent, accountable, and responsive to their constituents.

For a code of ethics to work, stakeholders in local governance should be consulted as part of its preparation, and the code should account for the sociocultural traditions of the country. Of course, having credible leaders in public service will help build a consensus on the meaning of ethics and integrity, and the exemplary values that result can help fight corruption. Furthermore, encouraging professional conduct through trade associations or professional bodies can be quite effective for members. Consideration should be given to mandating that local procurement officials belong to professional certification bodies, because not only can it increase the level of professional skills and knowledge, but the social network and shared values of professionalism help to curb corruption. Finally, attention might be paid to establishing ethics and integrity officers at the national level who can be deployed to local areas as needed.

Reliance on Standards, Regulations, and Statutes to Ensure Honesty

Although ethics are helpful in determining the correct purchasing decision, they are far from determinative. Thus, public procurement officials at all levels must rely on standards and regulations (sometimes in the form of statutory law but often detailed in a purchasing manual) to ensure efficiency in public procurement.[7] Effective purchasing procedures can be especially important at the local level in developing countries because of the acute scarcity of resources. One means of realizing this goal is through developing and using standard operating procedures (SOPs), which concentrate on standardizing goods, outlining how to order goods, determining what to buy, and detailing how to authorize payment. Using SOPs also has the effect of limiting the scope for ad hoc decisions and decreases the opportunities for corruption.

To take advantage of economies of scale and the lower prices that result, everyday equipment such as hand tools or computers, and other materials such as office supplies, are easily subject to standardization because they are like items that tend not to be asset specific nor specialized to any single agency or department. Obviously, standardization cannot be used when goods are highly specialized or used only by a single bureau.

Mirroring developed countries, elected officials should adopt regulations that govern the general duties and specify the procedures that should be followed for local procurement officials. An operating manual is often a good place to outline detailed administrative procedures, such as determining the limits on the use of petty cash for purchases. Among other things, regulations should specify procedures for conducting competitive bids—specifically the prequalification of potential bidders and the avoidance of illegal special preferences for vendors.[8] In addition, there should be clear procedures on how and under what conditions to purchase items not requiring bids (such as emergency purchases), and directives should be clear on how to acquire professional services. The regulations should spell out minimal requirements for entering into cooperative public purchasing agreements.

Local government regulations should also address inventory control policies that outline not only how and when to buy, test, and inspect ordered materials, but also how to maintain appropriate property records and how to dispose of obsolete equipment and materials. Celentani and Ganuza (2001) point out that in public procurement, when the procurement official has better information than the public about the price and the quality of the procured good, delegating the task of verifying procured quality to the procurement official introduces the possibility of misrepresenting the information in exchange for a positive payment from the vendor. Thus, as a general rule, all delivered equipment and materials should be inspected and tested at the time of delivery, and written standards should be used to tag materials as obsolete. Again, SOPs for this stage of procurement apply.

On the vendor side, a pledge against taking bribes should be made a condition for bidding, because they operate much as an explicit code of ethics and can be a powerful signal that the rules of the game have changed (World Bank 1997). Transparency should also be part of any code, and localities should encourage, if not mandate, that all government contractors establish corporate codes of conduct replete with compliance procedures that discourage bribery. However, officials should be sure that if such codes are required, the resulting pool of bidders will not restrict competition too tightly. A vendors' manual should also be formulated to help supplier representatives understand the rules and restrictions of public procurement. In general, confusion can be eliminated and corruption minimized by regulations that clarify the dos and don'ts in local procurement procedures. In the end, they give both general and specific performance guidance to both procurement officials and vendors alike.

Conclusion

By most accounts, the 2006 Hamas victory in the Palestinian Legislative Council elections was the result of an Arab backlash against the rampant corruption across the Palestinian National Authority. This is but one example of how open competition between political parties can lead to a change in government in developing areas, but it is still too early to tell whether corruption in local procurement can be addressed so easily. In the rest of the region, Carothers and Ottaway (2005) make it clear that democracy and openness in the Middle East have a long way to go by Western standards, and although many Middle East regimes are willing to become more liberal with some minimal degree of freedom of the press, they do so without seeing their power seriously challenged by institutional checks and balances. Consequently, there is little hope that bribery for public works contracts will diminish much under these circumstances.[9]

What is clear, however, is that even in conditions of operational pluralism, the lack of political will, low levels of transparency, and a weak civil society will have to be overcome before traditional strategies will significantly reduce corruption (World Bank 2000). One small step in this direction is to include multiple stakeholders in the local procurement process from the outset to help design and support a system of procurement planning, good contract administration, and appropriate standardized procedures.

This chapter shows why, in addition to the ever-present call for strengthening institutions of public procurement, training of the local procurement official is at least as important in developing countries. Indeed, much of the global effort to catch dishonest officials in the act of corruption and then punish these transgressions may neglect to account for the individual's propensity to engage in the act. This approach can be addressed only through state-of-the-art training and increased professionalism. Although no hard data back the point, very few local procurement officials in developing countries are likely to have completed certification courses such as those courses offered in developed nations by the National Institute of Government Purchasing for Certified Public Purchasing Officers and for Certified Public Purchasing Buyers.

It is argued here that anticorruption efforts should simultaneously target both the system and the individual, and that transparency should be the hallmark at both levels, because when a decision maker has discretion over what will be done and operates in private, the ability to hide corruption increases and accountability diminishes. Thus, to counter this fertile field for corruption, procurement decisions and the reasons for them should be publicized.[10] However, there is a fine line here, in that decision-making discretion should not be altogether eliminated, because, depending on the context, the costs in the form of increased bureaucracy and inflexibility might be greater than the benefits of minimizing discretion (see Klitgaard, Maclean-Abaroa, and Parris 2000; also see Huther and Shah 2000). Thus, there will be some discretion left to local public procurement officials, because they will inevitably be either solely determining who gets the privatized contract or they will be intimately involved in the decision. Again, it is easy to see that ongoing training and professionalization are essential no matter what other anticorruption strategies are pursued by governments in developing countries—as evidenced by the experiences of Hong Kong and Singapore (Shin 1999).

While ethical training is a requisite for any public procurement official, it is especially important in developing countries because of the context and temptations of wrongdoing. Moreover, clearly established procurement procedures cannot take the place of honest officials. Ongoing training continues to be one of the surest ways to minimize inefficiencies that commonly result from waste and abuses identified in this chapter, and that fact is probably truer today than at any other time, because of the increasingly technical and strategic nature of the responsibilities that go with the job. Properly buying goods and contracting out for services often requires designing highly technical specifications. Unfortunately, because of the cost and time needed for proper training, few training programs are available to local procurement officials, especially in developing countries. Because many bidding opportunities are associated with international agency project procurement in developing countries, it appears that international organizations such as the World Bank are filling the void left by insufficient training for local officials and suppliers.

There can be little doubt that training opportunities leading to professionalization of the field will help achieve reform of local public procurement systems in developing countries, and ongoing training programs will be required to leverage the expertise and experience of those already serving the public interest. Ultimately, however, reducing corruption requires political will, public confidence, adequate time, resources, dedication, and integrity by all parties involved. Without them, corruption reforms in local procurement are bound to fail.

Notes

The order of authorship for this chapter was determined by a coin toss.
1. The procurement planning model discussed below draws heavily from Hinson and McCue (2004). We attribute all material to them.
2. The remainder of this section is taken from Wikipedia's discussion of risk management. Since both practitioners and scholars update this open domain Web site regularly, the authors felt that given the current literature on risk management, this Web site is as good as any in stating current best practices and concerns in the field.
3. The Bribery Index is an aggregate of six indicators; incidence, prevalence, severity, frequency, cost, and bribe size. The first three indicators, incidence, prevalence, and severity, are percentages in the sample. The other three—frequency, cost, and size of bribes, which are actual values—are scaled by the highest value to obtain an index where the highest value equals 100. The aggregate index is the simple unweighted average of the six indexes.
4. The current discussion draws heavily from Coe (1976: 94–113).
5. Obviously, relying upon vendors' specifications can lead to both diminished competition and quality.
6. In the United States, an example would be the General Services Administration.
7. This section draws heavily from Coe (1976: 91–4).
8. Because transparency is key, the prequalification application procedures and evaluation criteria should be put in writing and made available to all potential suppliers.
9. For an example of Middle East bribery, see Lambsdorff (1998).
10. These prescriptions are similar to the strategies to reduce the discretion and monopoly power of government officials while improving transparency and citizen oversight outlined by the United Nations Development Programme (1997a).

References and Other Resources

Acemoglu, Daron, and Thierry Verdier. 1998. "Property Rights, Corruption and the Allocation of Talent: A General Equilibrium Approach." *Economic Journal* 108 (450): 1381–403.

ADB (Asian Development Bank). 2001. "Combating Corruption on All Fronts: National Efforts." In *Progress in the Fight against Corruption in Asia and the Pacific,* Conference Papers and Proceedings of the Joint ADB-OECD Conference on Combating Corruption in the Asia-Pacific Region in Seoul, Korea. ADB-OECD.

African Development Bank. 2003. "National Strategies for Combating Corruption: The Ghana Experience." Regional Learning Workshop, Addis Ababa, January 27–30.

———. 2003. "Enhancing the Asian Development Bank's Role in Combating Money Laundering and the Financing of Terrorism." Operations Manual Section 55, Asian Development Bank, Manila. http://www.adb.org/Documents/Manuals/Operations/om55.asp.

Banerjee, Abhijit V. 1997. "A Theory of Misgovernance." *Quarterly Journal of Economics* 112 (4): 1289–332.

Bardhan, Pranab, and Dilip Mookherjee. 2000. "Capture and Governance at Local and National Levels." *American Economic Review* 90 (2): 135–39.

———. 2003. "Decentralisation and Accountability in Infrastructure Delivery in Developing Countries." *The Economic Journal* 116 (508); 101–27. http://www.bu.edu/econ/workingpapers/papers/Dilip%20Mookherjee/ddinf.pdf.

———. 2006. "Decentralization, Corruption and Government Accountability." In *Handbook of Economic Corruption,* ed. Susan Rose-Ackerman. Northampton, MA: Edward Elgar.

Becker, Gary S. 1968. "Crime and Punishment: An Economic Approach." *Journal of Political Economy* 76 (2): 169–217.

———. 1994. "To Root Out Corruption, Boot Out Big Government." *Business Week,* January 31.

———. 1997. "Want to Squelch Corruption? Try Passing Out Raises." *Business Week,* November 3.

Becker, Gary S., and George J. Stigler. 1974. "Law Enforcement, Malfeasance, and Compensation of Enforcers." *Journal of Legal Studies* 3 (1): 1–18.

Bibhas, Saha. 2003. "Harassment, Corruption and Tax Policy: A Comment on Marjit, Mukherjee and Mukherjee [*Eur. J. Political Economy* 16 (2000) 75–94]." *European Journal of Political Economy* 19 (4): 893–97.

Bose, Gautam. 2004. "Bureaucratic Delays and Bribe-Taking." *Journal of Economic Behavior and Organization* 54 (3): 313–20.

Brunettia, Aymo, and Beatrice Weder. 2003. "A Free Press Is Bad News for Corruption." *Journal of Public Economics* 87 (7–8): 1801–24.

Callender, Guy, and Darin Mathews. 2000. "Government Purchasing: An Evolving Profession?" *Journal of Public Budgeting, Accounting & Financial Management* 12 (2): 272–90.

Carbonera, Emanuela. 2000. "Corruption and Decentralization." Working Paper 342/83, Dipartmento di Scienze Economiche, Università di Bologna.

Carothers, Thomas, and Marina S. Ottaway. 2005. "Getting to the Core." In *Uncharted Journey: Promoting Democracy in the Middle East,* ed. Thomas Carothers and Marina S. Ottaway, 251–68. Washington, DC: Carnegie Endowment for International Peace.

Celentani, Marco, and Juan-José Ganuza. 2001. "Organized vs. Competitive Corruption." Economic Working Paper No. 526, Department of Economics and Business, Universitat Pampeu Fabra, Madrid. http://www.anti-corr.ru/archive/Organized_vs_competitive.pdf.

———. 2002. "Corruption and Competition in Procurement." *European Economic Review* 46 (7): 1273–303.

Coe, Charles. 1976. *Purchasing for Local Government.* Athens: Institute of Government.

———. 1999. "Local Government Benchmarking: Lessons from Two Major Multi-government Efforts." *Public Administration Review* 59 (2): 110–23.

Compte, Olivier, Ariane Lambert-Mogiliansky, and Thierry A. Verdier. 2005. "Corruption and Competition in Procurement Auctions." *RAND Journal of Economics* 36 (1): 1–15.

Courtney, Robert H., Jr. 1970. "Security Risk Assessment in Electronic Data Processing Systems." Technical Report 21.700. Kingston, NY: IBM Corporation.

————. 1977. "Security Risk Assessment in Electronic Data Processing." In *AFIPS Conference Proceedings of the National Computer Conference*, 97–104. Arlington VA: AFIPS Press.

Doig, Alan, and Stephen Riley. 1998. "Corruption and Anti-Corruption Strategies: Issues and Case Studies from Developing Countries." In *Corruption and Integrity Improvement Initiatives in Developing Countries.* New York: United Nations Development Programme.

Engel, Eduardo, Ronald Fischer, and Alexander Galetovic. 2005. "Highway Franchising and Real Estate Values." *Journal of Urban Economics* 57 (3): 432–48.

Federal Acquisition Institute (FAI). 2004. *Contracting Officers Technical Representative (CORT), Training Blueprint.* Washington, DC: General Services Administration.

Federal Acquisition Regulation (FAR). 2005 (Issued March). Washington, DC: General Services Administration.

Fjeldstad, Odd Helge. 2003. "Decentralisation and Corruption: A Review of the Literature." Chr. Michelson Institute, Bergen, Norway. http://www.u4.no/document/showdoc.cfm?id=49.

Galtung, Fredrik. 1998. "Criteria for Sustainable Corruption Control." In *Corruption and Development,* ed. Mark Robinson, 105–28. London: Frank Cass.

Ganuza, Juan-José, and Esther Hauk. 2004. "Economic Integration and Corruption." *International Journal of Industrial Organization* 22 (10): 1463–84.

Guerrero, Manuel Alejandro, and Eduardo Rodríguez-Oreggi. 2005. "On the Individual Decisions to Commit Corruption: A Methodological Complement." Universidad Iberoamericana, Mexico. http://wwwtest.aup.edu/lacea2005/system/step2_php/papers/rodriguez_edupdf.

Gurgur, Tugrul, and Anwar Shah. 2005. "Localization and Corruption: Panacea or Pandora's Box?" Policy Research Working Paper No. 3486, World Bank, Washington, DC.

Hakobyan, Anna, and Marie Wolkers. 2004. "Local Corruption Diagnostics and Measurement Tools in Africa." Transparency International, Berlin. http://ww1.transparency.org/surveys/dnld/U4report_local_surveys_africa.pdf.

Hinson, Connie, and McCue, Clifford P. 2004 "Planning, Scheduling, and Requirement Analysis." National Institute of Governmental Purchasing, Herndon, Virginia. 2004.

Hunja, Robert R. 2003. "Obstacles to Public Procurement Reform in Developing Countries." Paper presented at the WTO–World Bank Regional Workshop on Procurement Reforms and Transparency in Public Procurement for Anglophone African Countries, Dar Es Salaam, Tanzania, January 14–17. http://www.wto.org/english/tratop_e/gproc_e/wkshop_tanz_jan03/hunja2a2_e.doc.

Huther, Jeff, and Anwar Shah. 2000. "Anti-Corruption Policies and Programs: A Framework for Evaluation." Policy Research Working Paper No. 2501, World Bank, Washington, DC.

International Monetary Fund. 1997. "Good Governance: The IMF's Role." International Monetary Fund, Washington, DC. http://www.imf.org/external/pubs/ft/exrp/govern/govern.pdf.

Johnston, Michael. 1993. "Social Development as an Anti-Corruption Strategy." Paper presented at Transparency International's 6th International Anti-Corruption Conference, Cancún, November 21–26.

Kaufman, Daniel. 1998. "Revisiting Anti-Corruption Strategies: Tilt towards Incentive-Driven Approaches?" In *Corruption and Integrity Improvement Initiatives in Developing Countries.* New York: United Nations Development Programme.

Klitgaard, Robert E. 1988. *Controlling Corruption.* Berkeley: University of California Press.

Klitgaard, Robert E., Ronald Maclean-Abaroa, and H. Lindsey Parris. 2000. *Corrupt Cities: A Practical Guide to Cure and Prevention.* Washington DC: World Bank and Institute for Contemporary Studies.

Lambsdorff, Johann Graf. 1998. "An Empirical Investigation of Bribery in International Trade." In *Corruption and Development,* ed. Mark Robinson, 40–59. London: Frank Cass.

Marjit, Sugata, Vivekananda Mukherjee, and Arijit Mukherjee. 2000. "Harassment, Corruption and Tax Policy." *European Journal of Political Economy* 16 (1): 75–94.

———. 2003. "Harassment, Corruption and Tax Policy: Reply." *European Journal of Political Economy* 19 (4): 899–900.

Marjit, Sugata, and Heling Shi. 1998. "On Controlling Crime with Corrupt Officials." *Journal of Economic Behavior and Organization* 34 (1): 163–72.

Matscheza, Philliat, and Constance Kunaka. 2000. *Anti-Corruption Strategies and Mechanisms in Southern Africa.* Harare, Zimbabwe: Human Rights Research and Documentation Trust of Southern Africa.

Monczka, Robert M., and Robert J. Trent. 1998. *Purchasing and Sourcing Strategy: Trends and Implications.* Tempe, AZ: Center for Advanced Purchasing Studies.

Mookherjee, Dilip, and I. P. L. Png. 1995. "Corruptible Law Enforcers: How Should They Be Compensated?" *Economic Journal* 105 (428): 145–59.

NBS (National Bureau of Standards). 1981. "FIPS PUB 87 (Federal Information Processing Standards Publication 87)." March 27, 1981. Springfield, VA: U.S. Department of Commerce.

Passas, Nikos. 1997. "Causes and Consequences of Corruption." Paper presented at the 8th International Anti-Corruption Conference, Lima, Peru, September 7–11.

Pope, Jeremy, ed. 1996. *National Integrity Systems: The TI Source Book.* Washington, DC: Transparency International and Economic Development Institute.

———. 2000. *TI Source Book 2000: Confronting Corruption, The Elements of a National Integrity System.* Berlin: Transparency International.

Prier, Eric. 2003. *The Myth of Representation and the Florida Legislature: A House of Competing Loyalties, 1927–2000.* Gainesville: University Press of Florida.

Queensland State Government. 2001. "Corporate Procurement Planning." Department of Public Works, Queensland Purchasing Division, Queensland.

Robinson, Mark. 1998. "Corruption and Development: An Introduction." In *Corruption and Development,* ed. Mark Robinson. London: Frank Cass.

Shankar, Raja, and Anwar Shah. 2003. "Bridging the Economic Divide within Countries: A Scorecard on the Performance of Regional Policies in Reducing Regional Income Disparities." *World Development* 31 (8): 1421–41.

Shin, Myoung-Ho. 1999. "Developing Effective Anticorruption Strategies in a Changing World." Paper presented at Transparency International's 9th International Anti-Corruption Conference, Durban, South Africa, October 10–15.

Shleifer, Andrei, and Robert W. Vishny. 1993. "Corruption." *Quarterly Journal of Economics* 108 (3): 599–617.

Tanzi, Vito. 1998. "Corruption around the World: Causes, Consequences, Scope, and Cures." Working Paper No. 98/63, International Monetary Fund, Washington, DC.

Transparency International—Kenya. 2004. "The Challenges of Reducing Corruption in a Changing Environment: The Case of Kenya." Presentation given to the World Bank / EC Core Course on Governance, May 25.

UNDP (United Nations Development Programme). 1994. *Human Development Report.* New York: Oxford University Press.

———. 1997a. "Corruption and Good Governance Discussion Paper 3." Management Development and Governance Division, Bureau for Policy and Programme Support, United Nations Development Programme, New York.

———. 1997b. "Reconceptualising Governance Discussion Paper 2." Management Development and Governance Division, Bureau for Policy and Programme Support, United Nations Development Programme, New York.

United Nations. 2001. "United Nations Manual on Anti-Corruption Policy." Draft. Global Programme against Corruption, Centre for International Crime Prevention, Office of Drug Control and Crime Prevention, United Nations Office at Vienna.

United Nations Economic and Social Commission for Asia and the Pacific. 2006. "What Is Good Governance?" United Nations Economic and Social Commission for Asia and the Pacific, Bangkok. http://www.unescap.org/huset/gg/governance.htm.

United Nations Office on Drugs and Crime. 2004. *The Global Programme against Corruption: UN Anti-Corruption Toolkit,* 3rd ed. Vienna: United Nations Office on Drugs and Crime.

University of Minnesota. 2004. "LRRB Knowledge—Building Priorities, #KB002, Construction: Contract Administration." www.cts.umn.edu/research/rfp/pdf.

USAID (U.S. Agency for International Development). n.d. "Democracy and Governance Goals." http://www.usaid.gov/our_work/democracy_and_governance/.

Vagstad, Steinar. 2000. "Centralized vs. Decentralized Procurement: Does Dispersed Information Call for Decentralized Decision-Making?" *International Journal of Industrial Organization* 18 (6): 949–63.

Van Rijckeghem, Caroline, and Beatrice Weder. 1997. "Corruption and the Rate of Temptation: Do Low Wages in the Civil Service Cause Corruption?" IMF Working Paper 97/73, International Monetary Fund, Washington, DC.

Wallace, Claire, and Christian W. Haerpfer. 2000. "Democratisation, Economic Development and Corruption in East-Central Europe: An 11-Nation Study." Institute for Advanced Studies, Vienna. http://www.ihs.ac.at/publications/soc/rs44.pdf.

Wikipedia contributors, "Risk Management." *Wikipedia, The Free Encyclopedia.* http://en.wikipedia.org/wiki/Risk_management (accessed on April 4, 2006).

———. "Statement of work." *Wikipedia. The Free Encyclopedia.* http://en.wikipedia.org/wiki/Statement_of_work (accessed on April 19, 2006).

World Bank. 1997. *Helping Countries Combat Corruption: The Role of the World Bank.* Washington, DC: World Bank.

———. 2000. "Designing Effective Anti-Corruption Strategies." In *Anti-Corruption in Transition: A Contribution to the Policy Debate.* Washington DC: World Bank.

———. 2004. *Guidelines Procurement Under IBRD Loans and IDA Credits.* Washington, DC: International Bank for Reconstruction and Development.

Wraith, Ronald, and Edgar Simpkins. 1978. "Nepotism and Bribery in West Africa." In *Political Corruption: Readings in Comparative Analysis,* ed. Arnold J. Heidenheimer, 331–40. New Brunswick: Transaction Books.

4

Local Debt Management

GERALD J. MILLER AND
W. BARTLEY HILDRETH

Using and managing government debt challenge administrators under any circumstances but even more so as decentralization of responsibility, fiscal stress, and pressure to privatize public services increase worldwide. This chapter explores the basic issues in subnational government debt management. Six questions help organize the discussion: How do local governments use debt? When do they use debt? How do they assess debt affordability? What forms of debt do they use? How do they issue debt? How do they manage existing debt? The chapter addresses each question through the discussion of debt policy making. The goal of the chapter lies in giving government managers the ability to produce debt policies tailored to their particular contexts.

Subnational governments borrow and accumulate debt following best practices in fulfilling their fiscal allocation function. Markets fail to provide certain goods, leaving governments and other nonmarket organizations the responsibility to provide "public goods." The division of responsibility between centralized and decentralized government provision of public goods depends on who benefits. The benefits of many public goods reach everyone in a nation. For some public goods, the benefits spread locally to the boundaries of subnational regions. National defense and cancer research, for example, may benefit the nation's residents as a whole, but firefighting and street lighting may benefit only local constituencies. Central governments invest in capital assets for defense or cancer research while subnational governments purchase the capital assets to pursue firefighting and street lighting (Musgrave and Musgrave 1989; Stiglitz 2000).

Subnational governments, therefore, acquire capital assets to pursue the functions deemed appropriate for the regions they represent. Localities finance capital investment through many imaginative arrangements, one of which is long-term debt. Why borrow to finance capital assets rather than pay for them with cash through operating budgets? Public finance best practices categorize capital investments as expenditures that will benefit future generations. The useful life—the benefit—of a fire station or streetlight system exceeds the typical one fiscal year of an operating budget financed with taxes. The investment transfers benefits across generations. Assuming those generations that benefit are the generations that should pay (another assumption from public finance best practices), governments borrow to purchase the capital assets, repaying the debt as the asset provides benefits over time. Intergenerational benefits match intergenerational responsibility for repaying debt.

When subnational governments accumulate debt, that debt represents the accumulation of assets, and the provision of high-performance public services, at the lowest cost. Debt stewards perform a major part of government financial management. In fact, one finance official defined public financial affairs as the activities related to the issues, "money-in-hand and money promised to be paid at a future date or dates" (Moak 1982: vii). Moak's "money promised" is the concern of this chapter and defines the idea of debt. A borrower's goal is to secure the greatest amount of money in hand for the payments agreed to be made in the future. To secure the greatest amount of payments in the future for the use of money, the borrower discloses data for an analysis of the risk of nonpayment. The borrower also approaches borrowing as a serial activity, leading to relationships with groups of lenders.

The debt management processes of local governments are regulated by law. Statutes and constitutions, as well as policies of governments in power, prescribe the functions local government must undertake. Higher-level governments may mandate these functions or permit them. The devolution of functions across countries suggests that national governments intent on shedding responsibilities do so through mandate and consent. Decentralization may or may not relate to some measure of subsidiarity—local government de jure fiscal autonomy and de facto willingness and ability to tap resources (Petersen and Freire 2004a: 12).

Debt management also depends on the willingness and ability of investors to lend money to local governments. The rule of law and property rights embedded in constitutions facilitate orderly lending. Lending depends on the willingness of investors and investment banks to advance amounts of money to local governments for a price—the interest rate adjusted for the risk—and according to a fixed repayment schedule. Whether a local government has the ability to borrow from a competitive capital market, or investors and investment banks to lend, stems from the level of privatization in an economy. All nations differ.

Local governments find borrowing efficiency and simplicity most often in domestic markets although the sizes of the domestic capital markets may differ. Domestic capital market size indicates the degree of transition away from a central government monopoly on lending or financing capital investment in another way (Petersen and Freire 2004b). This chapter assumes that local governments want to borrow from domestic and institutional investors. If domestic markets are lacking, local governments want to borrow through international markets in amounts denominated in the local government's own country currency to avoid foreign currency swings not reflective of their own fiscal and economic conditions. If either of these markets cannot or will not finance a local government's borrowing, domestic banks and higher-level governments, following their own procedures and policies, provide financing (Applegarth 2004; Christensen 2005).

Urban capital projects financed through long-term borrowing often presume access to capital markets in which they may offer bonds with 30 or so year maturities. Local governments without access to such markets can borrow with only short maturities of five years or less, similar to conventional bank loans. Transitional measures using bonds with loan or debt service guarantees by higher-level governments or banks may help local governments gain broader domestic market access to banks and investors with long-term savings. Planning and policy making as described in the first half of this chapter can help open domestic markets with the credibility that the plans and policies help create.

International aid agencies also play a role in capital investment. These international agencies include multilateral development banks, such as the World Bank, the Asian Development Bank, the African Development Bank, and the European Bank for Reconstruction and Development. The group also includes bilateral development aid programs, such as those managed by the EuropeAid Co-operation Office and Japanese Official Development Assistance overseen by the Japan International Cooperation Agency in the Japanese Ministry of Foreign Affairs. These agencies may lend, or lend in such a way that they subsidize credit. They may also condition lending on the reform of structures for debt policy and management.

How Do Local Governments Use Debt?

The most important influence on local government debt is the role local government leaders allow fiscal policy to play. Subnational debt management occurs within various frameworks, each limiting or exploiting the purposes of debt. National government statutes may or may not subsidize debt, leading to subnational policies that either limit or exploit the statutes' provisions. Many countries permit other structural opportunities, such as the public authority or quasi-autonomous nongovernmental organization, that subnational governments can exploit to gain greater leverage or an absolute increase in borrowing power (Allix and van Thiel 2005; Leigland 1994; van Thiel 2004).

Beyond constraints and opportunities, subnational governments have discretion to decide many fiscal actions through debt policies. Capital budget policy has become one of the most important of these. The budget for purchasing or constructing capital assets usually sparks the beginning of the process resulting in the search for the means to finance the capital improvements. Often, the search ends with the need to borrow to under-write the purchase or construction of the equipment, land, and buildings. Borrowing can include the sale of securities in a competitive capital market.

A capital budget and the policy to have one in the first place underline the subnational government leader's willingness to plan and to limit the uses for debt financing. The separation of a capital budget from an operating budget also segments the short-term and long-term fiscal and economic planning periods. The capital budget signals "creditworthiness" to attentive observers.

Capital improvements planning helps allocate resources and build consensus on public policies. As for allocation, one credit rater says the capital investment planning "is best viewed in the context of a comprehensive assessment of capital needs. Although a government may not have the financial or operational means to fund all desired projects, identifying those projects creates a basis for prioritizing, and seeking possible funding sources for them [as well as the role debt will play and] enables an entity to determine the scope and limits of immediate, medium-term, and long-term capital plans" (Laskey 2005: 1). More important, the policy on capital budgets can stimulate debate over a subnational government's existing debt, additional debt, and role in economic competition and stimulation, as well as tax levels, intergenerational tax burdens, and the need for certain capital assets.

The capital budget planning process precedes and binds borrowing decisions and debt management. The major force determining the requirement for debt is the group of capital needs subnational government leaders find. Consider the U.S. General Accounting Office study on practices that the authors consider best, in table 4.1.

First, vision encompasses the underlying purpose of the organization. The vision guides strategic planning and capital investment. Whose vision matters. Broad participation of subnational government stakeholders in "community visioning" creates a popular, durable reference point for planning and for later decisions on capital investments to pursue the goals of the

TABLE 4.1 Leading Practices in Capital Decision Making

Vision → Strategic Planning → Capital Budgeting ↓	
Principle	Practices
Integrate organizational goals into the capital decision-making process	1. Conduct comprehensive assessment of needs to meet results-oriented goals and objectives 2. Identify current capabilities, including the use of an inventory of assets and their condition, and determine if there is a gap between current and needed capabilities 3. Decide how best to meet the gap by identifying and evaluating alternative approaches (including noncapital approaches)
Evaluate and select capital assets using an investment approach	4. Establish a review and approval framework 5. Rank and select projects based on established criteria 6. Develop a long-term capital plan that defines capital asset decisions
Balance budgetary control and managerial flexibility when funding capital projects	7. Budget for projects in useful segments 8. Consider innovative approaches to full up-front funding
Use project management techniques to optimize project success	9. Monitor project performance and establish incentives for accountability 10. Use cross-functional teams to plan for and manage projects
Evaluate results and incorporate lessons learned into the decision-making process	11. Evaluate results to determine if organization-wide goals have been met 12. Evaluate the decision-making process; reappraise and update to ensure that goals are met

Source: U.S. General Accounting Office 1998.

plan (Miller and Evers 2002; Yankelovich 1991). Broad participation can overcome the parochial interests of some for economic development without community development, for immediate reelection, or for privileges accruing to the current official cadre.

Second, leaders translate this vision into functional, results-based goals and objectives for the government, department by department. If isolated to a single agency of subnational government, leaders ask, "If the agency or department did not exist today, how would our citizens, customers, and taxpayers best be served?" While the answer to "how best served" may require capital investment, other possible answers include transferring to another agency, privatizing, or eliminating the service requiring investment.

Organizing the capital budget process for those projects remaining after such an analysis brings up unique questions as well. One can ask, "Who will supervise and how much control or even responsibility will they be given?" as well as, "What's the timetable?" Someone must take charge of structuring this process. The law will do some of the structuring; the organization itself will do more. Obviously, because it is a budget activity, budgeters will participate, but planners and planning oversight boards, chief executives, legislators, and engineers or public works people will want influence and a voice.

The timetable is also often a matter of law. This capital investment process parallels and intersects the operating budget process.

The policies that guide the capital budgeting process are important. Many matters can be decided beforehand to help structure the process or focus attention or limit the scope of decisions. These are policies; nevertheless, notice the intent of those that appear in table 4.2—integrating planning policies with other financial policies, involving all interested parties, and disseminating policies early in the planning process. A set of debt policies, Tigue (1996) says, (a) enhances the quality of decisions by imposing order and discipline, and promoting consistency and continuity in decision making; (b) rationalizes the decision-making process; (c) identifies objectives for staff to implement; (d) demonstrates a commitment to long-term financial planning objectives; and (e) is regarded positively by the rating agencies in reviewing credit quality.

At the next and strategic point in capital investment planning, participants solicit analysis of capability and then needs. In line with the goals and objectives leaders set, analysis of capability reveals the human, information, and capital assets that exist, their condition, and what is needed to bring them up to the capability to serve their purpose. For capital assets, analysts conduct an inventory. They establish a baseline and from that track the use and performance of existing assets and facilities. They determine the

TABLE 4.2 Sample Policies for Capital Improvement Programming

"Annually, a six-year capital improvements program will be developed analyzing all anticipated capital expenditures by year and identifying associated funding sources. The plan will contain projections of how the city will perform over the six-year period in relation to policy targets for funding."

"The capital improvements program will incorporate in its projections of expenditures and funding sources any amounts relating to previous year's appropriations but which have yet to be expended."

"The first year of the six-year capital improvements program will be used as the basis for formal fiscal year appropriations during the annual budget process. Appropriations made in prior years for which expenditures have not been increased nor projects completed will be reevaluated and incorporated into appropriations for the new fiscal year."

"The government will maintain a capital projects monitoring committee composed of city staff to meet quarterly and review the progress on all outstanding projects as well as to revise spending projections."

"If new project appropriation needs are identified at an interim period during the fiscal year, the funding sources will be identified and the mid-year appropriations ordinance will be utilized to provide formal budgetary authority for the projects in question. At any governing board meeting during the fiscal year, the governing board may increase the appropriation for a given capital project provided a commensurate appropriation decrease is made for another project, so as not to alter the overall appropriations for the capital projects funds."

"Each year a closing resolution will be submitted to the governing board members and chief executive to obtain formal authorization to close completed capital projects."

Source: Tigue 1996: 31.

condition of those assets. They investigate whether previous budgets have allowed deferred maintenance. The analyst estimates what it will take to achieve vision and policies—the condition assets are in now in comparison with where the analyst interprets leaders desire them to be. The analyst then can calculate the gap between current condition and goal.

The analyst can propose alternative ways of filling the gap or rely on experts. The alternative projects required to fill the gap fall into a zero-base checklist for further analysis:

- Are the facilities necessary to achieve the agency's core functions?
- What existing assets are failing?
- What new facilities might increase performance?
- Does the existing agency have the specific expertise to fulfill its functions, to achieve its objectives with the capital assets proposed?

■ Could this function be privatized, contracted out, or otherwise outsourced, joint ventured, or eliminated so the local government does not have to invest in the assets?

Finally, capital improvement planning requires that leaders establish a method for review and approval of projects. Who will control the choice and how simple the choice process will be are strategic matters left to authoritative decision makers.

Those with the power to make strategic decisions on vision and goals earlier in the process might be expected to have the power to make capital allocation decisions. Customary ways of structuring choices include setting functional priorities, such as transportation over education, and discovering the urgency of each project—emergency over mandatory over necessary. The decision maker's information requirements are usually straightforward. The decision package might include the following:

■ How is the project or asset related to organizational objectives?
■ How does it solve organization needs?
■ How much does it cost initially and for operation over the asset's useful life?
■ How long will this asset's purchase or construction take before it is operational?
■ What are the asset's benefits and risks?

When Do Local Governments Use Debt?

Once the decision packages appear and decision makers prioritize the projects, the determination of how much of the list the subnational government can afford begins.

Matching Financing to Budgets

Debt is by no means the only way to finance capital improvements, so capital project financing derives from the sources leaders find most appropriate and economical. Consider the numerous sources of financing for different parts of a capital budget that emerged in one empirical study (Adams 1988) appearing in table 4.3.

Adams' analysis suggests that fees and charges cover an increasingly larger share of capital improvements. Taxes or other general government revenue finance a lesser portion. Tax-supported direct debt or higher-level government–subsidized debt, while important, is used less than ever before.

TABLE 4.3 Sources of Capital Investment Financing for a Capital Budget

Taxes and general revenues (decreasing in many subnational governments)	**Budget Part 1**	Cash for **pay-as-you-go** projects such as automobiles **matches** for federal and state grants **repayments** of state and federal loans financing capital investment **lease payments** private-public projects with **shared contributions**
	Budget Part 2	Tax- and general revenue–supported **debt**—the capital projects that will be paid for by general borrowing
Fees and charges (increasing in many subnational governments)	**Budget Part 3**	**Cash** through fees and charges for **pay-as-you-go** spending on such assets as smaller vehicles, machinery, and information technology equipment, office equipment, all with a relatively short economic life
	Budget Part 4	Fee-supported or revenue debt— water and sewer systems, highway systems, or any activity for which a government or government enterprise can charge a significant fee

Source: Adams 1988.

Leaders also rely less on the guaranteed debt that the revenue stream from taxes and government revenue supports. Instead, activities that generate user fees have become more important, and nonguaranteed debt has become a greater part of subnational debt.

Whether taxes or user fees support debt, debt reliance in financing capital assets is carefully scrutinized in government decision making. The details of the investigation by government leaders when scrutinizing the use of debt come from two different sources—the view of national and the view of subnational governments toward debt policy. From the national view we find,

It is recognized that in the interest of public debt management certain restrictions may be placed on the use of credit by local governments, but which still allow them a measure of local decision-making authority—"discretion." The key question to look at is: Who makes the key decisions regarding access to and use of credit by local governments? Sub-questions include but are not limited to:

- For what purposes may SNGs [subnational governments] borrow?
- Are there specific guidelines for long-term and short-term borrowing?
- Does the access to borrowing include the ability to issue bonds?
- Are there borrowing and debt service limits?
- What are the permitted sources for collateral for loans?
- Are there requirements to inform the State of borrowing by local governments?
- Are local governments required to obtain authorization from the State for all proposed credit or for certain types of borrowing?
- Are there specific rules for the settlement and repayment in the case where a local government is unable to meet its repayment obligations? (World Bank 2003: 13)

The subnational perspective gains structure from limits but also from the sound public finance principles and fundamentally coherent fiscal structure of local government defined in national constitutions and statutes. Chief among these principles and structures, coordinated decentralization of fiscal, borrowing, and expenditure powers allows localities to respond forthrightly to public and federal system expectations (White and others 1998: 10).

Techniques for Financing Capital Improvements

Capital budgets can be financed from four sources: operating budget revenues or "pay-as-you-go" financing; national or provincial government grants and loans; gifts and partnership income from public-private cooperative agreements; and debt, whether supported by taxes or revenue streams from fees charged for services. Petersen and Valadez (2004) introduce one strategy, used by the Philippines, to understand the subnational government choices in financing capital investment. Figure 4.1, a replica of the two-dimensional strategy, uses subnational government wealth and the revenue-generating potential of the project as axes for determining the financing strategy.

Poor governments and projects that will not produce revenue fall in the quadrant that suggests grant-only financing. Higher-level government support redistributes aid in such a way that poor governments can afford to provide social development projects, and the higher-level government achieves its equity goals. The greater the subnational government's wealth or the higher the probability that the project will produce adequate revenue support, the more likely the higher-level government will respond with

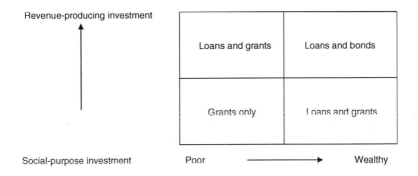

Source: Petersen and Valadez 2004: 54.

FIGURE 4.1 Matrix of Sources of Subnational Government Capital Investment Financing

loans. The development purposes of the strategy emerge, as Petersen and Valadez depict, "Government financial institutions were to facilitate the move to private capital as governments grew stronger and projects became self-financing" (2004: 55). At the greatest wealth and probability of revenue support from the project, subnational governments become independent of government financing. The higher-level government opts out of financing in favor of private credit markets.

Current Revenues

Paying for capital assets when purchased has several clear advantages. Pay-as-you-go financing avoids borrowing costs; makes the organization feel the costs immediately, often making the project more efficient because of the intense constraint; and appears appropriate for subnational governments with fully developed infrastructure systems. A plan for financing capital investments from current revenues forces higher fund balances or surpluses so that capital reserves can be accumulated in anticipation of investment. The higher fund balances force leaner funding for other current activities, causing routine operations to be run more efficiently. Finally, in an equity sense, pay-as-you-go financing does not bind future generations to the decisions made by the current generation.

Arguments against funding capital investments from current revenues exist as well. Pay-as-you-go financing may not be possible financially and may not be effective because projects are not completed when needed. Subnational governments facing population increases and economic growth problems must undertake immediate and large capital investments. The capital investment program needs are opposite current revenue patterns—the capital program at its peak and the current revenue pattern at a low point as revenues begin to grow. Therefore, growth pressure makes a subnational government less able to afford the investments that must accommodate need. Finally, pay-as-you-go financing violates the "golden rule" of capital investment by placing financial responsibility on current taxpayers, giving future taxpayers a free ride.

One major analytical point about pay-as-you-go financing comes from cost-benefit analysis of the discount rate used to evaluate public projects. If the discount rate used for investments is the opportunity cost of funds, either to the government or to society, low interest rates and low inflation will permit a larger capital budget, placing greater pressure on scarce current revenues. However, borrowing costs will roughly equal the opportunity cost of funds, and debt financing permits a large amount of capital investment. Should interest costs rise with stable inflation, capital investment, especially that permitted by debt financing, will fall.

Higher-Level Government Grants and Loans

National or provincial government aid can underwrite capital investment. Infrastructure financing ranks high among economic and social development tools. Few higher-level governments willingly neglect support for infrastructure investment. The support may come in the form of project grants, formula grants, general-purpose grants, interest cost subsidies, intergovernmental partnerships, loans, and loan guarantees (Salamon 2002).

Gifts

Gifts partially names a group of tools Cordes (2002: 255) refers to as "corrective taxes, charges, and tradable permits." Such regulatory tools corrects behavior by permitting some improvement through a payment enabling the subnational government to deal with the consequences. A common example involves a government negotiating greater housing densities in exchange for construction of low-income housing by a housing developer. Pollution taxes also contribute to environmental protection. These gifts may come in lump-sum form or annuities.

Debt

Finally, debt may finance capital investments. Debt policies, especially debt affordability policies, have gained prominence. The appropriate uses of debt for capital investing in these contexts appear in the discussion in the following sections.

How Do Local Governments Assess Debt Affordability?

Debt may be a subnational government's last resort. Debt may be the alternative only wealthy subnational governments can use to invest in revenue-producing facilities. Yet, anyone may ask about the subnational government's own policies toward debt, particularly those policies prescribing the assessment of debt affordability. All researchers agree that debt affordability must be part of debt policy, and that an analysis should determine the borrowing a subnational government can undertake and still retain access to the credit market on favorable terms.

Normative financial management also provides a rationale for calculating affordability, as professional practices are pursued in capital budgeting, in debt management, and in aggregate spending control. In capital budgeting, consensus has increasingly centered on a structured priority-setting process for long-term infrastructure, economic development, and other large projects. The criteria for setting priorities among projects appear frequently in textbooks (for example, Rabin, Hildreth, and Miller 1996) and in reference sources on debt management (for example, Hildreth 2003; Miller 1996). Once a project priority list exists, however, scarcity must come into play to enforce the priorities. Debt affordability studies provide that element of scarcity by establishing a means of aggregate spending control.

Debt affordability policies require sound empirical investigations of fiscal stress to determine what level of debt will produce stress. Credit-rating agencies have measured default through various means (Fitch IBCA 1999; Moody's Investors Service 2002; Standard & Poors 2001). Their studies suggest that general and even special tax-supported debt taken on by states has very low default rates (0.01–0.40 percent) and that the low risk associated with state tax–supported issues also relates to the high, positive recovery-from-default expectations investors hold. Studies of downgrades in U.S. state credit ratings have found that downgrades relate to increases in state per capita debt and resource declines during recessions (Johnson 1999; NASBO 1994).

The literature on credit-rating determinants also contains significant ideas about how much debt a subnational government can afford. Recently, a survey of this literature found important predictors of credit ratings, including both the type and level of economic diversification and the level of overlapping debt—that is, debt for which the taxpayer has responsibility through future taxes (Hildreth and Miller 2002). The spillover effects of economic growth and the debt competition among overlapping governments make intergovernmental, coordinated strategic planning necessary.

Process-oriented research on debt affordability has yielded a three-step method. For example, Simonsen, Robbins, and Brown (2003) propose that debt affordability analysis follow procedures involving ratio calculation, comparison of ratios to norms or standards, and forecasting. Ratio calculation has a crucial role in the definition of debt, which is the central component of the ratios. Tax-supported debt, direct debt, full-faith and credit debt, moral obligation or appropriation debt, and unfunded pension liabilities all find support for inclusion in that overall debt definition. Perhaps the key question when defining debt lies in the second analytical procedure for debt affordability—determining the norms or standards to use when defining debt. Because of the need to include norms and standards, the definition of debt may relate to prudent financial management, the capital budgeting process, or (less likely) the credit-rating process. In fact, some have argued that overlapping debt rather than direct debt might prompt more prudent debt issuance and higher credit ratings for all issuers in a given, overlapping jurisdiction (Hildreth and Miller 2002).

Nevertheless, the second analytical procedure calls for comparison to norms or standards. These norms or standards may be medians often calculated by the credit-rating agencies or cited by staff at these agencies as the description of relatively good or relatively poor credit. Often, these norms or standards are the result of establishing peer groups of subnational governments based on similar credit ratings, similar geographic regions, similar economic and demographic profiles, or financial management practices.

The selection of a group of measures or a single ratio or measure of debt capacity follows advice from the analyst managing debt or capital budgeting in a subnational government or from a regulator in a higher-level government. Along with the advice, the analyst provides a forecast of conditions represented in the ratios and the amount of debt that will exist for the foreseeable future. The forecast may include scenarios for different conditions (Miranda and Picur 2000) and a sensitivity analysis involving these scenarios.

Questions remain, however, about the definition of debt capacity and debt affordability. The primary question is what ratio do subnational governments choose and why.

The research for debt affordability ratios has centered on different levels of subnational government. One study covered worldwide subnational borrowing controls (Singh and Plekhanov 2005). Another studied U.S. states and their ratio choices (Miller and Hildreth 2003). The findings are discussed below in three parts. First, the cross-country comparisons appear followed by the entire list of states and their limitations on debt. Discussion follows. Second, the states that have completed debt affordability studies and the ratios these states used are revealed. Third, succeeding the survey, two cases get deeper attention, one case on the analytical use of the ratios in California, in forecasting, scenario building, and sensitivity analysis, and another on the analytical technique recommended to New York State by a budget watchdog group.

Cross-Country Comparison and U.S. State Studies

Worldwide Subnational Controls

The survey and analysis by Singh and Plekhanov (2005) covered 44 countries for the period 1982 to 2000. The panel and the type of constraint on subnational borrowing and the presence of a bailout during specific periods in which the constraint existed appear in table 4.4. Some countries, the "unrestricted regimes," let capital markets control debt. Other countries employed constitutional, statutory, or adminisitrative oversight rules determined by the central government. These debt affordability rules included ceilings on debt or borrowing, deficit targets for preventing off-budget borrowing, expenditure rules, rules related to debt repayment capacity, and a rule limiting subnational government borrowing to investment purposes. Other countries used self-imposed, subnational government rules of similar types. Finally, some governments used cooperative rules, defined later by one of the authors of the study as "Borrowing controls . . . designed through a negotiation process between the federal and lower levels of government. . . . on the overall deficit targets for the general government, as well as on the main items of revenue and expenditure [with specific limits] then agreed upon for the financing reqirements of individual subnational jurisdictions" (Ahmad, Albino-War, and Singh 2005: 16–7).

Singh and Plekhanov found few significant statistical relationships between constraint regimes and the resistance to a bailout. Cooperative controls were correlated with subnational surpluses. Vertical fiscal imbalance and cooperative constraint regimes were correlated with no bailout.

Singh and Plekhanov conclude as follows:

First, no single institutional arrangement seems to be superior to all the others under all circumstances. The appropriateness of any given borrowing constraint requires assessment in the light of other institutional characteristics, particularly the degree of vertical fiscal imbalances, the existence of any bailout precedents, and the quality of fiscal reporting.

Second, giving unconstrained borrowing authority to subnational governments is unlikely to be an optimal solution. At low levels of vertical fiscal imbalances, fiscal rules adopted by subnational governments themselves seem to lead to better fiscal outcomes.

Third, as vertical fiscal imbalances widen, however, the positive effect of self-imposed rules declines rapidly and centrally imposed fiscal rules seem to become the best option, both in the short and long runs, especially in emerging economies.

Fourth, for high vertical imbalances, administrative procedures may provide the central government with even tighter control over subnational government fiscal outcomes in the short run (compared to both fiscal rules and cooperative arrangements). However, the implicit guarantee of subnational debt related to these controls seems to undermine fiscal discipline in the long run.

TABLE 4.4 Subnational Borrowing Controls across the World

Country	Regime[a]	Bailout history	Years
Argentina	Self-imposed rules	Yes	1993–2000
Australia 1	Cooperative	Yes	1982–1990
Australia 2	Cooperative	No	1991–2000
Austria 1	Central rule	No	1982–1998
Austria 2	Cooperative	No	1999–2000
Belgium	Cooperative	No	1982–1998
Bolivia	Administrative	No	1986–2000
Brazil 1	Administrative	Yes	1989–1994
Brazil 2	Central rule	No	1997–1998
Canada (local)	Central rule	No	1985–2000
Canada (provinces)	Unrestricted	Yes	1982–2000
Chile	Administrative	Yes	1983–2000
Colombia	Central rule	Yes	1982–1986
Croatia	Unrestricted	No	1994–2000
Czech Republic	Unrestricted	No	1993–2000
Denmark	Cooperative	No	1982–2000
Estonia	Central rule	No	1991–2000
Finland	Unrestricted	No	1982–1998
France	Unrestricted	Yes	1982–2000
Germany 1	Central rule	Yes	1982–1991
Germany 2	Cooperative	Yes	1992–1998
Guatemala	Administrative	No	1990–1993
Hungary 1	Unrestricted	Yes	1982–1994
Hungary 2	Central rule	No	1995–2000

TABLE 4.4 Subnational Borrowing Controls across the World (*continued*)

Country	Regime[a]	Bailout history	Years
Iceland	Unrestricted	No	1983–1998
India 1	Administrative	Yes	1982–1998
India 2	Cooperative	Yes	1999–2000
Indonesia	Administrative	Yes	1982–1993
Ireland	Administrative	No	1989–1997
Israel	Administrative	No	1988–2000
Italy	Central rule	Yes	1985–1999
Latvia	Administrative	Yes	1994–2000
Lithuania	Central rule	No	1993–2000
Mexico	Administrative	Yes	1982–2000
Mongolia	Administrative	No	1992–2000
Netherlands	Unrestricted	Yes	1982–1997
New Zealand	Unrestricted	No	1992–2000
Nigeria	Unrestricted	No	1995–2000
Norway	Central rule	No	1982–1999
Peru	Administrative	No	1991–2000
Philippines	Administrative	No	1982–1991
Portugal	Unrestricted	No	1987–1998
Russian Fed.	Unrestricted	Yes	1995–2000
Slovak Rep.	Central rule	No	1996–2000
South Africa	Cooperative	No	1982–2000
Spain 1	Central rule	Yes	1982–1991
Spain 2	Cooperative	Yes	1992–2000
Sweden	Unrestricted	Yes	1982–1999
Switzerland	Self-imposed rules	No	1982–2000
United Kingdom	Administrative	No	1982–1998
United States	Self-imposed rules	No	1982–2000
Zimbabwe	Administrative	No	1982–1991

Source: Singh and Plekhanov 2005: 31.

Note: Data missing for Brazil 1995–96. The bailout history for Australia was reset to zero following a change in the mechanism of the enforcement of the decisions of the Loan Council.

a. Regime classifications come from Ahmad, Albino-War, and Singh (2005: 11–21):

• Unrestricted: "Some countries rely exclusively on capital markets to restrain subnational borrowing. In this case, the central government would not set any limits on subnational borrowing and local governments are free to decide amounts, sources, and uses of borrowing."

• Self-imposed rules: "Subnational governments may . . . decide on their own to adopt a fiscal rule in an attempt to enhance their credit standing in the market ."

• Central rule: ". . . The central government might try to contain subnational borrowing by imposing a fiscal rule . . . specified in the constitution or in laws. . . ."

• Administrative: ". . . The central government [has] direct control over the borrowing of subnational governments . . . including the setting of annual (or more frequent) limits on the overall debt [or components of debt such as external borrowing] of individual subnational jurisdictions . . . ; review and authorization of individual borrowing . . . ; and/or the centralization of all government borrowing. . . ."

• Cooperative: ". . . Borrowing controls . . . are designed through a negotiation process between the federal and lower levels of government. . . . Agreement is reached on the overall deficit targets for the general government, as well as on the main items of revenue and expenditure. Specific limits are then agreed upon for the financing requirements of individual subnational jurisdictions."

Fifth, the adoption of common standards of financial reporting is crucial for the success of cooperative arrangements and may increase the effectiveness of centrally imposed fiscal rules.

Finally, central governments should avoid bailing out subnational governments whenever possible, as bailouts significantly erode the effectiveness of borrowing controls. When considering a bailout, the central government should weigh carefully the short-term benefits against the long-term negative consequences. In the presence of bailout experiences, centrally imposed fiscal rules seem to be the most effective. (Singh and Plekhanov 2005: 24)

This research suggests that few hard rules have long-term effectiveness. Moreover, market discipline is not a barrier to a bailout, either. Only cooperative rule making with a set of procedures lasting only a short time yields the flexibility and discipline needed to assess debt affordability.

Studies of Debt Affordability Ratios Selected by States

In 1999, the (U.S.) National Association of State Budget Officers (NASBO) surveyed and provided information suggesting the pervasiveness of debt services limitation and debt limitation policies in the states. NASBO'S survey results appears in table 4.5.

TABLE 4.5 States and National Association of State Budget Officers (NASBO)—Classified Policies Limiting Debt Service and Debt

State	Policy to limit debt service (NASBO + updates)	Policy to limit authorized debt (NASBO)
Alabama	No	Statutory limits
Alaska	Targeted to unrestricted revenues	No
Arizona	Yes	General obligation debt limit of $350,000
Arkansas	General obligation debt approved by voters	No, but statutory limits can exist
California	Targeted	No
Colorado	No general obligation debt allowed	No general obligation debt allowed
Connecticut	No	Debt limited to 1.6 times general fund tax receipts in last year
Delaware	No	New authorizations limited to 5% of revenues in given year

TABLE 4.5 States and National Association of State Budget Officers
(NASBO)—Classified Policies Limiting Debt Service and Debt (*continued*)

State	Policy to limit debt service (NASBO + updates)	Policy to limit authorized debt (NASBO)
Florida	Targeted and capped	50% of tax revenue from preceding 2 years
Georgia	10% of general fund revenues	Working limits established
Hawaii	18.5% of general fund revenues in past 3 years	Total amount of principal and interest not to exceed debt limit
Idaho	No	No
Illinois	No	Authorization for general obligation debt set by statutes
Indiana	No	No general obligation debt allowed
Iowa	Yes	General obligation bond limit of $250,000
Kansas	No	$1 million general obligation debt limit without voter approval
Kentucky	No	General obligation bond limit of $500,000
Louisiana	10% of 3-year average revenues bond and redemption fund	2 times 3-year average bond revenues and redemption funds
Maine	5% of general fund and highway fund revenues	Net tax-supported debt at 3.2% of personal income
Maryland	8% of available revenues	Statutory limits on direct debt at 105% of previous FY (FY1991 base)
Massachusetts	Yes	Cap on bonds
Michigan	No	Limit debt of state agencies to 5% of personal income
Minnesota	3% of general fund unrestricted revenues	1.5 times largest revenue in preceding 4 years
Mississippi	5–8%	State constitution and statute
Missouri	No	No
Montana	No	No
Nebraska	No	2% of assessed value of property
Nevada	No	2% total reported assessed property valuation of state
New Hampshire	No, informal	Yes/general obligation; yes/revenues based on issuing authority
New Jersey	Yes	Yes
New Mexico	1% of taxable property subject to property tax	State constitution on general obligation bonds and statutory limits on authority issued

(*continued*)

TABLE 4.5 States and National Association of State Budget Officers (NASBO)—Classified Policies Limiting Debt Service and Debt (*continued*)

State	Policy to limit debt service (NASBO + updates)	Policy to limit authorized debt (NASBO)
New York	No	
North Carolina	No	Voter approval
North Dakota	10% of 1-cent sales tax	General obligation bond limit of $10 million
Ohio	5% of annual general fund expenditures	State constitution and statutes
Oklahoma	No	No
Oregon	Targeted	Statutory debt issuance authorization process, statutory and constitutional limits
Pennsylvania	Constitution	Outstanding debt limited to 1.75 times avg. 5-year tax revenues
Rhode Island	Limit debt service to 7.5% of general revenues	Limit debt to 6% of personal income
South Carolina	5% of prior year's revenues	Function of debt service
South Dakota	No	$100,000 limit on general obligation debt
Tennessee	Yes	Pledged revenues must be 150% of debt service requirements
Texas	Yes	Limit of 5% general fund revenues previous 3 years
Utah	No	Constitutional 1.5% of total fair market value of taxable property; statutory 20% of annual appropriation limit
Vermont	8% of general fund plus transportation fund revenues	Debt Affordability Committee reviews debt
Virginia	5% of taxable revenue	1.15% times average annual revenues
Washington	7% of general fund revenues	Legislative approval
West Virginia	Target	Legislative authorization
Wisconsin	3–4% of revenues	Yes—constitutional limit on debt issued
Wyoming	1% of assessed value of taxable property	1% of assessed value of taxable property

Sources: Council of State Governments 2002; NASBO 1999; NAST 2002. Original NASBO information (policy to limit debt service and policy to limit authorized debt) used with permission.

The survey reveals the fairly well-understood demand by voters to limit debt. Only six states have no policies limiting authorized debt. Limits on debt service, by either informal means, policy, statute, or constitutional provision, are less common. Nineteen states have no debt service limitations. Therefore, most of the states have some method of limiting either debt or debt service. Most require some analysis to back up the limits.

The rules requiring analytical backing for state debt policies, statutes, or constitutional provisions are sometimes flexible and sometimes not. The most flexible rules found in this research were those that rested on a study commission's recommendations that themselves were based on a thoughtful balancing of considerations, all of which reflected Peterson's directive (1998) to borrow only that amount that would ensure future access to the credit market on favorable terms.

States with Debt Affordability Studies

Debt affordability studies were found in 12 states. The studies recommended various combinations of ratios in building debt capacity and affordability models. However, one ratio—debt service to general revenues—stands out as the choice of all the states completing these studies. See table 4.6.

Why was the ratio of debt service to revenues used most often? According to the Florida State Division of Bond Finance (2002: 2), "The ratio . . . is used as the most important determinant of debt capacity because both tax rates and debt service are largely within the control of the State."

Moreover, several states used more than one measure. Consider the North Carolina ratios (Moore 2003). The treasurer advocated three ratios to guide establishing debt management policies: net tax-supported debt to personal income, debt service to revenues, and percentage of debt principal paid over the next 10-year period. The uncontrollable personal income established an environmental economic variable that policy makers could use as both a leading and concurrent indicator. The debt service ratio was chosen, as in Florida, because policy makers control both variables and because "this ratio reflects the State's budgetary flexibility to change spending and respond to economic downturns" (Moore 2003: 15). The 10-year payout ratio was considered a positive credit attribute, ensuring market access on favorable terms.

The target ratios seem to be within a similar range across the states. For the consensus target—the ratio of debt service to revenues—the range was quite tight, 4–5 percent. See table 4.7.

TABLE 4.6 State Debt Affordability Study—Recommended Ratios for Measuring and Monitoring Debt Capacity

Variables and measures	Number of states	Alaska	California	Florida	Louisiana	Maine[a]	Maryland	North Carolina	Oregon	Vermont	Virginia	Washington	West Virginia
Direct debt as % of assessed value of taxable property	1												X
Direct debt per capita	7		X	X		X					X		X
Direct debt as % of personal income (also per capita basis)	9		X	X		X	X			X	X		X
GO debt as % of market value of taxable property	1					X							
Debt service as % of general fund and special revenues	12	X	X		X[b]	X	X	X		X	X	X[c]	X[d]
Budget reserves as % of general revenues	1			X									
% of net debt paid in 10 years	2					X		X					
New debt authorizations not greater than redemptions	1						X						
Estimated market capacity	1		X										

Source: Miller and Hildreth 2003.

Note: GO = General obligation. Ratios used as targets or ceilings highlighted in table.

a. Includes accrued unfunded pension liability as part of debt.

b. Statutory requirement: debt service to taxes, licenses, and fees as estimated by the Revenue Estimating Conference.

c. Statutory requirement: debt service to 3-year mean of general state revenues, less than or equal to 7%.

d. Study recommends using all revenues and General Revenue Fund as denominator but targets debt service to General Revenue Fund.

TABLE 4.7 Targets and Ceilings

State	Target (% except where noted)	Ceiling (% except where noted)	Floor (%)	Method used	Peer group	Credit rater data used
Alaska						
Debt service as % of revenues[a]	5.0	8.0		"Historical policy"		
California						
Debt service as % of revenues[b]	5.0	6.0		Credit raters		Suggests all
Debt per capita						
Debt as % of personal income						
Estimated market capacity						
Florida						
Debt service as % of revenues[c]	6.0	8.0		Peer group, credit rater medians	10 most populous states: New York, Ohio, New Jersey, Illinois, California, Georgia, Pennsylvania, Michigan, Texas	Unknown, possibly Moody's
Debt per capita						
Debt as % of personal income						
Budget reserves as % of general revenues						

(continued)

TABLE 4.7 Targets and Ceilings *(continued)*

State	Target (% except where noted)	Ceiling (% except where noted)	Floor (%)	Method used	Peer group	Credit rater data used
Louisiana						
Debt service as % of revenues[d]		6.5		Statute		
Maine						
Debt service as % of revenues[e]		5.0		Peer group	Georgia, Nevada, New Hampshire, Vermont	Moody's, Standard & Poor's, Fitch IBCA
Maryland						
Debt service as % of revenues[f]	3.2			Unknown		
Debt as % of personal income[f]	8.0			Unknown		
New debt authorizations not greater than redemptions						
North Carolina						
Debt as % of personal income	2.5	3.0		Peer group	Highly rated states: Delaware, Georgia, Maryland, Minnesota, Missouri, South Carolina, Utah, Virginia	Moody's medians
Debt service as % of revenues	4.0	4.8				
% debt paid in 10 years		55.0	50.0			

		Peer group, credit raters	Moody's medians
Oregon[g]			
Debt service as % of revenues[h]	5.0	8.0	11 states rated higher: Delaware, Georgia, Indiana, Maryland, Michigan, Minnesota, Missouri, New Jersey, New Mexico, North Carolina, Ohio, South Carolina, Tennessee, Texas, Utah, Vermont, Virginia, Washington
Debt per capita			
Debt as % of personal income			
Vermont			
Debt per capita[i]	$818	$706	Unknown
Debt as % of personal income		5.0	All
Debt service as % of revenue		8.0	All
Virginia			
Debt service as % of revenues	5.0		Unknown
			AAA-rated states: Delaware, Georgia, Maryland, Minnesota, Missouri South Carolina, Utah
Debt per capita			Moody's medians and averages
Debt as % of personal income			Moody's medians and averages
Washington			
Debt service as % of revenues[j]	7.0		Unknown

(continued)

133

TABLE 4.7 Targets and Ceilings (continued)

State	Target (% except where noted)	Ceiling (% except where noted)	Floor (%)	Method used	Peer group	Credit rater data used
West Virginia						
Debt service as % of general revenue fund	5.0			GFOA publications, credit raters, various debt management reports from around the country	Similarly rated states: Alabama, Hawaii, Mississippi, Montana, Oklahoma, Rhode Island, Wisconsin	Moody's medians, Standard & Poor's
Debt service as % of revenues	4.0					
Debt as % of personal income	2.7					
Debt per capita	$700					
Debt as % of assessed value property	2.0					

Source: Miller and Hildreth 2003.

Note:

a. Range is 5–8%.

b. Uses scenarios with 4.25%, 5.00%, 6.00%; analyzes sensitivity using various conditions.

c. Also reports, but does not target, debt per capita, debt as % personal income, budget reserves as % of general revenues.

d. In 2003; in 2004–12, ceiling = 6%.

e. Also reports, but does not target, debt per capita, debt as % personal income, debt as % of full value property, term of debt.

f. Affordability criteria were developed and employed in the 1979 and subsequent reports.

g. Targets on debt service as % of revenues; others are comparisons.

h. 6–7% range, exceeds prudent capacity limits; 7–10% range, capacity limits reached.

i. 1995 dollars, adjusted for inflation.

j. Multiplied by the "arithmetic mean of general state revenues" as revenues are defined in statutes.

k. GFOA = Government Finance Officers Association.

The method of selecting the target ratio varied. Some used historical practices, others peer group states, and others medians that came from publications or conversations with credit-rating agency officials. These methods appear in table 4.7.

Case Studies

The California Case

California's use of the selected ratios involved at least six separate analyses. First, the analysts calculated the impact of authorized but unissued debt (net tax-supported debt or debt serviced by direct tax or special tax revenues, less truly self-liquidating obligations) for the horizon FY2003–10, assessing the incremental increase in debt service and then the ratio of debt service to current forecasts of revenue. (The debt service assumptions were 30-year general obligation and 25-year lease-revenue bonds, true interest cost of 5.75 percent, and level annual debt service payments.) Second, the group calculated the planned bond sales in FY 2003 and 2004 and the incremental increase in debt service and the debt service to revenues ratio. Third, the group examined the impact of bond proposals that were on the ballot for approval by voters and the incremental increase in debt service and debt service to revenues. Fourth, the group examined the impact of targeting the debt service to revenues ratio at various levels: 4.25 percent, 5.00 percent, and 6.00 percent. Fifth, the group created a market capacity scenario, establishing a $7 billion annual bond issuance ceiling (the estimated capacity of the market to absorb or buy bonds without demanding higher coupons), and comparing that ceiling with all previous bond issuance scenarios. Sixth, the group performed a sensitivity analysis on the most recent 10-year revenue forecast, comparing the three affordability target scenarios (4.25, 5.00, and 6.00 percent) with forecasts for 1 percent higher and 1 percent lower revenues. The scenarios, the study implies, were able to show the crowding-out impact of existing debt service forecasts on spending, if any.

The Alternative New York Citizens Budget Commision Method

A far more complicated method of determining state debt capacity and affordability comes from the New York City–based Citizens Budget Commission (2000). The complex method retains most states' emphasis on control, using ratios of variables that policy makers control, namely, debt and revenues. However, the method is much more sensitive to ranges of both variables.

The commission's method derives from work done by Tannenwald (1999) and the U.S. Advisory Commission on Intergovernmental Relations'

Representative Revenue System (RRS) (U.S. Advisory Commission on Inter-governmental Relation 1982, 1993).

First, the commission identified, in this case, New York State's relevant long-term debt, that is, that debt that is tax-supported but not self-liquidating. Unfunded pension liabilities were added to that long-term debt.

Second, the commission identified the resources available to repay debt through the RRS. (With this approach, the analyst calculates the national averages of state tax and other revenue source rates. The analyst then multiplies these average rates by the focal state's resource base values, producing a standardized revenue base. The analyst adjusts the standardized base for state versus local responsibilities, a division more pronounced toward New York City's responsibilities in New York.) According to the commission:

> A reasonable proxy for the division of functional responsibilities is the division of combined state and local revenues between the two levels of government [from Census Bureau figures on state and local government revenues and state-only revenues]. Relatively greater shares of combined revenues used by local governments indicate more spending responsibility at the local level; similarly a greater share of revenues used by states indicates that state governments have more financing responsibilities. The percentage shares, when indexed to the national average for the 50 states, is referred to as the Index of State Fiscal Responsibility. It can be used to adjust the revenue capacities of the states by multiplying the index by the representative revenue capacity. . . [yielding] a reasonable measure of available resources. . . . (Citizens Budget Commission 2000: 16)

Third, the commission calculated a square root of the ratio of debt to adjusted available resources in every state (the commission argued that such a square root would yield a normal distribution of debt capacity measures across the states), defining a "danger zone" as one standard deviation above the mean for the states. To make the danger zone even more meaningful, the commission calculated the loss in revenue from a recession as being about 2 percent for New York and advised that the danger zone for New York should be 2 percent less than the0 actual numbers.

Finally, the commission compared New York State debt with that yielded by the danger zone calculation and found New York debt within the danger zone.

Analysis of Debt Affordability Studies

Targeted debt ratios provide an effective debt limit, one more stringent than constitutional limits, U.S. state debt affordability studies suggest. The purpose of the target is certainly debt control, but the target also serves as the necessary scarcity factor in capital budgeting.

First, the target serves as the catalyst in forming certain debt policies. The target helps the government focus on defining the types of debt to bring under control. General obligation debt is certainly one type. Other tax-supported debt now falls under control as well, particularly that debt the public is only beginning to understand and fear—moral obligation, lease-related, or appropriation-backed debt. As a result, one source of fiscal illusion yields to transparency.

Second, the target ratio comes with assumptions, some more important than others. A credit rating, and the interest costs the rating suggests, underlies the comparison that subnational governments make in setting the target, indirectly best efforts to maintain that rating or upgrade it. The target ratio also assumes certain debt structures, particularly level principal and interest, and a level blend of old and new principal and interest, which puts game playing with structures out of reach.

Third, the target ratio boosts the centralizing forces in debt management. If there is an effective debt limit, some official must enforce it. The ability to limit debt almost certainly leads to central finance agency clearance of debt financing proposals. Such central clearance responsibilities make the capital budget a key part of the executive budget. Central clearance also places debt management alongside budget execution as centralized forms of financial control.

The following summarizes the results of the case studies:

- Targeted debt ratios have surfaced as one of the strongest and most crucial features of debt affordability policies and debt management. Debt ratios gained this importance because of the role debt affordability studies have played in creating transparency and an effective debt limit short of, and more flexible than, constitutional limits.
- The ratio of debt service to revenues as the preferred effective debt limit was targeted by 12 states. They have used the target as a mechanism for planning responses to various future conditions affecting the state.
- Debt affordability studies have shed new light on the dynamics of debt management. They have shown the degree of leverage debt managers can have over the capital planning process in the states and have revealed the incentives to follow best practices.

As a result of these studies, debt management has gain a systematic basis for analysis that has both theoretical and practical interest.

What Forms of Debt Do Local Governments Use?

Capital markets are capable of creating debt instruments to work with almost every viable economic opportunity. With this creative opportunity comes a downside. What might be feasible may not be wise. Therefore, the government finance officer has to weigh the opportunity against the cost because every transaction binds the government's financial affairs for some period.

As a borrower, the government's bottom line is to acquire funds at the lowest cost under the most preferred repayment terms. It is to be expected that the lender's goal is just the opposite: to loan money at the highest rate of return given the risks relative to other opportunities for the use of scarce money.

Basics of Borrowing

Term

The first fiscal policy consideration is the term of the loan, regardless of its form. Will the debt be short, intermediate, or long term? New borrowers find it difficult to borrow for long terms (say over 10 years). The goal may be to secure money for intermediate periods (1 or 2 to 10 years).

The two basic types of debt instruments are notes and bonds, with both being evidence of an obligation to repay money on the specified terms. Notes are usually issued for one year or less for various cash flow and temporary borrowing purposes. Bonds are generally issued for major capital improvement projects and are paid back over a long period.

Short-term borrowing using notes helps bridge the gap between the time an organization incurs expenses and the time when revenues are available. The term is often a year or less, and interest is usually paid at maturity. Notes are often issued to allow construction of major capital projects to proceed until permanent financing is available and final construction costs are known. Another common use is for short-term cash flow borrowing. If the government has major peaks and valleys in its revenue collection, adequate cash may not be available to meet spending requirements during certain periods. Because notes are outstanding for less than a year, interest rates are typically lower than longer-term borrowing,

Longer-term financing takes the form of municipal bonds. Bonds are typically issued for periods longer than seven years. These instruments are designed for capital projects.

Security

There are two general types of security, based upon the source of collateral. One is backed by the taxing power of the issuing government. This "full-faith and credit" obligation offers investors access to preferred collateral. Because of this potential call on taxpayers, higher levels of government, or citizens through a direct vote, or both, may impose limits.

The other general type of bond—the revenue bond—is backed by a dedicated source of funds. The projects for which these bonds are sold typically have specific users, instead of taxpayers in general. Therefore, the users of the new facility pay for the service.

However, if the charges are insufficient to cover debt service, the investors cannot access general taxes for repayment. For investors to accept such a narrow pledge, they have to have more details on the risk of the project and its ability to generate sufficient income. For assuming more risk, investors demand higher interest rates. The cost to allay investor concerns includes detailed covenants on how the debt proceeds will be used and timely and continuing disclosure on operations. Accordingly, administrative costs are higher as a result of the more complex structures.

In a double-barreled bond, the security pledge is ultimately a general obligation, but the first source of funds is a dedicated revenue source. An example of a double-barreled bond is one used to make utility improvements with the expectation that user charges will cover debt service as well as operating expenses instead of having to rely on general taxes.

Bonds

Bonds are the most common form of long-term capital financing by subnational governments.

Maturity and Repayment Structure

Bonds are repaid according to specified maturity dates. Interest is paid periodically (usually semiannually) according to a specific percentage of the face value of the bonds. The maturity of a bond issue should match the useful life of the facility or equipment it finances.

Term bonds consist of a single final maturity for all the bonds in the issue. A sinking fund is usually required to provide for the future payment of the bonds; annual payments are made into the fund instead of a balloon amount at the end.

An issue of serial bonds, in contrast, contains maturities scheduled over several years. This structure permits the issuer to repay part of the principal each year.

There are two basic forms of debt service maturity structures. In the *level principal* maturity approach, equal amounts of the bond issue are redeemed each year. Total debt service payments are higher in the earlier years, then subsequently decline. The other basic design is the *level debt service* approach, where the total of each annual principal and interest payment is held constant throughout the life of the issue. To achieve an annual level debt service requires that the annual principal maturities vary so total debt service requirements remain similar each year. The amount of principal that matures increases over time with this structure.

Variable Rate Bonds

In the typical interest rate environment, borrowing money for shorter periods is cheaper than borrowing money for several years. Therefore, variable rate bonds offer lower interest rates than fixed-rate securities because they have short maturities. In a variable rate bond, the interest rate paid to investors is allowed to fluctuate in response to market conditions, so it varies throughout the life of the issue. New rates are established periodically (usually weekly). Investors are allowed to either continue to hold their bonds, which now pay the new rate, or put the bonds back to the issuer. Issuers use a remarketing agent to manage this process and a letter-of-credit facility to provide liquidity if the governmental borrower cannot meet the liquidity demands. Because this procedure allows the investor more liquidity, risk and interest rates are lower than for fixed-rate obligations.

Realistic guidelines and procedures must be adopted to deal with risks. One guideline is to place limits on the amount of debt allowed to have floating rate interest. The willingness to accept the risk must be understood and accepted by the governing body. Also, the cost advantages of staying with the variable rate program instead of converting the debt into a fixed-rate security must be made at least annually.

Call Provisions

A call provision provides the borrower with the option to refund all or a portion of the bonds before the maturity date. With this option, issuers can refund higher-cost old debt with lower-cost new debt. Issuers are commonly restricted from exercising a call option for the first 10 years of the issue and are usually required to pay a premium to investors if bonds are subsequently redeemed.

Derivatives

Derivatives are instruments that derive their value from an underlying security or index. One common form is an interest rate swap, in which market bettors exchange floating and fixed interest rates. The original obligations and principal payments are unaffected because payments are made depending on which way the market has moved. Derivatives are complex mechanisms that require specialized knowledge combining financial and legal analysis.

Credit Enhancements

One way to obtain a lower cost of capital is to get another entity to guarantee payment. The price that a borrower pays to issue debt is reflected in the interest rate, which, in turn, depends on the borrower's perceived creditworthiness. Various means, known as credit enhancements, can be used to reduce the risk of default in the eyes of the investors—for example, bond insurance, letters of credit, reserves, and intergovernmental assistance.

Bond Insurance

Bond insurance is an unconditional pledge by a private insurance company to make principal and interest payments to the investors. Underwriters of bond insurance policies evaluate the creditworthiness of the borrower and charge an appropriate premium based on their review. The premier underwriters of bond insurance (those that obtain a top-rated triple-A bond rating themselves) provide only that type of service and thus are termed monoline insurers. Bond-rating agencies subject bond insurance firms to a stringent depression scenario stress test—insurers have to survive the scenario of a high default rate on all bonds held. Only a few private insurance firms have survived this demanding test. Thus, when a borrowing government obtains bond insurance, it is, in effect, renting the triple-A credit of the bond insurer. Another group of credit enhancement bond insurers cannot achieve the coveted triple-A standing, so they offer to rent out that lower rating for still lower-rated governmental entities.

Bond insurance offers certain advantages to the debt issuer. Renting a higher bond rating allows the borrowing governmental entity to borrow at a lower interest cost. Of course, the cost of the up-front insurance premium has to be weighed against the lower interest cost to be achieved. Bond insurance simplifies an otherwise complicated security arrangement, making it easier for investors to understand and evaluate the risks involved. Bond insurance allows investors to make decisions based on the bond insurance instead of the underlying bonds. This feature allows the bonds to have greater liquidity for trading in a secondary market. The most important feature is the bond issuer's unconditional and irrevocable promise to meet the principal and interest payment obligations of the issuer for the life of the insured bonds.

Letters of Credit

Letters of credit (LOCs) are financial instruments used by a government to substitute the credit risk of the provider of the letter of credit, usually a bank, for that of the weaker debt issuer. An LOC is an unconditional pledge of the bank's credit to make principal and interest payments of a specified amount on an issuer's debt for a specified time. Because the issue's rating is based on the bank's pledge to pay, issuers using LOCs are able to obtain more favorable interest rates on their issues than they would if their own creditworthiness were the basis for the rating. Variable rate debt requires the use of an LOC provider, also known as an LOC facility, as a backup in case the issuer of variable rate demand bonds faces a liquidity call. Many of the advantages of an LOC are the same as those for bond insurance. The disadvantages include the cost of a commitment fee and a draw-down fee if the LOC is actually drawn upon. Because the LOC is for a period shorter than the life of the bonds, the LOC must be renewed or replaced, opening up new risks, including nonreplacement, the acceleration of all debt, and the shortage of LOC providers.

Debt Services Reserves and Surety Policies

For certain bond transactions, such as revenue bonds, a debt service reserve must be established to increase the creditworthiness of the bond. At most, these dedicated cash funds are structured to cover one year's debt service payments in the event that revenues fall short. Although not long enough to protect investors against an issuer's default on its repayment obligation, this single year at least offers investors, and their fiduciary agents, the opportunity to intervene and have the issuer make changes that improve the chance of timely and full repayment by the original schedule.

Surety policies are a new product that substitute for debt service reserves. These insurance products guarantee the availability of funds and allow the issuer to avoid issuing additional bonds to initially fund debt service reserves.

Intergovernmental Support

Higher-level governments may create credit support mechanisms for municipal governments. One form is the direct guarantee of local debt. Another approach is the direct payment of all or part of the debt service on certain types of preferred projects, such as school projects. An intercept program is a contingent approach that is implemented only if the local unit encounters fiscal problems. An intercept agreement calls for the withholding of specific intergovernmental aid that normally flows to the local government and its diversion instead to pay off particular categories of debt owed by that local governmental unit.

Another form of intergovernmental assistance is the use of bond banks or loan pools. This mechanism allows several local bond issues to be aggregated into a single borrowing so as to benefit from lower transaction costs through economies of scale and lower interest rates as a result of the reduced individual risk.

Leases

In basic lease financing, an organization simply leases the use of property but does not acquire it. This is known as a true lease. A single lease conducted as a private placement may be divided into tranches, or shares, in the secondary market.

Lease-purchase agreements, by contrast, are actually contracts for purchase through installment payments. The government eventually acquires ownership of the leased property.

Certificates of participation are created when the lease payment obligation is divided into "participations" or pieces. This partition allows a variety of investors to share in the benefits of the lessee's payments while assuming part of the risk. Essentially, a trust is created with lease payments assigned to a trustee. The trustee represents the interests of the investors who hold the certificates of participation. Each certificate of participation is a marketable security, although most units are privately placed.

Before entering into a lease, it must be clear that the budget will cover the yearly lease requirements. Leases are entered into with the assumption that the proposed project is necessary and the benefits of this financial method outweigh its costs. The term of the lease should be no longer than the useful life of the asset. The lease must be subject to fiscal controls by the borrower, and the leaser must be held to performance standards regarding the asset. The governing body must understand both the lease terms and the risks associated with this form of financing.

Conduit Financing

Governments may serve as a conduit for borrowing by private enterprise— an activity fraught with danger if not handled carefully. For example, this type of financing has the government bestowing favor on one firm over others. It is important to establish strict guidelines to avoid legal, management, and political difficulties.

How Do Local Governments Issue Debt?

Debt is sold through financial intermediaries. A government sells the entire bond issue at wholesale to the intermediary (a financial firm that often goes by the name of "underwriter," "investment banker," or "fiscal agent," depending on the country) that then resells the individual bonds to ultimate investors at a retail price. For larger issues, many underwriters often combine to form a syndicate, which is led by one firm. The two basic methods of public sale are by competition or through negotiation. Another option is to sell through private placements.

Competitive Sales

In a competitive sale, the issuer determines the bond structure, solicits bids, then awards the sale to the financial intermediary that submits the lowest interest cost for the offered securities. Financial advisers and lawyers usually participate in these planning and management phases, but the financial intermediary becomes involved only after the public notice of sale has been made. Underwriters must evaluate the financial situation carefully to avoid lowering their profits when they attempt to resell the bonds to investors. Therefore, the underwriters have to set their bid to reflect both the interest rate that will be paid to investors and the overall compensation to be earned. Competitive bidding provides assurance that the bond issue has obtained the lowest market interest rate. However, competitive bidding works only when the market is familiar with the debt issuer and if there is an active secondary market for the issuer's bonds.

Negotiated Sales

The more common method of selling debt is to negotiate the price with the financial intermediary. The underwriter is actively involved in the bond structuring and marketing strategy. This early involvement allows underwriters to test the market and suggest structuring changes to maximize benefits to the sale. Negotiated underwritings also allow more flexibility in timing the sale date to take advantage of optimum conditions. Negotiated sales are generally more appropriate for complex issues because a greater sales effort is usually necessary. The underwriter's compensation is negotiated at the time the bonds are structured and offered. Following this negotiation, the issuer signs a bond purchase agreement.

Negotiated sales often require a syndicate of underwriters to purchase the entire issue. A senior managing underwriter takes the lead role and is responsible for structuring the issue and preparing bond documents in cooperation with the issuer's financial adviser and bond lawyers. The managing underwriter also allocates the bonds among the various participants in the syndicate according to rules established by the syndicate. Syndicates are seldom fixed groups of firms, but rather a tailored grouping for each particular underwriting.

Negotiated sales offer presale marketing to maximize investor demand and lower interest rates, with timing flexibility to meet changing market conditions. These advantages are offset by certain disadvantages, namely, no direct assurance that the debt has been sold at the best rates. The process is open to questions of fairness. Even though negotiated sales account for about 80 percent of the municipal bond market in the United States, political and accountability concerns remain. There are occasional "pay to play" allegations, and even legal proceedings, surrounding allegations that politicians exact payments (the "pay") from potential financial underwriters who want the business (the "play").

Private Placements

Bond issues are sometimes privately placed with institutional investors, rather than marketed more broadly through an underwriter, especially for small issuers selling their debt directly to a local bank. Private placements are most appropriate for smaller and more complex issues because they often require more direct negotiation with the investor. Because these securities tend to be less liquid, issuers usually pay higher interest rates on private placements.

Choosing the Best Method of Sale

No single method of bond sale is best in all circumstances. The decision is unique to each issuer and bond issue. One should always consider the relative advantages and disadvantages of each method. The best decision generally depends on market and credit conditions, and on the purpose and complexity of the bond issue.

A negotiated sale fits when there are unusual credit structures because it takes a premarketing campaign to explain the complex features to targeted investors. In contrast, bonds that are commonly seen and widely understood by the market are most appropriately sold through the competitive method. General obligation bonds or revenue bonds that are well known in the market and are structured with traditional serial and term maturities can be readily sold this way. Revenue bonds issued by government units that are not well known are better sold through the negotiated method, as are bonds containing unusual covenants or unique structures.

If the sale has risks that are better understood by sophisticated investors rather than the average retail bond buyer, it may be advisable to set the bond denominations at or above a large monetary value. For example, in the United States, such bonds are set in denominations of $100,000 or higher instead of the traditional $5,000 denomination of municipal bonds that attract relatively small-dollar investors. The higher denomination requires a level of financial wherewithal that increases the probability that the individual or institutional investor will undertake extra credit analysis.

A competitive sale is more easily conducted during stable market conditions. Not only will interest rates be more stable, but investor demand may be more predictable. However, during a volatile market, the issue must be brought to market at the optimum time. Uncertainty represents more investor risk, which translates into higher required investor rates of return. To navigate these uncertain periods, it helps to have expert advisers who can gauge market conditions.

It is preferable to issue debt when a low supply of competing instruments is likely. Low supply translates into high demand. Therefore, when many other issuers are coming to market, the timing flexibility afforded by a negotiated sale is more advantageous.

A government borrower with experience and credit quality should be able to use competitive sale of debt because its risk characteristics are well known to the market. In contrast, issuers with more questionable credit ratings, those undergoing significant budgetary stress, and those borrowing large amounts relative to their past experience, might find negotiated sales more appropriate.

Selecting Professionals Involved in the Issuance of Debt

Governments should select professional advisers using a competitive process. This process works whether the selection is for an external lawyer, the financial intermediary, or any other adviser to the debt sale.

A negotiated sale requires that the financial intermediary be selected with care and diligence. A competitive selection process can be used even if the debt sale will be negotiated. The government can issue requests for proposals to solicit interest and identify the firm most appropriate to plan and manage the sale. When searching for an underwriter, the burden can be placed on the underwriters to propose general ideas to demonstrate their understanding of the specific issue and market as well as the most appropriate marketing plan for the bond issue. The underwriter should clearly describe the experience of both the firm and the individuals who will be assigned to the financing team. Although the final cost will depend upon the sale itself, it is appropriate to ask for an indication of what the underwriting cost of the issue is expected to be.

The Pricing Process

Pricing determines the issuer's cost of capital. In a competitive sale, the price is set by separate bids (the more, the better) submitted to the issuer by a set time in an auction format. Because the goal of an issue is to achieve the lowest cost of capital, the lowest bid wins the sale. Embedded in the winning bid is the purchaser's "profit," calculated as the difference between the price paid for the bonds and the resale price paid by the ultimate investors. A negotiated sale, by contrast, requires the issuer to accept a price for the bonds that includes two components—the interest rate scale and the compensation for the underwriters. The interest rate scale is formed through a price discovery process using information on general market conditions, bond inventories, client demand, and the risk of holding unsold balances. The underwriter's compensation includes the sales commission, management fee, the risk of using the underwriter's funds to purchase the bonds, and expenses. A negotiated sale is, in essence, the discovery process of finding that point that balances the issuer's need to borrow money at the lowest cost possible and the purchaser's desire to loan the money at a profit.

Without care, the price discovery process in a negotiated sale can result in a higher price than required to actually place the bonds with investors. Therefore, issuers must be deliberate and careful in conducting a negotiated sale. This requires working with the underwriter in the lead up to the sale, during the pricing of bonds, and after the sale. Because the price is not set by auction, the issuer must get a "final pricing book" or report from the underwriter with details on the actual price scale of the bonds and a comparison to market benchmarks and to recent comparable sales.

The Ratings Process

Issuers know their affairs better than do potential investors. This asymmetric information situation creates the demand for independent certification agents to conduct extensive examinations of the relevant information about debt issuers. Credit rating agencies have an accepted role in capital markets as independent certification agents. They provide investors with an indicator of the issuer's credit quality—the long-term likelihood that their bonds will be paid. As such, rating agencies evaluate various factors that might affect the ability of the issuer to repay the debt, including the local economy, government regulations, financial condition of the borrower, and the structure of the bond issue itself.

When the bonds are secured by the full faith and credit of the government (as a general obligation bond is), the credit-rating agencies concentrate on the financial strength and economic health of the community and its underlying tax base. For revenue bonds, the evaluation focuses on the economic viability of the enterprise, with the pledge of revenues and bond covenants critical components because those specify the narrow security behind the bonds.

Bond ratings are for the direct benefit of the investor, but the issuer gains by attracting investors. More investors drive down the issuer's cost of capital. To achieve this benefit, issuers must pay a fee for the opportunity to have one or more rating agencies rate the proposed debt issuance. This fee increases with the size and complexity of the planned debt. Most issuers seek at least two credit ratings because research indicates that a second rating tends to lower an issuer's borrowing costs, even if the ratings are different. Moreover, some institutional investors can only invest in an instrument if it has two credit ratings.

Credit-rating firms often have an advisory service that will give a preliminary assessment of an issuer's credit quality. This confidential rating is subject to change before an actual sale.

Ratings are assigned for the life of the bond obligation, but rating agencies reserve the right to change the rating as conditions warrant. Rating agencies expect to be informed of any changes that might affect the credit quality of the specific issue, as well as the overall government unit.

Basis of Award

Regardless of the sale method, the preference is to award the sale based upon the true interest cost (TIC) method of calculation. The TIC is based on the time value of money, which reflects the fact that interest payments made today have more value than payments made in the future. The TIC is the discount rate that produces a present value equal to the amount of money received by the issuer in exchange for the bonds (when it is used to discount all the future debt service payments).

Post Sale

The closing of a bond sale involves the delivery of the bonds to the wholesale purchaser and, of course, the receipt of the sale proceeds. The issuer has a continuing interest in the management of the debt obligation until the bonds are completely retired. First, bond proceeds must be invested in a way that ensures that the funds will be available as the project needs the funds. It is important to maintain contact with investors and their representatives throughout the life of the issue. Events that might affect trading in the secondary market should always be disclosed so the issuer can maintain credibility in the capital markets for future needs.

How Do Local Governments Manage Existing Debt?

Debt issuance carries the obligation for debt management. Issuers have to establish monitoring and reporting mechanisms to ensure timely availability of market-relevant information for current or potential investors. Of course, investors expect issuers to avoid interruptions in the repayment of debt.

Best Practices in Management

Management is one of the credit-rating factors, even if it is not as easy to quantify as fiscal condition, debt profile, and tax base. It is relevant because many of the problems facing seasoned borrowers emerge from poor practices, such as inadequate accounting and control practices, overspending and inadequate fiscal planning, and the overuse of off-budget liabilities.

Best practices dictate certain actions, with each one suggesting the need for a set of prescribed fiscal policies. Some of these best practices are discussed below.

Balanced budgets convey strong fiscal management. Financial statements should be prepared on the basis of generally accepted accounting practices so the results can be compared over time and against comparable governments. Establishing and maintaining a budget stabilization account or working capital reserves provide a stock of resources that can be tapped in the event of liquidity problems. Avoiding one-time revenues as a way to balance the budget is another good step to take. A multiyear financial plan provides a preview of identified capital project needs with the plan for their financing. A similar approach for the operating budget can identify any structural gaps in which revenue growth is slower than the growth rate for expenses. By focusing on the near future, the government can avoid surprises through better planning for contingencies.

Accountability mechanisms, such as interim financial reports and timely end-of-year audited financial statements, are vital. Debt must be monitored, and a complete record of all debt must be kept because its repayment affects the operating budget. If the jurisdiction has a Web site, the information should be updated and not allowed to become stale. Debt affordability must be monitored to preserve borrowing capacity. This means that some capital projects should be financed by current revenue flows instead of borrowing.

Debt should not be issued for longer than the economic life of the asset. Credit-rating services look for fast retirement of debt. To one agency, an aggressive payment of 65 percent or more of principal during a 10-year span is a positive credit feature while payment below 40 percent is considered a weak fiscal practice.

The ability to repay a debt obligation is tied to the economic base that will generate the public resources for public debt repayment. Therefore, a well-defined and coordinated economic development strategy is necessary, with a close examination of the costs and benefits of each proposed project involving public-private cooperation. Higher bond ratings accrue to those communities with diverse economies rather than those with concentrated economies. Effective economic development strategies convey a long-term perspective toward achieving diversification.

Investor Relations

An active secondary market means that holders of current debt can sell their investments to other investors at a price that incorporates the current and future risks of that credit instrument. The original issuance of new debt benefits from the secondary market tradability of the issuer's outstanding securities. Therefore, it is important to actively manage investor relations.

Management and governing body officials must know, and follow, all borrowing policies and laws. A single contact person should serve as the official spokesperson for dealing with market-relevant information. The provision of audited annual financial reports to interested parties conveys transparency and financial accountability. Maintaining open communication with credit-rating agencies facilitates the exchange of credit-relevant information.

Changing Old Debt

Depending upon the legal agreement entered into when the debt was originally issued, there may be opportunities to refund the debt before its original maturity date. Issuing new debt to replace old debt is one option. The refunding of outstanding debt can advance economic or legal needs, or both. If the existing debt carries high coupon interest rates, retiring that debt with new debt at a lower rate would be beneficial. It is best to approach any refunding with a targeted savings amount in mind. Absent an economic rationale, refunding may be used to change the legal terms of borrowing. Perhaps the old debt carries onerous legal restrictions that no longer apply, which may be a compelling reason to refund the old debt and borrow again.

Debt that carries an embedded call option provides the issuer with the option, but not the obligation, to redeem the bonds at the agreed-upon call date instead of the later maturity date.

Any redemption before scheduled maturity may be contrary to the economic interest of bondholders.

Financial Emergencies

Bondholders expect principal to be repaid, and the agreed-upon interest paid, on time and in full. Any failure to pay troubles investors and materially impairs the issuer from borrowing money in the future. Default means the loss of money or the opportunity that the money represents. A delay of payment by even a day causes concern, with the economic burden on investors growing with each passing day. Defaults seldom happen suddenly, but instead are the culmination of legal, economic, political, managerial, and financial problems over time. Defaults, therefore, reflect underlying problems that, left unresolved, can impose a burden on investors.

Bond documents often define default as more than the mere nonpayment of money on time, but also the failure to follow agreed-upon procedures. Borrowers often must agree to detailed legal obligations, duties, and responsibilities, with the details documented in lengthy bond covenants. Violating any one of these provisions is a technical default as opposed to an economic default. Yet, a technical default turns into an economic default if the issuer does not correct the covenant violation. Therefore, the full definition of default means an omission or failure to keep a promise or meet an obligation.

The ultimate financial emergency is bankruptcy, leading the issuer to restructure its finances. A restructuring can lead to repudiation of existing debt. Of course, this type of action freezes the issuer out of the capital markets for an extended period, and is not advisable.

Conclusion

This chapter explored the basic issues in subnational government debt management. Six questions framed the discussion: How do local governments use debt? When do they use debt? How do they assess debt affordability? What forms of debt do they use? How do they issue debt? How do they manage existing debt? The chapter addressed each question through the discussion of debt policy making and stressed the goal of giving government managers the ability to produce debt policies tailored to their particular contexts.

References and Other Resources

Adams, Carolyn Teich. 1988. *The Politics of Capital Investment: The Case of Philadelphia.* Albany: The State University of New York Press.

Ahmad, Ehtisham, Maria Albino-War, and Raju Singh. 2005. "Subnational Public Financial Management: Institutions and Macroeconomic Considerations." International Monetary Fund Working Paper/05/108, IMF, Washington, DC. http://www.imf.org/external/pubs/cat/longres.cfm?sk=18225.0.

Alaska, State of, Department of Revenue. 2002. "Alaska Public Debt 2001–2002." Treasury Division, Department of Revenue, Juneau. http://www.revenue.state.ak.us/treasury/debtbook/2002_public_debt_revised.pdf.

Allix, Marine, and Sandra van Thiel. 2005. "Mapping the Field of Quasi-Autonomous Organizations in France and Italy." *International Public Management Journal* 88 (1): 39–55.

Angelides, Philip. 2002. "The State of California's Debt Affordability Report." State Treasurer, Sacramento. http://www.treasurer.ca.gov/publications/2002dar.pdf.

Applegarth, Paul V. 2004. "Capital Market and Financial Sector Development in Sub-Saharan Africa." Center for Strategic and International Studies, Washington, DC.

Bahl, Roy. 1984. *Financing State and Local Government in the 1980s.* New York: Oxford University Press.

Bahl, Roy, and William Duncombe. 1993. "State and Local Debt Burdens in the 1980s: A Study in Contrast." *Public Administration Review* 53 (1): 31–40.

Christensen, Jakob. 2005. "Domestic Debt Markets in Sub-Saharan Africa." *IMF Staff Papers* 52 (3): 518–38.

Citizens Budget Commission. 2000. "An Affordable Debt Policy for New York State and New York City." New York. http://www.cbcny.org/debt1018.pdf.

Clingermayer, James C., and B. Dan Wood. 1995. "Disentangling Patterns of State Debt Financing." *American Political Science Review* 89 (1): 108–20.

Coleman, Henry A. 2003a. "Fiscal Stress: It's Not Just a Big City Problem." New Jersey Policy Perspective, Trenton. http://www.njpp.org/fiscalstress.html.

———. 2003b. Personal interview, September 4.

Cordes, Joseph J. 2002. "Corrective Taxes, Charges, and Tradable Permits." In *The Tools of Government: A Guide to the New Governance,* ed. Lester M. Salamon, 255–81. New York: Oxford University Press.

Corsetti, Giancarlo, and Mervyn Kin, eds. 1997. *The Debt Burden and Its Consequences for Monetary Policy: Proceedings of a Conference Held by the International Economic Association at Deutsche Bundesbank, Frankfurt, Germany.* Hampshire, UK: Palgrave Macmillan.

Council of State Governments. 2002. *CSG State Directory: Directory III—Administrative Officials 2002.* Lexington, KY: Council of State Governments.

Croce, Enzo, and V. Hugo Juan-Ramon. 2003. "Assessing Fiscal Sustainability: A Cross-Country Comparison." Working Paper 03/145, IMF, Washington, DC. http://www.imf.org/external/pubs/cat/longres.cfm?sk=16610.0.

Fitch IBCA. 1999. "Municipal Default Risk." Fitch, New York. http://www.fitchibca.com.

Florida, State of, Division of Bond Finance. 2002. "State of Florida Debt Affordability Study Update: 2002 Report." Tallahassee. http://www.fsba.state.fl.us/bond/pdf/publications/DARrpt02.pdf.

Hackbart, Merl M., and James Leigland. 1990. "State Debt Management Policy: A National Survey." *Public Budgeting and Finance* 10 (1): 37–54.

Hildreth, W. Bartley. 2003. *State and Local Government Debt Issuance and Management Service.* Austin, TX: Sheshunoff Information Services, Inc., updated yearly.

Hildreth, W. Bartley, and Gerald J. Miller. 2002. "Debt and the Local Economy: Problems in Benchmarking Local Government Debt Affordability." *Public Budgeting and Finance* 22 (4): 99–113.

Johnson, Craig L. 1999. "State Government Credit Quality: Down, but Not Out!" *Public Administration Review* 59 (3): 243–9.

Larkin, Richard, and James C. Joseph. 1996. "Developing Formal Debt Policies." In *Handbook of Debt Management*, ed. Gerald J. Miller, 277–82. New York: Dekker.

Laskey, Amy R. 2005. "To Bond or Not to Bond: Debt Affordability Guidelines and Their Impact on Credit." Tax-Supported Special Report, Fitch Ratings, Public Finance, New York.

Leigland, James. 1994. "Public Authorities and the Determinants of Their Use by State and Local Governments." *Journal of Public Administration Research and Theory* 4 (4): 521–44.

Louisiana, State of, State Bond Commission. 2003. "Status Report: Net State Tax Supported Debt." Louisiana Department of Treasury, Baton Rouge. http://www.treasury.state.la.us/divisions/bondcommission/agendas_ect/2003nstsdrpt.doc.

Maine, State of, State Treasurer's Office. 2003a. "Debt/Bonds." Office of State Treasurer, Augusta. http://www.state.me.us/treasurer/debts_bonds/index.html.

———. 2003b. Presentation to Standard & Poor's. Office of State Treasurer, Augusta. http://www.state.me.us/treasurer/2003Rating-Agency Presentation.pdf.

Maryland, State of, Capital Debt Affordability Committee. 1996. "Understanding and Forecasting Condition or Ability to Repay Debt: Report of the Capital Debt Affordability Committee on Recommended Debt Authorizations for Fiscal Year 1993." In *Handbook of Debt Management*, ed. Gerald J. Miller, 283–322. New York: Dekker.

Maryland, State of. 2003. "$500,000,000 General Obligation Bonds, State and Local Facilities Loan of 2003, Second Series." Treasurer, State of Maryland, Annapolis. http://www.treasurer.state.md.us/reports/MDState2-OS.pdf.

Miller, Gerald J., ed. 1996. *Handbook of Debt Management.* New York: Dekker.

Miller, Gerald J., and Lyn Evers. 2002. "Budgeting Structures and Citizen Participation." *Journal of Public Budgeting, Accounting & Financial Management* 14 (2): 233–72.

Miller, Gerald J., and W. Bartley Hildreth. 2003. "State Debt Affordability Studies and the Results They Produce." Paper presented at the national conference of the Association for Budgeting and Financial Management, Washington, DC, September 18.

Miranda, Rowan A., and Ronald D. Picur. 2000. *Benchmarking and Measuring Debt Capacity.* Chicago: Government Finance Officers Association.

Mizruchi, Mark S., and Linda Brewster Stearns. 1994. "A Longitudinal Study of Borrowing by Large American Corporations." *Administrative Science Quarterly* 39 (1): 118–40.

Moak, Lennox. 1982. *Municipal Bonds.* Chicago: Municipal Finance Officers Association.

Moody's Investors Service. 2002. "Special Comment: Moody's US Municipal Bond Rating Scale." Moody's Investors Service, New York.

Moore, Richard H. 2003. "State of North Carolina Debt Affordability Study." State of North Carolina, Durham, NC.

Musgrave, Richard A., and Peggy B. Musgrave. 1989. *Public Finance in Theory and Practice*, 5th ed. New York: McGraw-Hill.

NASBO (National Association of State Budget Officers). 1994. "Debt Management Practices in the States." NASBO, Washington, DC.

———. 1999. "Capital Budgeting in the States." NASBO, Washington, DC. http://www.nasbo.org/ publications.php.

NAST (National Association of State Treasurers). 2002. State Debt Management Network (Web site address list). http://www.nast.net/debtnet/Debt2002/statelinks.htm.

North Carolina, State of. 2003. "Debt Affordability Study." Department of State Treasurer, State of North Carolina, Raleigh. http://www.nctreasurer.com/NR/rdonlyres/D80A0D06-C6D3-47D8-88F2-156D6CE337D3/0/debtstudycoverletter.doc.

Oregon, State of, State Debt Policy Advisory Commission. 2002. "Report." State Debt Policy Advisory Commission, Oregon State Treasury, Salem. http://www.ost.state. or.us/divisions/dmd/sdpac.

Perdue, John. 2003. "Debt Capacity Report, State of West Virginia, Fiscal Year 2003." State Treasurer's Office, Charleston. http://www.wv.gov/OffSite.aspx?u= http://www.wvsto.gov/.

Petersen, John E. 2003. "Rating the Body Politic." *Governing Magazine*, January. http://66.23.131.98/archive/2003/jan/finance.txt.

Petersen, John, and Mila Freire. 2004a. "Fiscal Devolution." In *Subnational Capital Markets in Developing Countries*, ed. Mila Friere and John Peterson, 11–27. New York: Oxford University Press.

———. 2004b. "Market Setting and Legal Framework." In *Subnational Capital Markets in Developing Countries*, ed. Mila Friere and John Peterson, 29–45. New York: Oxford University Press.

Petersen, John, and Miguel Valadez. 2004. "Subnational Governments as Borrowers." In *Subnational Capital Markets in Developing Countries*, ed. Mila Friere and John Peterson, 49–62. New York: Oxford University Press.

Peterson, George E. 1998. "Measuring Local Government Credit Risk and Improving Creditworthiness." World Bank, Washington, DC. http://www.worldbank.org/html/fpd/urban//mun_fin/toolkit/tools.PDF.

Rabin, Jack, W. Bartley Hildreth, and Gerald J. Miller. 1996. *Budgeting: Formulation and Execution*. Athens, GA: Vinson Institute of Government.

Regens, James L., and Thomas P. Lauth. 1992. "Buy Now, Pay Later: Trends in State Indebtedness, 1950–1989." *Public Administration Review* 52 (2): 157–61.

Salamon, Lester M. 2002. *The Tools of Government*. New York: Oxford University Press.

Simonsen, Bill, Mark D. Robbins, and Raymond Brown. 2003. "Debt Affordability." In *Encyclopedia of Public Administration and Public Policy*, ed. Jack Rabin, 308–12. New York: Dekker.

Singh, Raju, and Alexander Plekhanov. 2005. "How Should Subnational Government Borrowing Be Regulated? Some Cross-Country Empirical Evidence." International Monetary Fund Working Paper/05/54, IMF, Washington, DC. http://www.imf.org/external/pubs/cat/longres.cfm?sk=18077.0.

Smith, Charles. 1998. "Measuring and Forecasting Debt Capacity: The State of Oregon Experience." *Government Finance Review* 14 (6): 52–4.

Standard & Poors. 2001. "Default Research: Municipal Rating Transitions and Defaults." Standard & Poors, New York.

Stiglitz, Joseph E. 2000. *Economics of the Public Sector*, 3rd ed. New York: W. W. Norton.

Tannenwald, Robert. 1999. "Fiscal Disparity among the States Revisited." *New England Economic Review* July/August: 3–25.

Tigue, Patricia. 1996. *Capital Improvement Programming*. Chicago: Government Finance Officers Association.

Trautman, Rhonda Riherd. 1995. "The Impact of State Debt Management on Debt Activity." *Public Budgeting and Finance* 15 (2): 33–51.

U.S. Advisory Commission on Intergovernmental Relations. 1982. "Tax Capacity of the Fifty States: Methodology and Estimates." Washington, DC.

———. 1993. "State Fiscal Capacity and Tax Effort." Washington, DC.

U.S. General Accounting Office. 1998. "Leading Practices in Capital Decision-Making." GAO/AIMD-99-32, GAO, Washington, DC.

———. 2001. "Debt Management: Insights and Tools from Selected Nations." GAO-02-14. GAO, Washington, DC.

van Thiel, Sandra. 2004. "Why Politicians Prefer Quasi-Autonomous Organizations." *Journal of Theoretical Politics* 16 (2): 175–201.

Vermont, State of, State Treasurer. 2003. "State Treasurer's Annual Report." State Treasurer's Office, Montpelier. http://www.tre.state.vt.us/Download/2002Annual%20 Report.pdf.

Virginia, State of. 2002. "Debt Capacity Advisory Committee: Report to the Governor and General Assembly, December 23, 2002." Office of the Governor, Richmond. http://www.trs.state.va.us/debt/dcac.htm.

Washington, State of. 1996. "State Finance Committee: Debt Issuance Policy." Office of the State Treasurer, Olympia. http://tre.wa.gov/BondDebt/dipolicy.htm.

White, Roland, Roy Bahl, Junald Ahmad, and Matthew Glasser. 1998. "Policy Framework for Municipal Borrowing and Financial Emergencies." Republic of South Africa, National Treasury, Department of Finance, Pretoria. http://www.info.gov.za/otherdocs/ 2000/mun_fin.pdf .

World Bank. 2003. "Financial Management and Creditworthiness: Module F Trainers' Manual." World Bank, Washington, DC.

Yankelovich, Daniel. 1991. *Coming to Public Judgment*. Syracuse, NY: Syracuse University Press.

5

Local Government Internal Controls to Ensure Efficiency and Integrity

JESSE HUGHES

The statutory and regulatory basis for internal controls varies from government to government. This chapter sets out the principles that underlie internal controls and the rules that must be followed to account for and to use the resources that are received and expended through the budget. Examples are given of internal controls; these examples can assist managers in ensuring that internal control systems are comprehensive and effective.

All personnel within government are responsible for assessing risk in their areas of responsibility and establishing those internal control procedures necessary to minimize risk. The basic rule is that management is responsible for establishing and enforcing internal controls. Auditors are responsible for checking the adequacy and effectiveness of those controls.

Corruption and Money Laundering

Effective internal controls can help prevent, detect, and correct the risk of corruption. Corruption can be difficult to avoid—the checkpoint police officer who is reluctant to return a passport, the clerk behind the desk who pushes someone's papers to the bottom of the pile, the customs officer who is painfully slow to use his rubber stamp—but it is not easy to measure. Vast amounts of money flow through public hands. How much is diverted into private pockets? In an attempt to measure the degree of corruption, Transparency International has developed a Corruption Perception Index that it publishes annually for about 150 countries. The index is based on in-country surveys and expert evaluations. Some lessons identified by the United Nations Development Programme on ways to tackle corruption are as follows (UNDP 1998: 11–12):

> First, it is clear that cross-border corruption indicates the need to attack corruption on an international and regional basis. The sustainability of such efforts depends heavily on the support of and co-ordination with solid, domestic anti-corruption policies. Efforts should not only focus on cross-border and "grand corruption," but "petty corruption" as well, which directly affects the living conditions of the majority. While the scale of these illegal transactions may be small, cumulatively they can do considerable economic and political damage to civil society.
>
> Second, there is no single recipe for fighting corruption. Causes and logics of corruption vary, and the resulting differences among situations need to be taken into account in the design of anti-corruption strategies. However the following points can be generally considered:
>
> ▨ Exceptional political and managerial will is necessary to promote and maintain anti-corruption reforms;
> ▨ As much as possible, strategies should combine three components for action: enforcement of law, prevention through institutional reforms, and mobilisation of the population;
> ▨ In addition to institutional improvements, enhancing professionalism, ensuring independence and honing technical skills should strengthen capacity in key activities (law, accounting/auditing and investigative journalism);
> ▨ Enhanced professional skills, as well as political and managerial will to control corruption, are more likely to be seen in democratic societies where the pressure of political competition often forces politicians to act. Democratisation is thus a necessary but not a sufficient condition for the reduction of corruption; and
> ▨ Although economic liberalisation is not a panacea for public-sector corruption, reducing the size of the state reduces the size of the potential corrupt "take" and enables the public sector to improve its efficiency.
>
> Third, more attention still needs to be given to questions of timing and sequencing, to the identification of short-term priorities and initial actions, to the consistency in approach and to the way in which to foster the political and managerial will, all necessary to promote and sustain reform.
>
> Finally, there is a need for caution in relying on civil society activism in the fight against malfeasance, as it would be too optimistic to believe that the inclusion of "civil society" is a sufficient guarantee of either the sustainability of anti-corruption measures or of their developmental consequences. The objective of development has to be foremost when preparing an anti-corruption agenda.

Money laundering is diverting monies illegally obtained (drug money, for instance) into legal channels. The Financial Action Task Force is an intergovernmental body established to set standards, as well as develop and promote policies to combat money laundering and terrorist financing. To meet this objective, the Financial Action Task Force has published 49 recommendations.[1] These recommendations are too numerous to list here but they have been recognized by the International Monetary Fund and the World Bank as the international standards for combating money laundering and the financing of terrorism.

Objectives and Scope of Internal Controls

This section is reprinted with permission from "Internal Control—Integrated Framework: Executive Summary" (COSO 1992)

> Senior executives have long sought ways to better control the entities they run. Internal controls are put in place to keep the entity on course toward . . . [its] goals and achievement of its mission, and to minimize surprises along the way. They enable management to deal with rapidly changing economic and competitive environments, shifting demands and priorities, and restructuring for future growth. Internal controls promote efficiency, reduce risk of asset loss, and help ensure the reliability of financial statements and compliance with laws and regulations.
>
> Because internal control serves many important purposes, there are increasing calls for better internal control systems and report cards on them. Internal control is looked upon more and more as a solution to a variety of potential problems.

What Internal Control Is

Internal control means different things to different people. This causes confusion among legislators, regulators and others. Resulting miscommunication and different expectations cause problems within an entity. Problems are compounded when the term, if not clearly defined, is written into law, regulation or rule.

This concept deals with the needs and expectations of legislators, management and others. While internal control can help an entity achieve its objectives, it is not a panacea. It defines and describes internal control to

- Establish a common definition serving the needs of different parties.
- Provide a standard against which governmental bodies, businesses, and other entities—large or small, in the public or private sector—can assess their control systems and determine how to improve them.

Internal control is broadly defined as a process, effected by an entity's . . . [legislative body], management, and other personnel, designed to provide reasonable assurance regarding the achievement of objectives in the following categories:

- Effectiveness and efficiency of operations
- Reliability of financial reporting
- Compliance with applicable laws and regulations

The first category addresses an entity's basic objectives, including performance goals and safeguarding of resources. The second relates to the preparation of reliable published financial statements, including interim and condensed financial statements and selected financial data derived from such statements, such as budgetary control releases that are reported publicly. The third deals with complying with those laws and regulations to which the entity is subject. These distinct but overlapping categories address different needs and allow a directed focus to meet the separate needs.

Internal control systems operate at different levels of effectiveness. Internal control can be judged effective in each of the three categories, respectively, if the . . . [legislative body] and management have reasonable assurance that

- They understand the extent to which the entity's operational objectives are being achieved.
- Published financial statements are being prepared reliably.
- Applicable laws and regulations are being complied with.

Internal control consists of five interrelated components. These are derived from the way management runs . . . [its activities], and are integrated with the management process. Although the components apply to all entities, small and . . . [medium entities] may implement them differently than large ones. Its controls may be less formal and less structured, yet a small company can still have effective internal control. The components are:

Control environment

The control environment sets the tone of an organization, influencing the control consciousness of its people. It is the foundation for all other components of internal control, providing discipline and structure. Control environment factors include the integrity, ethical values and competence of the entity's people; management's philosophy and operating style; the way management assigns authority and responsibility, and organizes and develops its people; and the attention and direction provided by the . . . [legislative body].

Risk assessment

Every entity faces a variety of risks from external and internal sources that must be assessed. A precondition to risk assessment is establishment of objectives, linked at different levels and internally consistent. Risk assessment is the identification and analysis of relevant risks to achievement of the objectives, forming a basis for determining how the risks should be managed. Because economic, industry, regulatory and operating conditions will continue to change, mechanisms are needed to identify and deal with the special risks associated with change.

Control activities

Control activities are the policies and procedures that help ensure [that] management directives are carried out. They help ensure that necessary actions are taken to address risks to achieving the entity's objectives. Control activities occur throughout the organization, at all levels and in all functions. They include a range of activities as diverse as approvals, authorizations, verifications, reconciliations, reviews of operating performance, securing of assets, and segregation of duties.

Information and communication

Pertinent information must be identified, captured and communicated in a form and timeframe that enable people to carry out their responsibilities. Information systems produce reports containing operational, financial and compliance-related information that make it possible to run and control the business. They deal not only with internally generated data, but also information about external events, activities and conditions necessary to informed . . . decision-making and external reporting. Effective communication also must occur in a broader sense, flowing down, across and up the organization. All personnel must receive a clear message from top management that control responsibilities must be taken seriously. They must understand their own role in the internal control system, as well as how individual activities relate to the work of others. They must have a means of communicating significant information upstream. There also needs to be effective communication with external parties, such as . . . suppliers, . . . and shareholders.

Monitor internal control systems

Internal control systems need to be monitored—a process that assesses the quality of the system's performance over time. This is accomplished through ongoing monitoring activities, separate evaluations or a combination of the two. Ongoing monitoring occurs in the course of operations. It includes regular management and supervisory activities, and other actions personnel take in performing their duties. The scope and frequency of separate evaluations will depend primarily on an assessment of risks and the effectiveness of ongoing monitoring procedures. Internal control deficiencies should be reported upstream, with serious matters reported to top management and the ... [legislative body]. [An internal auditing function is often established within an entity to assist in monitoring the effectiveness and efficiency of internal control systems.]

There is synergy and linkage among these components, forming an integrated system that reacts dynamically to changing conditions. The internal control system is intertwined with the entity's operating activities and exists for fundamental business reasons. Internal control is most effective when controls are built into the entity's infrastructure and are a part of the essence of the enterprise. "Built in" controls support quality and empowerment initiatives, avoid unnecessary costs and enable quick response to changing conditions.

There is a direct relationship between the three categories of objectives, which are what an entity strives to achieve, and components, which represent what is needed to achieve the objectives. All components are relevant to each objectives category. When looking at any one category—the effectiveness and efficiency of operations, for instance—all five components must be present and functioning effectively to conclude that internal control over operations is effective.

The internal control definition—with its underlying fundamental concepts of a process, effected by people, providing reasonable assurance—together with the categorization of objectives and the components and criteria for effectiveness, and the associated discussions, constitute this internal control framework.

What Internal Control Can Do

Internal control can help an entity achieve its performance [goals] ... and prevent loss of resources. It can help ensure reliable financial reporting. And it can help ensure that the entity complies with laws and regulations, avoiding damage to its reputation and other consequences. In sum, it can help an entity get to where it wants to go, and avoid pitfalls and surprises along the way.

What Internal Control Cannot Do

Unfortunately, some people have greater, and unrealistic, expectations. They look for absolutes, believing that

> Internal control can ensure an entity's success—that is, it will ensure achievement of basic . . . objectives or will, at the least, ensure survival.

Even effective internal control can only help an entity achieve these objectives. It can provide management information about the entity's progress, or lack of it, toward their achievement. But internal control cannot change an inherently poor manager into a good one. And, shifts in government policy or programs, . . . or economic conditions can be beyond management's control. Internal control cannot ensure success or even survival.

> Internal control can ensure the reliability of financial reporting and compliance with laws and regulations.

This belief is also unwarranted. An internal control system, no matter how well conceived and operated, can provide only reasonable—not absolute—assurance to management and the . . . [legislative body] regarding achievement of an entity's objectives. The likelihood of achievement is affected by limitations inherent in all internal control systems. These include the realities that judgments in decision-making can be faulty, and that breakdowns can occur because of simple error or mistake. Additionally, controls can be circumvented by the collusion of two or more people, and management has the ability to override the system. Another limiting factor is that the design of an internal control system must reflect the fact that there are resource constraints, and the benefits of controls must be considered relative to their costs.

Thus, while internal control can help an entity achieve its objectives, it is not a panacea.

Roles and Responsibilities

Everyone in an organization has responsibility for internal control.

Management

The chief executive officer is ultimately responsible and should assume "ownership" of the system. More than any other individual, the chief executive sets the "tone at the top" that affects integrity and ethics and other factors of a positive control environment. In a large . . . [entity], the chief executive fulfills this duty by providing leadership and direction to senior managers and reviewing the way they're controlling the operation. Senior managers, in turn, assign responsibility for establishment of more specific internal control policies and procedures to personnel responsible for the unit's functions. In a smaller entity, the influence of the chief executive . . . is usually more direct. In any event, in a cascading responsibility, a manager is effectively a chief executive of his or her sphere of responsibility. Of particular significance are financial officers and their staffs, whose control activities cut across, as well as up and down, the operating and other units of an entity.

. . . [Legislative body]

Management is accountable to the . . . [legislative body], which provides governance, guidance and oversight. Effective . . . members [of the legislature] are objective, capable and inquisitive. They also have knowledge of the entity's activities and environment, and commit the time necessary to fulfill their . . . responsibilities. Management may be in a position to override controls and ignore or stifle communications from subordinates, enabling a dishonest management which intentionally misrepresents results to cover its tracks. A strong, active . . . [legislative body], particularly when coupled with effective upward communications channels and capable financial, legal and internal audit functions, is often best able to identify and correct such a problem.

Internal auditors

Internal auditors play an important role in evaluating the effectiveness of control systems, and contribute to ongoing effectiveness. Because of organizational position and authority in an entity, an internal audit function often plays a significant monitoring role.

Other personnel

Internal control is, to some degree, the responsibility of everyone in an organization and therefore should be an explicit or implicit part of everyone's job description. Virtually all employees produce information used in the internal control system or take other actions needed to effect control. Also, all personnel should be responsible for communicating upward problems in operations, noncompliance with the code of conduct, or other policy violations or illegal actions.

A number of external parties often contribute to achievement of an entity's objectives. External auditors, bringing an independent and objective view, contribute directly through the financial statement audit and indirectly by providing information useful to management and the . . . [legislative body] in carrying out their responsibilities. Others providing information to the entity useful in effecting internal control are . . . those transacting business with the . . . [entity, such as] financial analysts, bond raters and the news media. External parties, however, are not responsible for, nor are they a part of, the entity's internal control system.

COSO Framework on Risk Management

"Over a decade ago, the Committee of Sponsoring Organizations of the Treadway Commission (COSO) issued 'Internal Control—Integrated Framework.' . . . [That document, as outlined in its executive summary reprinted above, has helped] businesses and other entities assess and enhance their internal control systems. That framework has since been incorporated into policy, rule, and regulation, and used by thousands of enterprises to better control their activities in moving toward achievement of their established objectives" (COSO 2004: v).

As a result of many high-profile business scandals and increased awareness of the level of corruption in many countries as noted by the Corruption Perception Index published by Transparency International, calls were made for enhanced corporate governance and risk management, with new laws, regulations, and listing standards. The need for an overall risk management framework for the entity as a whole, providing key principles and concepts, a common language, and clear direction and guidance, became even more compelling. Thus, COSO published "Enterprise Risk Management—Integrated Framework" in 2004 to fill this need. This framework "expands on internal control, providing a more robust and extensive focus on the broader subject of enterprise risk management. While it is not intended to and does not replace the internal control framework, but rather incorporates the internal control framework within it, entities may decide to look to this framework both to satisfy their internal control needs and to move toward a fuller risk management process" (COSO 2004: v).

"Among the most critical challenges for management is determining how much risk the entity is prepared to and does accept as it strives to create value" (COSO 2004: v). Based on these integrated frameworks, legislation has been enacted or is being considered by many local governments to extend the long-standing requirement to maintain systems of internal control as well as require management to certify and the independent auditor to attest to the effectiveness of those systems. All local governments are encouraged to adopt similar legislation based on these frameworks to provide fuller risk management and internal control processes.

To assist in achieving the goal of improving their risk management processes, many local governments are establishing or enhancing an internal audit function within their governmental units. The professional practice of internal audit is supported by a framework published by the Institute of Internal Auditors (2004). This framework provides for a code of ethics, internal auditing standards, development and practice aids, and practice advisories. All local governments are further encouraged to enhance their internal audit function and to adopt this professional practices framework for internal auditors.

The remainder of this section is reprinted with permission from COSO's 2004 document, "Enterprise Risk Management—Integrated Framework: Executive Summary."

Overview

The underlying premise of enterprise risk management is that every entity exists to provide value for its stakeholders. All entities face uncertainty, and the challenge for management is to determine how much uncertainty to accept as it strives to grow stakeholder value. Uncertainty presents both risk and opportunity, with the potential to erode or enhance value. Enterprise risk management enables management to effectively deal with uncertainty and associated risk and opportunity, enhancing the capacity to build value.

Value is maximized when management sets strategy and objectives to strike an optimal balance between growth and return goals and related risks, and efficiently and effectively deploys resources in pursuit of the entity's objectives. Risk management encompasses

- *Aligning risk appetite and strategy.* Management considers the entity's risk appetite in evaluating strategic alternatives, setting related objectives, and developing mechanisms to manage related risks.
- *Enhancing risk response decisions.* Enterprise risk management provides the rigor to identify and select among alternative risk responses—risk avoidance, reduction, sharing, and acceptance.
- *Reducing operational surprises and losses.* Entities gain enhanced capability to identify potential events and establish responses, reducing surprises and associated costs or losses.

- *Identifying and managing multiple and cross-enterprise risks.* Every enterprise faces a myriad of risks affecting different parts of the organization, and enterprise risk management facilitates effective response to the interrelated impacts, and integrated responses to multiple risks.
- *Seizing opportunities.* By considering a full range of potential events, management is positioned to identify and proactively realize opportunities.
- *Improving deployment of capital.* Obtaining robust risk information allows management to effectively assess overall capital needs and enhance capital allocation.

These capabilities inherent in enterprise risk management help management achieve the entity's performance . . . targets and prevent loss of resources. Risk management helps ensure effective reporting and compliance with laws and regulations, and helps avoid damage to the entity's reputation and associated consequences. In sum, enterprise risk management helps an entity get to where it wants to go and avoid pitfalls and surprises along the way. . . ."

Enterprise Risk Management Defined

Enterprise risk management deals with risks and opportunities affecting value creation or preservation, defined as follows:

> Enterprise risk management is a process, effected by an entity's . . . [legislative body], management and other personnel, applied in strategy setting and across the entity, designed to identify potential events that may affect the entity, and manage risk to be within its risk appetite, to provide reasonable assurance regarding the achievement of entity objectives.

. . . This definition is purposefully broad. It captures key concepts fundamental to how . . . organizations manage risk, providing a basis for application across . . . [all sectors]. It focuses directly on achievement of objectives established by a particular entity and provides a basis for defining enterprise risk management effectiveness.

Achievement of Objectives

Within the context of an entity's established mission or vision, management establishes strategic objectives, selects strategy, and sets aligned objectives cascading through the enterprise. The enterprise risk management framework is geared to achieving an entity's objectives, set forth in the following categories:

- *Strategic*, high-level goals, aligned with and supporting its mission
- *Operations*, effective and efficient use of its resources
- *Reporting*, reliability of reporting
- *Compliance*, compliance with applicable laws and regulations

This categorization of entity objectives allows a focus on separate aspects of enterprise risk management. These distinct but overlapping categories—a particular objective can fall into more than one category—address different entity needs and may be the direct responsibility of different executives. This categorization also allows distinctions between what can be expected from each category of objectives. Another category, safeguarding of resources, used by some entities, also is described.

Because objectives relating to reliability of reporting and compliance with laws and regulations are within the entity's control, enterprise risk management can be expected to provide reasonable assurance of achieving those objectives. Achievement of strategic objectives and operations objectives, however, is subject to external events not always within the entity's control; accordingly, for these objectives, enterprise risk management can provide reasonable assurance that management, and the . . . [legislative body] in its oversight role, are made aware, in a timely manner, of the extent to which the entity is moving toward achievement of the objectives.

Components of Enterprise Risk Management

Risk management consists of eight interrelated components. These are derived from the way management runs an enterprise and are integrated with the management process. These components are

- *Internal environment*—The internal environment encompasses the tone of an organization, and sets the basis for how risk is viewed and addressed by an entity's people, including risk management philosophy and risk appetite, integrity and ethical values, and the environment in which they operate.
- *Objective setting*—Objectives must exist before management can identify potential events affecting their achievement. Enterprise risk management ensures that management has in place a process to set objectives and that the chosen objectives support and align with the entity's mission and are consistent with its risk appetite.
- *Event identification*—Internal and external events affecting achievement of an entity's objectives must be identified, distinguishing between risks

and opportunities. Opportunities are channeled back to management's strategy or objective-setting processes.

▓ *Risk assessment*—Risks are analyzed, considering likelihood and impact, as a basis for determining how they should be managed. Risks are assessed on an inherent and a residual basis.

▓ *Risk response*—Management selects risk responses—avoiding, accepting, reducing, or sharing risk—developing a set of actions to align risks with the entity's risk tolerances and risk appetite.

▓ *Control activities*—Policies and procedures are established and implemented to help ensure the risk responses are effectively carried out.

▓ *Information and communication*—Relevant information is identified, captured, and communicated in a form and timeframe that enable people to carry out their responsibilities. Effective communication also occurs in a broader sense, flowing down, across, and up the entity.

▓ *Monitoring*—The entirety of risk management is monitored and modifications made as necessary. Monitoring is accomplished through ongoing management activities, separate evaluations, or both.

Enterprise risk management is not strictly a serial process, where one component affects only the next. It is a multidirectional, iterative process in which almost any component can and does influence another.

Relationship of Objectives and Components

There is a direct relationship between objectives, which are what an entity strives to achieve, and enterprise risk management components, which represent what is needed to achieve them. The relationship is depicted in the three-dimensional matrix [figure 5.1].

Figure 5.1 portrays the ability to focus on the entirety of an entity's enterprise risk management, or by objectives category, component, entity unit, or any subset thereof.

Effectiveness

Determining whether an entity's enterprise risk management is "effective" is a judgment resulting from an assessment of whether the eight components are present and functioning effectively. Thus, the components are also criteria for effective enterprise risk management. For the components to be present and functioning properly there can be no material weaknesses, and risk needs to have been brought within the entity's risk appetite.

When risk management is determined to be effective in each of the four categories of objectives, respectively, the . . . [legislative body] and

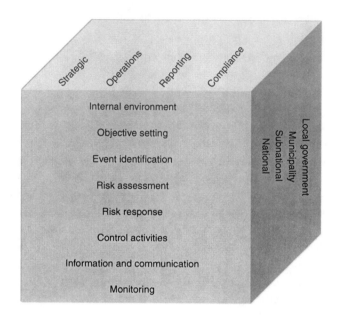

Source: Adapted from COSO (2004).

FIGURE 5.1 Risk Management Model

management have reasonable assurance that they understand the extent to which the entity's strategic and operations objectives are being achieved, and that the entity's reporting is reliable and that applicable laws and regulations are being complied with.

The eight components will not function identically in every entity. Application in small and mid-size entities, for example, may be less formal and less structured. Nonetheless, small entities still can have effective enterprise risk management, as long as each of the components is present and functional properly.

Limitations

While enterprise risk management provides important benefits, limitations exist. In addition to factors discussed above, limitations result from the realities that human judgment in decision making can be faulty, decisions on responding to risk and establishing controls need to consider the relative costs and benefits, breakdowns can occur because of human failures such as simple errors or mistakes, controls can be circumvented by collusion of two or more people, and management has the ability to override risk management decisions. These limitations preclude a . . . [legislative body] and management from having absolute assurance as to achievement of the entity's objectives.

Internal Control

Internal control is an integral part of enterprise risk management. This enterprise risk management framework encompasses internal control, forming a more robust conceptualization and tool for management. Internal control is defined and described in "Internal Control—Integrated Framework." Because that framework has stood the test of time and is the basis for existing rules, regulations, and laws, that document remains in place as the definition of and framework for internal control. . . . [Consequently,] the entirety of that framework is incorporated by reference into this one.

Roles and Responsibilities

Everyone in an entity has some responsibility for enterprise risk management. The chief executive officer is ultimately responsible and should assume ownership. Other managers support the entity's risk management philosophy, promote compliance with its risk appetite, and manage risks within their spheres of responsibility consistent with risk tolerances. A risk officer, financial officer, internal auditor, and others usually have key support responsibilities. Other entity personnel are responsible for executing risk management in accordance with established directives and protocols. The . . . [legislative body] provides important oversight to enterprise risk management, and is aware of and concurs with the entity's risk appetite. A number of external parties . . . often provide information useful in effecting enterprise risk management, but they are not responsible for the effectiveness of, nor are they a part of, the entity's enterprise risk management.

International Federation of Accountants Standards Applicable to the Private and Public Sectors

In recent years, many developed and developing countries have embarked on a thorough reevaluation of the role of government in their societies. Flowing from this, a redefinition of the political-administrative relationship has evolved, designed to ensure greater accountability and a greater devolution of power to managers. With regard to internal control, the International Federation of Accountants (IFAC) has recognized that governing bodies of public sector entities need to ensure that a framework of internal control is established and operates in practice, and that a statement on its effectiveness is included in the entity's annual report (IFAC 2001). Specific comments by IFAC on internal control were as follows (IFAC 2001: 45–6):

▪ Although internal control is a process, its effectiveness is a state or condition of the process at one or more points in time. Internal control systems operate at different levels of effectiveness. Control is effective to the extent that it provides reasonable assurance that the entity will achieve its objectives reliably.

▪ In reporting on the effectiveness of the entity's framework of internal control, governing bodies need to include in the annual report a statement to the effect that the framework of internal control they have established is both appropriate to the nature of the organization and effective in practice. The statement outlines the arrangements that they have established to enable them to make the required statement. These may take the form of a review of the various systems, risks and opportunities, as well as monitoring of the key control processes and procedures. The criteria against which the system is measured are thus identified, as well as the date on which the conclusion is made.

▪ Care needs to be taken to provide staff with the skills required to implement and maintain an internal control system, and to ensure that staff responsible for securing major changes in the system are suitably experienced.

▪ Objectives change over time and therefore management needs to periodically assess the effectiveness of control in the entity and communicate the results to the governing body.

▪ Procedures and control activities need to be revised from time to time to ensure their continuing relevance and reliability, especially at times of major change.

▪ The effectiveness of internal control needs to be reviewed and tested regularly. The review covers all control activities, including those related to financial, operational, budgetary, compliance and risk management. The primary responsibility for this rests with management.

IFAC has established the following International Standards on Auditing (ISAs) specific to the evaluation of internal control (IFAC 2006a).

"*ISA 315—Understanding the Entity and Its Environment and Assessing the Risks of Material Misstatement.* The auditor should obtain an understanding of the entity and its environment, including its internal control, sufficient to identify and assess the risks of material misstatement of the financial statements whether due to fraud or error, and sufficient to design and perform further audit procedures" (IFAC 2006a: 350).

"*ISA 330—The Auditor's Procedures in Response to Assessed Risks.* In order to reduce audit risk to an acceptably low level, the auditor should determine overall responses to assessed risks at the financial statement level, and should design and perform further audit procedures to respond to assessed risks at the assertion level" (IFAC 2006a: 404).

Institute of Internal Auditors Standards Applicable to the Private and Public Sectors

The IIA has established the following standards specific to risk, control, and governance assessments in the performance of their assurance (A) and consulting (C) activities (IIA 2004: 7–9):

2110—Risk Management

The internal audit activity should assist the organization by identifying and evaluating significant exposures to risk and contributing to the improvement of risk management and control systems.

2110.A1—The internal audit activity should monitor and evaluate the effectiveness of the organization's risk management system.

2110.A2—The internal audit activity should evaluate risk exposures relating to the organization's governance, operations, and information systems regarding the

■ Reliability and integrity of financial and operational information
■ Effectiveness and efficiency of operations
■ Safeguarding of assets
■ Compliance with laws, regulations, and contracts

2110.C1—During consulting engagements, internal auditors should address risk consistent with the engagement's objectives and be alert to the existence of other significant risks.

2110.C2—Internal auditors should incorporate knowledge of risks gained from consulting engagements into the process of identifying and evaluating significant risk exposures of the organization.

2120—Control

The internal audit activity should assist the organization in maintaining effective controls by evaluating their effectiveness and efficiency and by promoting continuous improvement.

2120.A1—Based on the results of the risk assessment, the internal audit activity should evaluate the adequacy and effectiveness of controls encompassing the organization's governance, operations, and information systems. This should include

- Reliability and integrity of financial and operational information
- Effectiveness and efficiency of operations
- Safeguarding of assets
- Compliance with laws, regulations, and contracts

2120.A2—Internal auditors should ascertain the extent to which operating and program goals and objectives have been established and conform to those of the organization.

2120.A3—Internal auditors should review operations and programs to ascertain the extent to which results are consistent with established goals and objectives to determine whether operations and programs are being implemented or performed as intended.

2120.A4—Adequate criteria are needed to evaluate controls. Internal auditors should ascertain the extent to which management has established adequate criteria to determine whether objectives and goals have been accomplished. If adequate, internal auditors should use such criteria in their evaluation. If inadequate, internal auditors should work with management to develop appropriate evaluation criteria.

2120.C1—During consulting engagements, internal auditors should address controls consistent with the engagement's objectives and be alert to the existence of any significant control weaknesses.

2120.C2—Internal auditors should incorporate knowledge of controls gained from consulting engagements into the process of identifying and evaluating significant risk exposures of the organization.

2130—Governance

The internal audit activity should assess and make appropriate recommendations for improving the governance process in its accomplishment of the following objectives:

- Promoting appropriate ethics and values within the organization
- Ensuring effective organizational performance management and accountability

▧ Effectively communicating risk and control information to appropriate areas of the organization

▧ Effectively coordinating the activities of and communicating information among the board, external and internal auditors and management

2130.A1—The internal audit activity should evaluate the design, implementation, and effectiveness of the organization's ethics-related objectives, programs and activities.

2130.C1—Consulting engagement objectives should be consistent with the overall values and goals of the organization.

International Organization of Supreme Audit Institutions Identification of Organization Need for Internal Controls in the Public Sector

This section includes portions of INTOSAI documents, which are reprinted with permission.

A working group on audit manuals from the European Court of Accounts and select supreme audit institutions from Central and Eastern European countries and Cyprus, Malta, and Turkey was assigned the task to address audits of internal control systems (INTOSAI n.d.). They adopted the frameworks developed by COSO and identified the following key components of an ideal public internal financial control system in their report (INTOSAI 2004: 10):

1. Management awareness and responsibility to establish sound and efficient financial control systems
2. A strong central institution/organization (preferably Ministry responsible for finance) responsible for the direction and co-ordination of public finances
3. Centrally established standards (preferably by the same institution/organization as stated above) for accounting, financial statements and reporting and controls including internal audit
4. Clear procedures and transparent lines of responsibility and accountability in internal and external control environment
5. Risk assessment based systems and procedures of preventive, detective and directive controls, such as public procurement, countering of fraud and corruption, programming and selection of projects, etc.
6. Clear and transparent rules for financial and performance reporting by the government and other public sector entities

7. An effective internal audit function
8. Strong and continuing external oversight (by parliament and supreme audit institutions) and sound professional relationship between internal and external audit

The Working Group further identified the following key internal and external audit functions (INTOSAI 2004: 7):

1. Management is responsible to establish and organize internal audit as a "supervisory function" within the organization's internal control system and connection between management, stakeholders and external audit. Internal audit also has a role in risk management, and can help in realization of the basic goals of an organization. In effect, internal audit is independent and objective, and provides assurance and consulting activity designed to add value and improve effectiveness of risk management, control and governance processes.
2. The role of the external auditor will be to assess the work undertaken by internal audit and where possible rely on it. The external auditor may gain audit assurance from an effective internal control system, but to do so will need to ensure that it has operated correctly during the financial period. The external auditor will make a judgment on this following an assessment on the effectiveness of the internal control system, and also an assessment of the reliance that can be placed in the work of internal audit.
3. Internal audit is an important aspect of an internal control structure. The management of public entities should be clearly responsible for defining the role of internal audit and ensuring that it has an appropriate level of authority and independence, including the right to report to the highest level of management. A crucial instrument in developing and providing effective internal audit services should be the Central Harmonization Unit (CHU)—as a center of excellence and experience.[2] They should be responsible for developing and harmonizing . . . control and audit methodologies based on international best practice, coordinating the further development of sound financial management by promoting best public internal financial control . . . practice and quality assessment/ compliance testing including internal control system and internal audit throughout the public sector.
4. In evaluating the effectiveness of internal control, the external auditor can use the work of their internal audit colleagues, who form one part of the internal control structure, and are well placed to provide the external auditor with guidance as to the effectiveness of the systems that are in place. The external auditor must always remember, however, that responsibility

for the overall conclusion drawn is ultimately that of the external auditor based on an examination of the systems in place, the quality of the internal audit unit, and the attitudes towards internal control and risk management of the entity under review. To allow the work of internal audit to be effectively assessed, the external auditor has to understand [the] purpose (role), procedures and methods of internal audit's work, as well as [consider] the quality of staff and the independence and objectivity that they bring to their work."

The separate roles and responsibilities were summarized as follows (INTOSAI 2004: 84):

Managers' Internal Control Roles and Responsibilities

- Create a positive control environment by
  — Setting a positive ethical tone,
  — Providing guidance for proper behavior,
  — Removing temptations for unethical behavior,
  — Providing discipline when appropriate,
  — Preparing a written code of conduct for employees.
- Ensure that personnel have and maintain a level of competence to perform their duties.
- Clearly define key areas of authority and responsibility.
- Establish appropriate lines of reporting.
- Establish management control policies and procedures that are based on management's analysis of risk.
- Use training, management communications, and day-to-day actions of managers at all levels to reinforce the importance of management control.
- Monitor the organization's control operations through annual assessments and reports to top management.

Auditors' Roles and Responsibilities

- Maintain independence in fact and appearance.
- Ensure professional competence of audit staff.
- Advise management on areas at risk.
- Establish auditing strategic plans and goals.
- Perform audits of operations.
- Evaluate information technology systems.
- Recommend ways to improve operations and strengthen controls.
- Follow up to ensure recommendations are fully and effectively implemented.

- Coordinate audit activities with external auditors.
- Implement an audit quality assurance system.
- Periodically evaluate effectiveness of internal control practices.
- Continually monitor operation of internal control practices throughout the organization and modify them as appropriate.

INTOSAI Framework

INTOSAI also provided a framework for establishing and maintaining internal control that could be used to determine if the concepts for risk management, internal control, and audit had been fully implemented (INTOSAI 2001). See figure 5.2.

The following Checklist for Managers is recommended for establishing and maintaining effective internal control (INTOSAI 2001: 7):

In Establishing Your Framework, Have You

- Assessed the risks the organization faces?
- Identified control objectives to manage the risks?
- Established control policies and procedures to achieve the control objectives?
- Created a positive control environment?
- Maintained and demonstrated personal and professional integrity and ethical values?
- Maintained and demonstrated a level of skill necessary to help ensure effective and efficient performance?
- Maintained and demonstrated an understanding of internal controls sufficient to effectively discharge responsibilities?

For Implementing Internal Control, Have You

- Adopted effective internal control throughout the organization?
- Based the organization's internal control on sound internal control standards?
- Included in the organization's internal control structure appropriate and cost-effective control practices?
- Prescribed control practices through management directives, plans, and policies?
- Established a means of continually monitoring the operation of the organization's internal control practices?

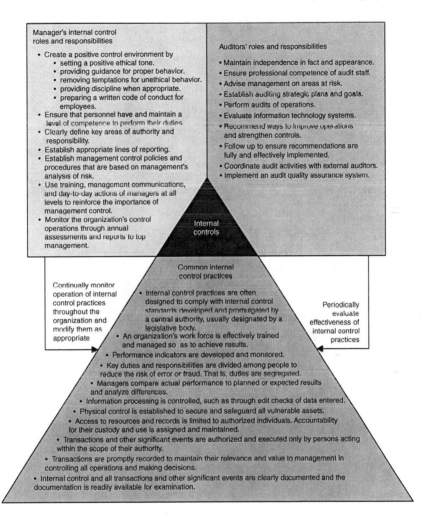

Manager's internal control roles and responsibilities

- Create a positive control environment by
  - setting a positive ethical tone.
  - providing guidance for proper behavior.
  - removing temptations for unethical behavior.
  - providing discipline when appropriate.
  - preparing a written code of conduct for employees.
- Ensure that personnel have and maintain a level of competence to perform their duties.
- Clearly define key areas of authority and responsibility.
- Establish appropriate lines of reporting.
- Establish management control policies and procedures that are based on management's analysis of risk.
- Use training, management communications, and day-to-day actions of managers at all levels to reinforce the importance of management control.
- Monitor the organization's control operations through annual assessments and reports to top management.

Auditors' roles and responsibilities

- Maintain independence in fact and appearance.
- Ensure professional competence of audit staff.
- Advise management on areas at risk.
- Establish auditing strategic plans and goals.
- Perform audits of operations.
- Evaluate information technology systems.
- Recommend ways to improve operations and strengthen controls.
- Follow up to ensure recommendations are fully and effectively implemented.
- Coordinate audit activities with external auditors.
- Implement an audit quality assurance system.

Internal controls

Common internal control practices

Continually monitor operation of internal control practices throughout the organization and modify them as appropriate

Periodically evaluate effectiveness of internal control practices

- Internal control practices are often designed to comply with internal control standards developed and promulgated by a central authority, usually designated by a legislative body.
- An organization's work force is effectively trained and managed so as to achieve results.
- Performance indicators are developed and monitored.
- Key duties and responsibilities are divided among people to reduce the risk of error or fraud. That is, duties are segregated.
- Managers compare actual performance to planned or expected results and analyze differences.
- Information processing is controlled, such as through edit checks of data entered.
- Physical control is established to secure and safeguard all vulnerable assets.
- Access to resources and records is limited to authorized individuals. Accountability for their custody and use is assigned and maintained.
- Transactions and other significant events are authorized and executed only by persons acting within the scope of their authority.
- Transactions are promptly recorded to maintain their relevance and value to management in controlling all operations and making decisions.
- Internal control and all transactions and other significant events are clearly documented and the documentation is readily available for examination.

Source: INTOSAI 2001: 2.

FIGURE 5.2 Framework for Establishing and Maintaining Effective Internal Control

Concerning the Audit Function, Have You

▨ Shown an understanding of the difference between internal control and audit?

▨ Recognized that an audit function is integral to your organization's internal control?

▨ Established an audit function?

■ Ensured the audit organization's independence?
■ Given the audit organization responsibility for evaluating the effectiveness of the audited organization's internal control practices?
■ Established a system to monitor the organization's progress in implementing internal and external auditor recommendations?

Public Internal Financial Control

Public internal financial control (PIFC) is the term used in the European Union (EU) for an integrated internal control system for the entire public sector (EC 2005). A basic feature of the EU model of an effective PIFC system is the clear demarcation between financial management and control on the one hand and internal audit on the other. All public income and spending centers should be subject to PIFC and all control and audit systems should be integrated into the system. The PIFC model consists of three principle elements as listed below.

■ *Managerial accountability:* being the responsibility of management for adequate financial management and control systems, including ex ante approval procedures for commitments, disbursements, tendering and contracting, as well as recovery for unduly paid amounts.
■ *Independent internal audit:* being a function that is responsible only for the assessment of the adequacy of the financial management systems through traditional financial audits as well as systems-based and performance audits.
■ *Centralized harmonization:* being an organization responsible for the coordination and harmonization of the implementation of PIFC throughout the entire public sector. Typically, there are two central harmonization units: one for managerial accountability and another for internal audit.

The commission assesses the progress of PIFC development through monitoring a series of steps to be taken by the central authority responsible for the development of PIFC. The first step is the drafting and adoption of a PIFC policy or strategy paper in which a gap analysis is provided of the present control systems that leads to a number of recommendations for upgrading the systems, taking into account internationally accepted control and audit standards. The second step is the drafting and adoption of framework and implementation laws relating to internal control and internal audit. The third step is the establishment of operational and well-staffed organizations like decentralized internal audit units, adequate financial services in income and spending centers, and central harmonization units for both functions (financial management and control and internal audit). The fourth step is the establishment of sustainable training facilities for financial controllers and internal auditors.

Best Practices in Control and Management Systems for European Union Membership (SIGMA Baselines)

SIGMA (Support for Improvement in Governance and Management in Central and Eastern European Countries) (2001) identified the following needs for internal and external auditors in their six baselines (financial control, public procurement management systems, civil service, public expenditure management systems, external audit, and policy-making and coordination machinery) for public sector financial control:

- A functionally independent internal audit or inspectorate mechanism with relevant remit and scope has to be in place. It could have the form of one or several organizational entities, but should meet the following criteria: be functionally independent, have an adequate audit mandate (in terms of scope and types of audit), use internationally recognized auditing standards.
- Whether appropriate coordination and supervision of the applied audit standards and methodologies are in place should also be considered.
- One of the six baselines applies to external audit. It states that the general financial control standards for the management of European Union funds and own resources in the candidate countries as well as in the member states require an effective external audit of all public sector resources and assets, and that this should be carried out in a continuous and harmonized manner. The external audit could also have a crucial role in the evaluation of and reporting on how the financial control systems are implemented and function.

Relevance and Feasibility of Internal Controls for Local Governments in Developing Countries

Each budget institution should implement its own systems of internal control appropriate to its organizational structure. All internal control systems should be documented. Along with the annual report on accounts, each institution should obtain from its management an assurance statement on the operation of its system of internal controls. The statement should certify that all approved systems of internal control have been reviewed and continue to operate effectively.

This chapter does not specify the precise nature of the systems because the circumstances of each institution will differ. In particular, large organizations will need more complex control systems. However, all systems should meet the principles set out below and auditors will judge the effectiveness of an institution's systems by reference to those principles. Once implemented, systems should be reviewed annually. Negative answers to these general principles of control will require management to review the effectiveness of that particular area of operation.

General Principles of Control

Organizational structures

- Work should be organized to maximize efficiency, avoid duplication, achieve objectives, and maintain a disciplined control environment.
- Good internal communication is needed to ensure that systems continue to be adequate to meet changing circumstances.

Management review and monitoring

Financial performance should be monitored to ensure that

- Personnel understand the systems;
- Records and systems are maintained accurately and effectively;
- Policies, timetables, and targets are met;
- Areas of weakness are identified for action;
- Errors and fraud are deterred and detected; and
- Appropriate anticipatory and remedial action are taken.

Management supervision and control

Procedures should ensure that

- Internal checks are performed effectively, and
- Weakness in controls are identified and reported to senior management.

Segregation of duties

Roles and responsibilities should be defined to ensure that

- Areas of activity involving risk are separated, for example, the person responsible for authorizing a payment should not be the person inputting the data, making the payment, checking the transaction, or destroying documents;
- Every area of work is independently supervised, validated, or reconciled;
- The opportunities for collusion are reduced; and
- Unintentional errors have a higher chance of being detected.

Authorization and approval

Appropriate authorization and approval procedures should ensure that

- Management policies are adhered to,
- Only legitimate activities are performed,
- There is clarity about what approvals are needed for what levels of expenditure,
- The use of systems and assets are controlled, and
- The operation of authority is documented and a clear management and audit trail is maintained.

Physical safeguards

Appropriate physical safeguards should

- Limit access to systems, assets, and records;
- Establish clear control of the use of assets and custodial responsibility for them; and
- Enable records to be reconstituted in the event of a system failure.

Specific Internal Control Principles

The general principles set out above should be applied in the areas that follow. Each section refers to certain specific applications of those principles that are relevant to each area. They are designed to be appropriate to large institutions. Smaller institutions may require simpler internal control systems, but they still should conform to the general principles listed above and to the specific application of those principles as set out below. The inability to provide adequate segregation of duties because of small numbers of staff may be offset by close involvement of supervisors. Control risks may be accepted because improvements in control might cost more than the losses they are aiming to prevent.

Accounting and budgetary systems

Accounting staff should not be involved in other finance-related operational tasks. Procedures should ensure the following:

- Statutory requirements are observed to maintain proper books of account.
- Balances and reconciliation procedures are carried out to ensure transactions are correctly recorded and processed with agreement between the general ledger and subsidiary records.

- The status of accounts in the statement of assets and liabilities should be externally verified.
- Systems provide the information to enable source documents to be traced to financial statements and vice versa.
- Journal vouchers are authorized and bear appropriate explanatory narrative.
- Financial regulations should specify budget preparation methods, approvals needed for changes in budgets, system of budget execution reports, need for financial implications reports for revenue and capital projects.
- Every budget head should be administered by one, and only one, named budget holder.
- Senior managers should supervise the budgetary management of those reporting to them.

Fixed assets

- Records of fixed assets should contain an identifying description, responsible budget holder, value, date of purchase, and expected life.
- Proper arrangements should be made for physical security.
- Periodic physical checks against records should be carried out.
- Proper utilization of the assets should be achieved.

Stores

- Full stores records should be maintained of orders, receipts, issues, returns, and write-offs.
- Stores document should be signed by all parties to the transaction.
- Storekeeper should not be solely responsible for ordering new stocks or writing off stocks.
- Periodic checks of physical stores against stores records should be made by persons other than the storekeeper.
- Security should be reviewed at least annually.

Salaries

- Control should be exercised by designated persons on the number of employees, their gradings, their duties, hours worked, and so forth.
- All staff should have written job descriptions.
- Personnel records should be comprehensive.
- Written authorization must be obtained to start payments to all new employees. All timesheets and changes in the amounts to be paid to employees must be authorized in writing.
- A record of the signatures of all authorizing officers must be maintained.

- Pay calculations should be checked independently.
- Employees should be properly identified before payment by cash is made and receipts obtained.
- Independent verification of the existence of payees should be obtained from time to time.
- Payroll staff should take no part in payment of salaries.

Ordering goods and payment of invoices

- Only authorized officers may order goods and ordering procedures must be controlled.
- Before payment, all invoices must have an authorizing signature and a signature for goods received.
- Persons responsible for processing invoices for payment must not also be authorizing officers.
- Payment procedures must provide for checks on quantities delivered, quality, delivery of services, part orders, duplicate payments, and taking of discounts.

Cashiers and income

- Two persons must be present when the post is opened and cash received and recorded.
- All cash paid out must be authorized by someone other than the cashier and must be signed for.
- The person responsible for raising accounts receivable must not be responsible for the receipt of the cash.
- A maximum amount of cash to be held by a cashier must be specified.
- Arrangements for the physical security of the cash must be agreed on and documented.
- Periodic checks on cash should be carried out by independent persons.
- Systems must be in place to record all types of income due.
- There must be written procedures for raising accounts for income due and following up on debts.
- The maximum amount of cash to be held overnight must be specified.
- The public must be informed at sales point that receipts must be obtained.
- Ticket stocks must be independently ordered and controlled.
- Reconciliation of ticket sales to cash should be done by an independent person.

Information technology

The use of computers in accounting and budgeting should always be subject to strict security and control principles because the scope for error and fraud is much greater than with manual systems. Systems of physical security should cover the following:

- Secure accommodation for computers
- Alarm systems
- Minimization of risk from fire and water
- Separate storage of backup files
- Comprehensive inventories of hardware and software
- Staff training

Operating systems must undertake the following:

- Log all transactions by user and terminal;
- Record user's identification as part of the transaction record;
- Limit access to data files and programs both through the system and through access methods external to the system;
- Prevent alteration of financial data except through the posting of transactions that are entered through the normal update processes;
- Allow detection, reporting, and investigation of unauthorized access to data;
- Prevent malicious or accidental destruction or misuse of data; and
- Allow a limit to be placed on the number of unsuccessful or unauthorized attempts at a particular operation and provide an audit trail of such attempts.

User identification passwords must have the following attributes:

- Be controlled
- Not be obvious—no names, birth dates, and so on
- Not be left lying in the open or in desks
- Not be shared by more than one person
- Be changed periodically (preferably every 90 days)

Application programs controls should include the following:

- Full system documentation
- Validity checks on input data
- Audit trails for all transactions
- Access authorization controls
- Recording and authorization process for program changes

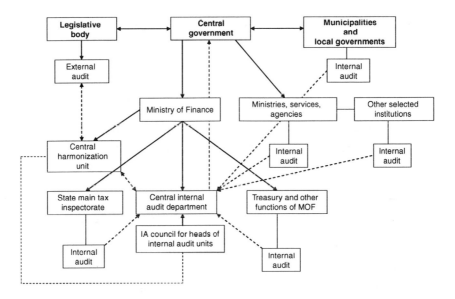

Source: Author.
Note: MOF = Ministry of Finance.

FIGURE 5.3 Recommended Organizational Structure for Implementing Internal Controls

Organizing to Implement Internal Controls

Within local government, it is recommended that the organizational structure depicted in figure 5.3 be established to implement the concepts and principles identified earlier in the chapter by COSO, IFAC, the Institute of Internal Auditors, INTOSAI, the Organisation for Economic Co-operation and Development, and the working group from the Central European countries and the Supreme Audit Institutions.

The external audit function is performed by the Supreme Audit Office. It is an independent function that reports directly to the legislative body. When the International Standards on Auditing are fully adopted, the Supreme Audit Office will be primarily responsible for expressing an opinion on the fair presentation of the financial statements published by the local government. Supplements to the ISAs have been issued by INTOSAI and the European Union as noted in this chapter. To meet international standards, the financial statements would be prepared following the International Accounting Standards and International Financial Reporting Standards as prescribed by the International Accounting Standards Board[3] for government business enterprises and the International Public Sector Accounting Standards prescribed by IFAC (IFAC 2006b) for other government operations. To express an audit opinion on the fair presentation of the financial statements, the external auditor will perform an evaluation of the adequacy of internal controls and the degree of compliance with laws and regulations.

It is proposed that the internal audit function be initially established as the Central Internal Audit Department with responsibility for coordinating all internal audits within the local government in line with the IIA's international standards. Initially, internal audits would be performed within the Ministry of Finance until the Central Internal Audit Department's staff is fully qualified to train others on these professional skills. At that point, the internal audit function would be established within the line ministries, municipalities, *rayons,* and local governments and report directly to them.

It is further proposed that a Central Harmonization Unit (CHU) be established as desired by the Public Internal Financial Control (PIFC) Expert Group. Although there is some argument for two CHUs to be established, only one is needed at the early stages of implementation to perform the coordination and harmonization function. It is felt that a CHU is so fundamental a condition to the successful introduction and development of PIFC that in reality the concept has become part of PIFC itself: indeed, PIFC is being defined as having three pillars: managerial accountability through the financial management control systems, functionally independent internal audit, and a CHU for methodologies and standards.

Each institution should have both a set of standing orders that specify how business is to be conducted and a set of financial regulations that govern financial management. Both standing orders and financial regulations should state the maximum period between formal review and updating of the orders and regulations. Significant changes in circumstances may, of course, require them to be updated at any time.

Standing orders should cover

- The methods by which financial and operational policy decisions are made,
- Rules for the conduct of meetings,
- The delegation of authority to individuals,
- Method of identifying and managing risk, and
- Responsibilities for reviewing performance.

Financial regulations should cover

- Responsibilities for budgetary matters, including preparation of budgets, authorization of variation between budget heads, reporting on budget execution, and need for financial implications report in specified circumstances;
- Rules on the letting of contracts and the placing of orders for goods and services;
- Responsibilities for the operation of each financial process, for example, salaries, cashiers;
- Rules on inventories and physical security; and
- Limits on borrowing and lending.

A sample action plan for improvement, as used in Latvia, could be as follows (World Bank n.d.):

Action item	Responsibility	Due date	Done?
			[Yes/no]
Develop a statement of philosophy about responsibility for public resources, employee accountability, and personal ethics.			
Teach an internal control training course to administrative officials.			
Issue a Management Responsibilities Handbook to administrative officials.			
Communicate information about internal control using official notices, newsletters, electronic mail, annual report, and so forth.			
Issue an annual statement of responsibility and accountability for internal controls to administrative officials.			
Provide an internal control awareness pack for new administrative officials.			
Revise ministry rules and regulations to specify the state secretary's (or chief executive's) overall responsibility for internal controls in the organization.			
Revise job descriptions of administrative positions to specify primary responsibility for internal controls at the department level.			
Include an evaluation of internal control performance in personnel evaluations or appraisals.			

(continued)

(continued)

Action item	Responsibility	Due date	Done?
Take appropriate disciplinary action when an employee disregards his or her internal control responsibilities, including acts of omission.			
Require every department to complete a risk assessment and implementation plan, updated every two years, to be provided to the head of internal audit.			

Notes

1. These recommendations are listed on the FATF Web site at http://www.fatf-gafi.org.
2. CHUs are described in Annex 6 to INTOSAI (2004).
3. The International Accounting Standards Committee issued International Accounting Standards from 1973 to 2000. The International Accounting Standards Committee was replaced by the International Accounting Standards Board in 2001. The International Accounting Standards Board issues International Financial Reporting Standards, and amends and supplements previously issued International Accounting Standards.

References and Other Resources

COSO (Committee of Sponsoring Organizations of the Treadway Commission). 1992. "Internal Control—Integrated Framework: Executive Summary." http://www.coso.org/publications/executive_summary_integrated_framework.htm.

———. 2004. "Enterprise Risk Management—Integrated Framework: Executive Summary." http://www.uta.fi/~kulaou/COSOERMsummary.pdf.

EC (European Commission). 2005. Chapter 28, *Financial Control: The Acquis and Public Sector Financial Management*. Brussels.

IIA (Institute of Internal Auditors). 2004. "International Standards for the Professional Practice of Internal Auditing." Institute of Internal Auditors, Altamonte Springs, FL. http://www.theiia.org.

IFAC (International Federation of Accountants). 2001. *Governance in the Public Sector: A Governing Body Perspective*. New York: IFAC.

———. 2006a. *Handbook of International Auditing, Assurance, and Ethics Pronouncements*. New York: IFAC.

———. 2006b. *Handbook of International Public Sector Accounting Pronouncements*. New York: IFAC.

International Accounting Standards Board. 2006. *International Financial Reporting Standards*. London: IASB. http://www.iasb.org.

INTOSAI (International Organization of Supreme Audit Institutions). http://www.intosai.org.

————. n.d. "Guidelines for Internal Control Standards for the Public Sector." Internal Control Standards Committee, Brussels.

————. 2001. "Internal Control: Providing a Foundation for Accountability in Government." INTOSAI, Vienna. http://www.intosai.org/Level3/Guidelines/3_Internal ContrStand/3_INT_Ae.pdf.

————. 2004. "Internal Control Systems in Candidate Countries." Vol. 1 and Vol. 11 (Annex 6 and 13), Working Group on Audit Manuals, Report to Supreme Audit Institutions of Central and Eastern European Countries, Cyprus, Malta, Turkey, and European Court of Auditors, Vienna.

SIGMA (Support for Improvement in Governance and Management in Central and Eastern European Countries). 2001. "Public Sector Financial Control Baselines." Organisation for Economic Co-operation and Development and the European Union, Paris. http://www.oecd.org/dataoecd/56/58/36579529.pdf.

Transparency International. n.d. http://www.transparency.org.

UNDP (United Nations Development Programme). 1998. "Corruption and Integrity Improvement Initiatives in Developing Countries." UNDP, Management Development and Governance Division, New York.

World Bank. n.d. "Latvia Internal Control System Handbook." Unpublished, World Bank, Washington, DC.

6

Internal Control and Audit at Local Levels

MUSTAFA BALTACI AND SERDAR YILMAZ

An internal control and audit framework aims at improving financial and administrative management capacity by limiting fiscal behaviors that result in waste, misallocation, and corruption. While common in both the public and the private sectors, these financial management tools have been widely overlooked in the context of decentralization in developing countries. This chapter argues that to achieve efficiency and effectiveness at the local or subnational governmental level—that which is below the central level—internal control and audit should be among the key components of a fiscal decentralization program.

In recent years, fiscal decentralization programs implemented in many developing countries have given local governments additional service responsibilities and access to more public funding, either in the form of intergovernmental transfers or through the authority to raise taxes from a wider variety of local sources. However, expanding their expenditure responsibilities and spending authority without improving public financial management systems has had little impact on service delivery outcomes. The absence of effective public financial management systems at both central and local levels has sometimes resulted in fiscal imbalances, weak accountability, political capture, and deterioration in public services. In some cases, the consequent weaknesses in local governments' financial management have posed threats to their national economies. Fiscally distressed local governments in Argentina, for example, significantly increased the country's vulnerability to external shocks by maintaining far too much borrowing with poor fiduciary management. Similarly, Brazil, Colombia, and India have experienced excessive fiscal deficits caused by their subnational governments because of such factors as weak local political capacity, lack of internal control and external oversight, and expectation of bailouts when localities borrow beyond their means. Therefore, a grave need exists to keep local governments fiscally on track and to hold local government officials accountable for results. A contemporary internal control and audit framework could help achieve both objectives.[1]

A number of good examples of contemporary internal control and audit systems exist. Both the United States and the United Kingdom have championed internal control and audit at all levels of government. Similarly, the European Union (EU) has heavily invested in developing internal control and audit systems, particularly in candidate countries. Support for Improvement in Governance and Management (SIGMA), a joint entity of the EU and the Organisation for Economic Co-operation and Development, has been singled out as the catalyst to encourage the transition countries to build effective internal control and audit systems.

However, examples of internal control and audit at the subnational level are rare, particularly in developing countries. In many cases, reformers have placed more emphasis on improving capacity and building control mechanisms at the central government level. Regrettably, establishing internal control and audit practices at the local government level has received little or no attention, even in countries where decentralization programs devolve more responsibilities to local governments.[2]

This chapter is an attempt to close this implementation gap by developing a conceptual framework for internal control and audit for use at the local level. The following section introduces a series of factors that creates weak local government accountability structures. The succeeding section introduces the concept of internal control, particularly focusing on contemporary internal control systems, and is followed by a section that discusses internal audit as part of a broader control framework, highlighting the differences between internal control and internal audit. The concluding section summarizes the main points and their relation to public financial management. There are five annexes to this chapter, which illustrate the general points of the discussion with country examples.

The Need for Improving Accountability in Decentralization

Fiscal decentralization is a broad concept relating to intergovernmental institutions, budgetary processes, and financial arrangements underlying the central-local relationship in a country. With the implementation of a decentralization program, the legal and political authority to plan projects, make decisions, and manage public functions is transferred from the central government and its agencies to local governments. Although the motivation behind decentralization is different in each country, the underlying goal has always been to improve the quality of public services and the effectiveness of the public administration system.

A close review of previous decentralization efforts indicates that they frequently have failed to deliver the expected outcomes in local service provision and improved public administration. Many developing countries have reported that decentralization cultivated weak fiscal discipline and poor expenditure management, attributable to a combination of weak managerial capacity in local governments, pervasive capture by local elites, widespread mismanagement or misallocation of public resources or both, and rampant corruption. To counter the impact of these influences, the decentralized structure must ensure conformity with rules and regulations, expenditure controls, and performance monitoring. A contemporary internal control framework accompanied by an effective internal audit process could both aid the external audit process and assist central governments in their monitoring efforts over local governments with regard to effectiveness, corruption, waste, and misuse.

In many countries, however, local governments lack control and audit procedures. Using selected countries as examples of current decentralization reforms, table 6.1 provides a brief summary of internal control systems and issues arising from inadequacy or lack of such systems altogether.

For example, Bosnia and Herzegovina is a federalist state with a highly decentralized government structure where, in the absence of modern internal control and audit systems, governments at all levels have failed to develop sound budget practices (World Bank 2003a). The lack of control systems makes safeguarding against abuse, misuse, fraud, and irregularities impossible. In Bosnia and Herzegovina, widespread corruption is coupled with low public morale and distrust toward public institutions (World Bank 2003a). At least one report on the country concludes that without establishing an effective control system at the subnational level, detection and control of misconduct in public procurement are next to impossible (World Bank 2002b).[3]

TABLE 6.1   Local Governments and Internal Controls in Selected
Countries

Country	Characteristics of internal control system at the local level	Issues arising from lack of internal controls
Argentina	Lack of legal instruments and no political willingness to improve internal control and audit systems	High level of indebtedness in local governments and failures in providing urban services
Bosnia and Herzegovina	Lack of contemporary internal control and audit systems	Impaired safeguarding measures against abuse, misuse, fraud, and irregularities; widespread corruption; misconduct and misuse of public funds; and public disaffection against government institutions
China	Ex ante expenditure control and compliance audits	Common problems in compliance with laws and regulations; unlawful tax practices
Colombia	Unclear legal framework defining the functions and responsibilities of the fiscal control agencies; ineffective internal control mechanisms	Negligence, corruption, and misuse of public funds
India—Karnataka State	Inefficient control and audit practices; old-fashioned rule books; lack of timely and reliable information; focus on compliance audits; and inadequate follow-up with audit findings	Frequent cases of abuse, misuse, and fraud; irregularities and malpractices in procurement; lack of adherence to the stated rules and procedures
Indonesia	Weak internal control and audit systems	Unethical and uneconomic operations due to pervasive corruption, inefficient cash management, and collusive practices in procurement
Philippines	Weak internal control environment; nonexistent internal audit; and lack of timely financial information	Lack of compliance with laws, rules, and regulations; fraud and irregularities; overpaid public purchase and procurement

Source: Author's compilation.

In the Philippines, despite enactment of the 1991 Local Government Code to devolve more responsibilities to subnational governments, the internal control environment and institutional arrangements for financial accountability remain extremely weak at the local level (Commission on Audit 2003; World Bank 2004d). The absence of key control mechanisms is one of the factors for weak governance in local government units (World Bank 2003c, 2004d). Fraud, irregularities, lack of compliance with regulations, and the inability of local governments to produce timely, accurate financial information are the major impediments to fulfilling accountability obligations.

Similarly, Indonesia has recently devolved decision-making power for major service delivery items from the central to the subnational level. Yet, diagnostic studies report that the lack of fraud and corruption detection and prevention systems is a major snag in improving local accountability (World Bank 2003b). Inefficient cash management, collusive practices in procurement, and weaknesses in internal control and audit, among other demanding issues, have remained constant concerns to the country's decentralization program. It is reported that only 5 percent of budgetary transactions of local governments are audited by the regional and provincial internal audit bodies and only 50 percent of the local authorities are checked periodically by the external audit institution (Khan and Sondhi 2005).

In India, the constitutional amendments of 1993 aim for strengthening citizen participation in local government decision-making processes. However, the subnational fiscal crisis of the late 1990s revealed a number of accountability flaws in the public finance framework (World Bank 2005c). Many Indian states have now adopted financial management reform programs and have passed fiscal responsibility acts. In Karnataka State, for example, irregularities and malpractice in the public procurement system have resulted in public mistrust of the system. To reform the public procurement system, the state government enacted the Karnataka Transparency in Public Procurement Act to enhance transparency in the tendering process and minimize opportunities for manipulation and corrupt practices (World Bank 2004b).

In Argentina, the decade of the 1990s was marked by recurring deficits and indebtedness at all levels of government. Recent efforts have been made to enhance local government finance (World Bank 2002a). Only with the enactment of the Fiscal Responsibility Laws in 1999 and 2004 have subnational governments begun to implement fiscal reforms that ensure citizen control over their operations and predictability of their fiscal policy performance. However, recent diagnostic studies show that legal instruments and political willingness to improve the internal control system at the sub-national level are lacking (Arlia 2005).

In China, subnational governments accounted for about 70 percent of government spending in 2002 (World Bank 2005b). However, internal control and auditing remains a weak link in subnational expenditure management (Mountfield and Wong 2005: 94). Subnational governments have their own audit bureaus, but they are "under the direct authority of the executive branch, compromising their independence" (Mountfield and Wong 2005: 94), and the focus is mostly on compliance audits. According to a recent report by China's National Audit Office, the external audit institution, local governments engage in unlawful tax practices by granting tax cuts or exemptions (or both) or implementing tax rebate policies (National Audit Office of China 2004).

Colombia has been engaged in a major decentralization experiment for the past 15 years. However, the legal framework is still unclear in defining the functions and responsibilities of the entities involved in subnational fiscal control. In the present situation, fiscal control is highly centralized, and provincial comptroller offices have little autonomy. Additionally, a multilayer bureaucracy often makes the control process sluggish (World Bank 2005a). Such factors lead to a vulnerable internal control environment where fraud, negligence, and corruption remain significant risks to local governance (World Bank 2005a).

These examples and others like them lead to the conclusion that local governments have to improve their administrative and financial management capacities for decentralization to produce better outcomes. The success of a fiscal decentralization program depends on strengthening the ability of sub-national governments to manage revenues and expenditures more efficiently and to provide services more effectively. Furthermore, in countries where corruption, waste, and inefficiencies in public services are widespread, these problems are usually compounded at the local level. Contemporary internal controls and well-functioning internal audit systems are meant to deliver key assurances to all stakeholders against these problems. In the absence of a contemporary internal control system, with internal audit as a safeguard for checking efficiency and effectiveness of that system, local governments are vulnerable to waste, corruption, and inefficiencies.

Contemporary Internal Controls

An internal control framework is a set of organizational policies and proce-dures to ensure reliable record keeping, to safeguard assets, to promote oper-ational efficiency, and to monitor adherence to policies and directives.[4] The functional and broader definition of internal control includes such actions as supervising management to ensure they have an adequate level of funding to deliver services; ensuring all transactions comply with legal frameworks; and ensuring practices are consistent with stated policies, organizational objectives, and performance criteria. Internal control means establishing a system in which all actions are monitored proactively, irregularities are corrected, and deficiencies are reported to top management. According to the International Organization of Supreme Audit Institutions (INTOSAI), it is not about "one event or circumstance, but a series of actions that permeate an entity's activities. These actions occur throughout an entity's operations on an ongoing basis" (2004: 6).[5] The lack of such organizational policies and procedures—internal controls—may result in such problems as (a) unethical, uneconomic, inefficient, and ineffective operations; (b) weak accountability links; (c) unlawful actions; and (d) lack of safeguarding measures against waste, abuse, mismanagement, errors, fraud, and irregularities.[6]

Until recently, "control" has been viewed as a system of ex ante financial and compliance controls that generally are operated by a central government agency, usually the Ministry of Finance. Lately, the control paradigm in the public sector has witnessed a conspicuous shift from classic ex ante expenditure checks to contemporary financial and nonfinancial internal controls. The contemporary definition of internal control includes a broader context, which not only refers to the traditional role of financial expenditure controls, but also provides management with the capability to supervise service delivery effectiveness. Therefore, contemporary internal control is a management tool to ensure that an institution's leadership is functioning in accordance with stated policies and procedures; delivering services efficiently and effectively; protecting assets and properties from improper use; keeping timely and precise accounts; and producing fiscal and nonfiscal information accurately.

The goal of a contemporary internal control framework is to ensure that resources are managed properly and accountability is maintained. In this framework, the tools that management can employ range from ex ante expenditure controls to compliancy checks, inventory controls, record keeping, reporting, and monitoring (see figure 6.1). However, a contemporary internal control framework is more than a set of traditional financial and compliance controls. It is based upon a system of management information, financial regulations, and administrative procedures for assessing such activities as revenue collection, accounting, and procurement practices; policy- and decision-making processes; expenditure effectiveness; and human resources management. It encompasses a variety of tools for ensuring that policies and

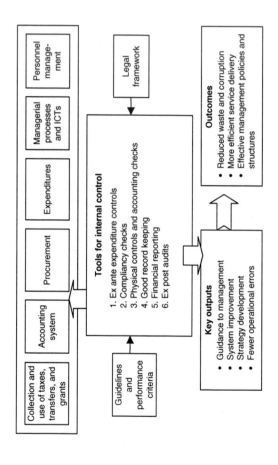

Source: Author's compilation.
Note: ICT = information and communication technology.

FIGURE 6.1   Internal Control Processes

procedures comply with the legal framework, as well as for ensuring effective and efficient service delivery.[7]

Contemporary control activities include a wide range of involvement such as approvals, verifications, and reviews of operating performance. These control activities can be organized as follows:

- *Accounting controls* are aimed at covering the procedures and documentation concerned with safeguarding assets and the reliability of financial records. A strong internal control system with coherent accounting checks enables the accountants and managers to check for errors and misuse of public resources.
- *Administrative controls* are applied to the procedures and records concerning the decision-making processes that lead employees to carry out authorized activities in achieving the organization's objectives. For example, physical check is an important administrative tool by which staff that are in charge of control processes undertake regular checks on the goods and removable items owned by the entity. Physical checks help ensure that the organization's property is used appropriately.
- *Management controls* are used to cover all the plans, policies, procedures, and practices needed for employees to achieve the entity's objectives. In this context, for example, hierarchical checks provide a powerful tool to make sure that responsibilities are handled in accordance with policies and procedures. These controls help to build a bottom-to-top trust with functioning communication among managerial levels while it diminishes the opportunity for corruption and misuse (INTOSAI 2004).

In a traditional financial control framework, such tools are usually underemployed and the institutional arrangements have relevant shortcomings. The responsibility for controls, for example, rests with the Ministry of Finance (MOF) instead of the public institution in question. As the sole practitioner of budgeting and fund allocation, the MOF exercises control functions on subnational governments as well as line agencies. Financial and compliance checks are usually carried out by financial controllers who are posted to public sector institutions by the MOF. Controllers report perceived irregularities to the MOF rather than to the public institution in question. The MOF may conduct ex ante controls from the headquarters in the event that no individual controller is assigned. In this centralized control model, the MOF authorizes a broad range of departmental activities, such as providing clearance for purchases, procurement, and personnel recruitment. As shown in figure 6.2, in a centralized internal control model, the MOF independently

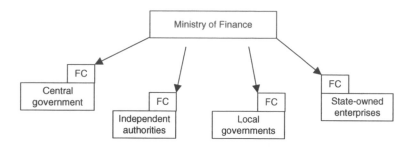

Source: Author's compilation.
Note: FC=financial controller.

FIGURE 6.2 Centralized Internal Control Model

dispatches its financial controllers to the spending institutions—including local governments—to oversee public financial management practices.

The paradigm of contemporary internal control, however, holds every single public institution accountable. It requires each public institution to administer the internal control program itself rather than an outsider. It is based on the premise that each institution is in charge of managing its finances in delivering outputs. Thus, public institutions are required to assemble a financial control department. The controller's job is not only financial controls but also participation in the decision-making processes of public financial management transactions. This participation includes, for example, a permanent seat on the procurement committee. Contemporary internal controls are embedded in an entity's managerial processes as checks and balances performed at all layers. Norms and values are internalized rather than externally imposed. More emphasis is given to horizontal and hierarchical interactions within the institution. Contemporary internal control, therefore, assigns responsibilities to all staff, not only to budget and accounting officials.

In a decentralized control model, the MOF is given only limited power because internal controls are task aligned with individual organizations. Limited power does not mean that the central government has no role. Indeed, the central government should set the standards and monitor the effectiveness of the local-level internal control systems. In the United Kingdom, for example, local authorities apply their own systems but through a framework of generally accepted rules and procedures endorsed by professional bodies such as the Chartered Institute of Public Finance and Accountancy and the Treasury. In Albania, each budget institution has a finance office that is responsible for first-level controls in budget execution. The finance officer ensures completeness of documentation, availability of budget allocation, and compliance with departmental rules. The Council of Ministers ensures that an effective internal control framework is in place and maintained. This process enhances the ministers' understanding of the state's management and provides positive incentives for ministries to correct any deficiencies reported by the internal control system (OECD/PIFC Expert Group 2004). In the United States, the Single Audit Act designates a control framework for centrally funded earmarked transfers to local authorities. Accordingly, the White House Office of Management and Budget is legally assigned to issue circulars to delineate the framework and to coordinate the control works. See annex 6A.1 for examples in other countries.

A decentralized contemporary control approach is desirable when a decentralization program devolves more fiscal responsibilities to local governments. In a fiscally decentralized structure, local governments are invested with budget preparation and execution power, so they should also be in charge of managing the internal control systems to strengthen downward accountability links. A decentralized contemporary control approach will mandate that local governments keep reliable records of resources and properties; develop results-oriented policies; be effective, efficient, and economic in service delivery; and be proactive in taking necessary measures for perceived risks. Furthermore, the decentralized model helps to achieve "subsidiarity" in local governments by building internalized values and principles. See annex 6A.2 for a discussion of issues in establishing contemporary internal control frameworks at the local level.

Contemporary internal control systems offer a golden opportunity for stakeholders to be more informed about the day-to-day activities of a public sector entity. However, the success of an internal control system is profoundly affected not only by the attitudes of management and employees but also by the establishment of safeguards. The following features of a management system for internal controls are important to its efficacy:

- Decisive leadership that is responsible for designing, implementing, supervising, maintaining, and documenting the internal control system
- Well-considered internal control design aligned with the organizational objectives
- Committed personnel who perform their jobs in accordance with the prestated policies, procedures, regulations, and ethical rules
- Effective risk identification and system monitoring mechanisms
- Internal audit and independent internal auditors, as part of the internal control system that provides a set of sound safeguarding processes

Internal Audit: A Key Module in Control Systems

"Internal control" and "internal audit" are close and commonly intertwined terms, often used interchangeably. However, there are functional and operational distinctions between internal control and internal audit. Internal controls are the systems put in place to ensure sound financial management and service delivery, whereas internal audit is the check of those systems. Internal control processes are intended to provide generic assurances to mitigate the probable risks via ex ante expenditure checks, whereas internal auditors are engaged in ex post compliance, performance, and financial audits. The feature that most distinguishes internal audit from internal control is that internal audit operates independently from the entity's administration and internal control structure.[8]

An effective control system should be composed of both financial and nonfinancial controls applicable to each phase of the decision-making process, as figure 6.3 illustrates. Such a system has three main components: risk identification, development of internal control systems and procedures to counter the perceived risks, and establishment of an internal audit procedure for checking internal control efficiency and effectiveness (Allen and Tommasi 2001). It includes independent internal auditors as a safeguard to oversee managerial decisions, activities, and program results. In an organization, it is the leadership team's responsibility to develop an operating method for the control system. The management team should oversee the functioning of the control system and ensure that the information floats smoothly across the main actors, especially the management team, internal auditors, and external auditors.

The goal of internal audit should be to add value and improve an organization's operations and control structure. Internal audit provides both governments and related parties with a powerful tool for understanding the

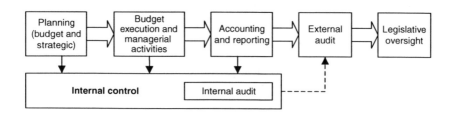

Source: Author's compilation.

FIGURE 6.3 Public Financial Management Cycle

extent to which the public institution has delivered on-budget and effective services. Therefore, internal audit is "a well-defined activity and a recognized profession" (Madsen 2003: 5) that is performed by professionals who determine whether the organization's decision making is sound and effective. Ideally, internal auditors are excluded from day-to-day management activities, and are not allowed to intervene in decision-making circles. This limited scope suggests shifting the internal audit from ex ante to ex post reviews, which means that auditors should engage in testing the conformity and effectiveness of completed transactions and expenditures.

From a *functional* point of view, internal audit assists the effectiveness of internal control as a supporting element in overseeing the proper use of revenues and authority. Internal audit, in this sense, is viewed as an integral part of the entire control system. It is the last step before the external audit checks whether decision making was proper, effective, and compliant with policies and procedures. However, internal audit needs to be *operationally* independent and separately situated from the administration. Figure 6.4 illustrates these links.

Although there is a degree of continuing communication between audit and administration, there should be no intervention by the administration to affect the audit results. The mandate, scope, methodology, and results should be determined by the internal auditors (that is, by the chief auditor or the audit committee) by seeking only guidance from senior management. Internal auditors usually communicate with the administration at two points: first, when handing over the audit reviews and second, when discussing the audit results.

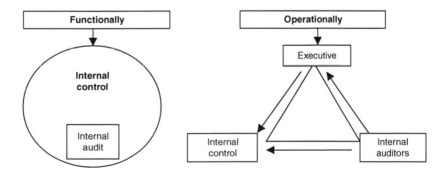

Source: Author's compilation.

FIGURE 6.4 Functional and Operational Links in Internal Control and Audit

If an audit committee is assembled to facilitate communication between top management and the auditors, the auditors can submit their reports to this committee. There should also be a link between internal auditors and external auditors (supreme audit institutions). By definition, external auditors independently, and usually on behalf of a legislative body, inspect public institutions for their financial and nonfinancial activities. In assessing the effectiveness of an institution's control framework, the external auditor may use the work of internal auditors, who are a part of the internal control system and are more apt to provide guidance on the system in place. Annex 6A.3 presents a brief discussion on the process of building an internal audit unit.

In many countries, the scope of the internal audit function is limited to ex ante expenditure controls and compliance, both at the central and subnational levels. Box 6.1 defines and discusses three different types of audits.

However, in certain countries, auditing has evolved to cover all aspects of governance. Table 6.2 illustrates the changing character of internal audit. In these countries, the internal audit embarks on a mandate to evaluate programs

---

BOX 6.1   Three Types of Audit

A *compliance audit* consists of the checks carried out to evaluate how well the organization complies with and adheres to relevant policies, laws, directions, plans, and procedures. The compliance audit emerges as the basic element of conducting an audit.

The *financial audit* assesses the internal control systems that ensure the quality of accounting information and financial reporting. Financial audits include financial statements, accounts, accounting, receipts, and other financially related issues. Financial statement audits provide reasonable assurance about whether the financial statements of an audited entity present fairly the financial position, results of operations, and cash flows in conformity with accounting standards. Financial audits also determine whether (a) financial information is presented in accordance with established or stated criteria, (b) the entity has adhered to specific financial compliance requirements, or (c) the entity's internal control structure over financial reporting and safeguarding assets is suitably designed and implemented to achieve the control objectives.

Finally, a *performance audit* aims to review whether a particular activity is completed in a way that has produced effective, efficient, and economic results. It is viewed as an objective examination of evidence for providing a reasonable assessment of an organization's performance.

Source: Adapted from U.S. GAO (1999).

TABLE 6.2   Evolution of Internal Audit

Traditionally perceived role	Defined modern role
Police	Partners in the organization
Financial focus	Governance focus
Focus on tangible assets	Focus also on intangible assets
Compliance based	Performance and risk based
Reactive	Proactive
Ex ante	Ranges from ex ante to ex post

Source: Adapted from OECD/PIFC Expert Group (2004).

in light of established performance criteria and organizational objectives. That is, the internal audit systems in these countries add value to the effectiveness of public sector operations by enabling objective scrutiny. Internal auditing in the province of Ontario in Canada, for example, experienced a cultural and functional transformation in the late 1990s. In 1998, as a first step toward improving its internal audit service, the provincial government combined small units that provided auditing services to the province's 23 ministries and created an integrated internal audit division under the direction of a chief internal auditor. Over the course of a year, the division undertook a strategic planning exercise to develop its vision, mission, values, and strategic goals. The strategic plan that emerged from this exercise established a client-focused vision for the division and provided a framework for serving the needs of the province. The transformation process has gained support from senior management and the cabinet approved an internal audit directive to serve as the division's most important tool for ensuring sound corporate governance. After the transformation was complete, the client satisfaction rating rose steadily, from 75 percent in 1999 to 88 percent in 2003. The staff and clients now see the auditors as business partners and valuable contributors to effective, efficient program delivery rather than as adversaries (Lapointe 2004).

Internal auditing, however, is a demanding task in local governments. Annex 6A.4 discusses the basic elements of internal auditing. Establishing an audit body requires answers to a set of critical questions, such as where to start, how to organize audit work, its scope, and how to achieve integrity and independence at the same time (see annex 6A.5). As discussed above, clear-cut examples of local governments with both sound internal control and audit systems often exist in affluent countries, where decentralization is in place at virtually all lower levels. In developing countries, however, capacity problems prevail to such an extent that local governments either are negligent in committing to accountable financial management or are weak in their capacity to develop such management.

Yet, examples of good practices are apparent in a number of countries that have acted to promote fiscal accountability and internal audit mechanisms in local government. For example, Argentina, Hong Kong (China), and Singapore have created ethics offices for their cities. Supreme audit institutions in many developing countries have started to include local governments in their audit work. Others recently initiated internal audit systems at the local level. In Pakistan, for example, the North-West Frontier Province has made positive strides in the establishment and operation of internal audit units. Internal audit units are established in four main departments—health, education, police, and public works. The North-West Frontier Province government has now determined to establish internal auditors in all other provincial departments (World Bank 2004c). In India's Orissa State, audits of urban local bodies are conducted annually by the local fund auditors of the state finance department. Audits successfully cover all local transactions. When embezzlement is detected, the auditor has the power to allow the errant employee to replace the stolen amount. Serious irregularities are reported to the appropriate authorities for necessary action (Subramanian 2005).

Conclusion

This chapter argues that the success of a fiscal decentralization program depends on strengthening the ability of subnational governments to manage revenues and expenditures more efficiently and to provide services more effectively. Local governments in many developing countries have been affected adversely by decentralization policies because they have not been provided the necessary instruments to enhance the monitoring of local government performance and to perform accountability checks. Under circumstances in which no accountability programs exist, the misuse and waste of public funds is inevitable. As a result, countries need to highlight the need for transparent financial systems with effective internal control and audit structures in local governments.

The chapter identifies internal control and audit as key components of public financial management (PFM) systems for increasing efficiency and effectiveness in local government operations. An effective, efficient, transparent, and rules-based PFM system is an essential tool for a government implementing a fiscal decentralization program. Within the PFM framework, internal control and audit functions support the fiscal decentralization process by promoting transparency and accountability in the use of public resources, ensuring allocation of public resources in accordance with citizens' priorities, and supporting aggregate fiscal discipline. A well-functioning internal control and audit system provides all stakeholders with broader outputs and outcomes as it seeks to deliver better guidance to management by mitigating and eliminating risks, helping in the design of effective strategic development plans, removing inherent errors and inconsistencies within the system, and strengthening integrity through multiple checks. Thus, effective decentralization strategies require that the subnational government strengthen its internal control and audit instruments while more power is devolved to local governments.

In addressing control and audit reforms, local government practitioners need to account for the different dynamics of internal control and internal audit. Neither internal control nor internal audit systems are complete or magical solutions on their own. They do not necessarily resolve all challenges in a PFM apparatus. Instead, improving governance structures and accountability frameworks requires a broader strategy encompassing the whole spectrum of PFM issues, which include planning, budgeting, accounting, procurement, public debt, asset management, reporting, external audit, and legislative oversight. Regardless of the coverage of a decentralization program, we believe an effort to reform intergovernmental fiscal systems should include internal control and audit because of the crucial role they play in enhancing accountability and effectiveness of local government operations.

Annex 6A.1: Internal Control and Audit in Local Governments across the World

The United States is one of the countries that champions internal control in local government. With the help of its greatly decentralized public sector structure, the United States has adopted an understanding of modern internal control practices, particularly in local agencies. According to the present legal construction of the United States, local governments are responsible for designing internal control systems while being invested with the power to audit if risks are encountered, according to the Government Accountability Office (GAO) standards on governmental auditing. The GAO, along with state auditors, ensures that a local government has not failed to revisit its risks through designing effective internal controls and audits. The Governmental Accounting Standards Board promulgates accounting guidelines and financial reporting standards for state and local governments, whereas the White House's Office of Management and Budget sets the internal control standards for the use of federal funds. According to these standards, every local government official has responsibility regarding the condition of management controls. For example, a city's management is responsible for setting up and maintaining an adequate system of internal controls. It is critical that management set the right tone at the top by clearly stating management's expectations for integrity, honesty, and impartiality; by prescribing a code of ethics and conflict of interest guidelines; and by periodically assessing whether appropriate controls are in place. Management, however, is accountable to the city council, which provides policies, guidance, and oversight. The council asks departments questions about their controls. The city auditor plays an important role in evaluating the effectiveness of control systems and contributes to the ongoing effectiveness of management controls by making relevant recommendations. Also, all other staff members are made aware of their responsibility to contribute to the city's management controls.

The subnational audit system in the United States is also unique. State auditors are assigned to oversee both state departments and some programs of lower-tier governments. For example, in Pennsylvania, the auditor general of state, who is an elected official, leads a team carrying out performance and financial audits in the state departments. In addition, he or she initiates audit programs to ensure that pension plans established by municipalities for their police officers, paid firefighters, and nonuniformed employees are properly funded and that they are administered in compliance with applicable laws, regulations, contracts, procedures, and policies.[9] The state auditor plays a dual role as the internal auditor of the state's operations and the external auditor of selected municipal programs. At the municipal level, the city usually has its own auditor.

In Philadelphia, a major Pennsylvania city, an elected city controller has broad authority and responsibility for protecting the public's interest in the handling of the city's money. The controller's office performs annual financial and performance audits of every city officer, department, board, and commission, and any agency receiving appropriations from the city. An annual financial audit and other reviews of the School District of Philadelphia are also performed, as are special audits whenever the controller deems them necessary, or as requested by the mayor. The controller acts as internal auditor to the city's activities while becoming an external auditor to the school districts.[10]

As an elected official, the New York City comptroller serves as the chief financial officer and controller of the city. The mission of the comptroller's office is to ensure the financial health of New York City by providing periodic information to the mayor, the city council, and the general public. The comptroller advises on city programs and operations, fiscal policies, and financial transactions. In addition, the comptroller manages pension funds, performs budgetary analysis, audits city agencies, oversees budget and contract authorization, and prepares warrants for payment. The comptroller's office employs a great number of staff, including accountants, attorneys, information technology analysts, economists, engineers, and budget, financial, and investment analysts.[11]

In *Sweden*, the mandate of auditors is set forth in national legislation and in local regulations, such as the Local Government Act and the Companies Act. In local governments (municipalities and county councils), the ultimate decision-making powers are exercised by the assembly while responsibility for preparing matters and for administration and execution rests with elected representatives in committees and assembly-drafting committees. Auditing is the assembly's instrument for inspecting the activities of committees and assembly-drafting committees. The Local Government Auditing Inquiry (Swedish Government Official Reports 1998) emphasizes that auditing is the instrument of the entire assembly and that the citizens' priorities should be its primary focus. The assembly elects the auditors for a period of four years. All auditors fulfill their individual mandates independently. The auditors' inspection and determination should follow "generally accepted auditing standards in local governments," which are published by the Swedish Association of Local Authorities and the Swedish Federation of County Councils (Swedish Government Official Reports 2004).

In *France*, the Decentralization Law of 1982 assigned a new court, the regional audit chamber, to be responsible for ex post auditing of local authority accounts. This court's duty is to verify accounts of public accountants of these territorial communities and their public institutions; review management of these communities as well as the management of their public institutions, which directly or indirectly depend on or receive financial assistance from them; and help in verifying budgets of communities and their public institutions through advice, formal notice, or proposals under certain circumstances and according to procedure set by the law. The court has the power to verify whether there are any irregularities in management by expenditure-sanctioning authority or managing authority, and to verify the efficiency of management. However, the French model does not necessarily fit into the modern definition of internal auditing in local governments. Rather, the audit chamber acts like a miniaturized court of accounts for that region.[12]

In New South Wales (NSW) in *Australia*, the Independent Commission Against Corruption found that 80 percent of general managers considered internal audit to be important. However, the same research found that only about 20 percent of councils had an audit charter, internal auditor, or audit committee as of 2001. The Local Government Act, Local Government (Financial Management) Regulation (1999), and the Local Government Code of Accounting Practice and Financial Reporting establish requirements for financial audit. State government agencies are bound by Section 11 of the Public Finance and Audit Act (1983) requiring the establishment of a system of internal audit where practicable. The NSW Treasury also issued a supporting "Best Practice Guide—Internal Control and Internal Audit" in June 1995. In the Victoria jurisdiction, the Local Government Act (1989) included the requirement for councils to have audit committees. Audit committees should comprise at least three members, including two who are not members of the council. The guidelines require councils to have and review the Internal Auditor's Charter, qualifications, and resources; have an approved audit plan; and monitor management's response to audit reports (NSW Department of Local Government 2005).

In the *United Kingdom*, the "Code of Practice for Internal Audit in Local Government" was issued by the Chartered Institute of Public Finance and Accountancy in 2000. The institute updated the code and released a consultative report in 2003. Major accounts and audit legislation require that all principal local government organizations in England, Wales, Scotland, and Northern Ireland should make provision for internal audit in accordance with the Code of Practice. Internal auditors of local governments are appointed by the Audit Commission, an independent public body responsible for ensuring that public money is spent economically, efficiently, and effectively in the areas of local government, housing, health, criminal justice, and fire and rescue services.[13]

Annex 6A.2: Establishing Effective Internal Control in Local Governments

Not all local agencies have the capacity and professional staff to undertake the primary responsibilities associated with internal controls. Many local governments are struggling to cope with ineffective budgetary processes along with outdated accounting and planning techniques. Variations in the size of local organizations present different obstacles toward building effective local government internal control systems. For example, local governments in major cities seem to be more prepared to engage in modern internal control practices and procedures because they have greater access to revenues and stronger capacity. Smaller local governments (measured in total financial capacity and population) continually grapple with basic problems such as unsustainable revenues and budget deficits, unpaid public employees, and indebtedness. Major metropolitan governments can shift more readily to full-framed internal control systems, while relatively smaller ones may be capable of only a certain system upgrade level. Small local governments unable to build effective internal control systems may consider an alternative. For example, a local agency with no or few budgeting personnel may consider unifying its control procedures with a neighboring local authority facing similar shortcomings. Employing a group of accounting officials and internal auditors jointly may help reduce burdensome personnel costs.

Presented below is a straightforward, five-step strategy for creating internal control systems in a local government.

Step 1: Understand the Current Structure

A local government must first review the control system currently in place. A detailed analysis of what does and does not work within the existing administrative and financial (budgetary and accounting) processes would provide useful hints for the next steps. In brief, some of the typical problems that contemporary local government organizations face are (a) lack of clear objectives and organizational goals; (b) lack of, or ambiguous, legal frameworks governing the control structure; (c) lack of ethical integrity rules and professionalism; (d) pervasive individual misconduct; (e) high risk of fraud, misuse, and waste; (f) inefficient accounting and cash management; (g) lack of existing accountability systems, which lead to clutter and delay in major projects; and (h) inertia and lack of motivation. Perceived risks and monitoring procedures also need to be included in the assessment. Such extensive work usually is done by a professional consultant who is hired by the local government.

Step 2: Design a Control Framework

According to the weaknesses and strengths indicated by the preliminary analysis, an appropriate control framework needs to be designed. Devising a proper structure is certainly challenging and requires advanced knowledge of financial management. However, a local government can adopt a ready-made control assessment design by making minor adjustments to the generally accepted internal control guidelines. COSO's "Internal Control–Integrated Framework" (COSO 1992) and INTOSAI's "Guidelines for Internal Controls Standards for the Public Sector" (INTOSAI 2004) have been recognized as the most common in both defining and evaluating internal controls.[14] The two guidelines provide a clear-cut framework consisting of five interrelated components: (a) control environment, (b) risk assessment, (c) control activities, (d) information and communication, and (e) monitoring.

The *control environment*, the foundation for all other components of internal control, provides discipline and structure. It incorporates ethical values, management's tone (willingness) and operating style, and the hierarchy of authority (the level of interaction among the managerial layers). *Risk assessment* refers to the ability of an organization to address relevant risks to achieve stated objectives. *Control activities* are the policies and procedures that help ensure that management directives are performed properly. They include a wide range of activities, such as approvals, verifications, and reviews of operating performance. It is important that pertinent *information* be identified, captured, and *communicated* in a certain form that enables staff to perform their responsibilities on a timely basis. An effective communication stream with internal and external parties also is a key factor. *Monitoring* is a way of assessing the quality of the system's performance over time. It requires that flaws in internal control be reported upward to top management. This responsibility is partly addressed by the internal auditors. However, after decisions are made, management must perform ongoing monitoring.

The central government can play a role in setting the standards for internal control and monitoring its implementation by local governments, as in the United Kingdom. This achieves a certain level of standardization for local governments, and makes it easier for external oversight to evaluate the effectiveness and efficiency of internal control systems.

Step 3: Prepare and Revise the Legal Framework

A strong legal basis in local governments is needed to clearly define duties, responsibilities, policies, processes, and objectives. A clear definition of the main mission, responsible parties, and authorities helps streamline internal control. A cohesive legal framework also enables management to compare results with the intended objectives.

The proposed legislation should particularly include the designation of related financial actors and their responsibilities. Three significant actors for control activities are the authorizing official (senior manager or designees), program manager (department heads or project managers), and accounting officer. The program manager proposes an activity (for example, purchase, procurement, and consultancy payments); the senior manager clears the demand (or signs the proposal); and finally the accounting officer makes the payment from the related budget allocation. This *segregation of duties* in financial management is built upon the fact that no actor can assume any responsibility of the other two.[15] Some instances, however, include other individuals, such as procurement officer or procurement committee members; they lie between the program manager and the senior manager in the decision-making hierarchy. The senior manager, in any case, has the power to veto the requested purchase. In local governments, the top official (mayor, governor, or secretary) typically is designated as the senior manager although the authority is often delegated to an individual in the next lower tier.

Step 4: Explore the Instruments to Practice Internal Control

Although the duties of modern internal control permeate all layers of government, tangible tools are still required. The common practices of control provide some practical instruments, such as physical checks, accounting checks, and horizontal checks. Thus, staff members who are in charge of control processes undertake regular *physical checks* on the goods and removable items owned by the entity. Physical checks help ensure that the organization's property is used appropriately. In many instances, each unit is required to maintain an inventory of public properties to account for all items. A discovery of a missing item may cause both a disciplinary measure and reimbursement by the person responsible for the loss.

Governments are expected to double-check accounting activities. Engaging in fast-flowing financial activities might make some public accountants and cashiers vulnerable to quantitative errors in the accounts. Indeed, checks are not always cashed in the right amount, cash receipts may go unrecorded, and payments may not be posted to the right person. A strong internal control system with coherent *accounting checks* enables the accountants and managers to rely more on existing data and records in managing the programs.

Similarly, *hierarchical controls* provide a powerful tool to make sure responsibilities are handled in accordance with policies and procedures. These controls help build bottom-to-top trust with functioning communication among managerial levels while it diminishes the opportunity for corruption and misuse. Likewise, some activities require cooperation among different operational departments. The countercontrols, in this case, are called *horizontal checks*, which enable managers to correct intentional or unintentional errors. In a construction project cycle, for instance, as a capital management unit oversees the progress of the construction, the contractor's entitlements are sent to accounts payable with a clearance. If the accounts payable assessment considers the payment request improper, it might need either to deny the request or to return it to the constructions unit for a careful reexamination.

Finally, *internal audit* emerges as a sound safeguard to ensure that the internal controls are effective and to give accurate guidance to management.

Step 5: Implement the Proposed Framework

Implementation is unquestionably the most significant part of an internal control action. It takes unrelenting sustainability, leadership, patience, and devotion. It requires that internal control be owned by those who have a decisive influence upon it. Executive bodies, the legislature, and taxpayers play a role in this ongoing process; legislative bodies cannot be considered in isolation from the executive bodies. Legislative bodies are meant to give guidance to management while being in charge of establishing the legal framework.

Annex 6A.3: Starting from Scratch: Building an Audit Unit in Local Government

Establishing an audit body does not need to open a Pandora's box of unknown issues. However, some critical questions must be answered in the process of audit formation. For example, one needs to know where to start and what to do, how to organize audit work and its scope in a local government, and how to build the necessary integrity and independence criteria. The following analysis demonstrates the requirements of instituting internal audit in a local government.

A Straightforward Agenda

Having a clear agenda mandated by a decisive political driver is a significant feature when assembling an audit body. Thus, a local government is often given an agenda in connection either with the external pressures (for example, a mandatory regulation of central government, budgetary requirements, and donors' recommendations) or with internal demands (locally adopted legislation, updates in accounting and budgetary policies, and political executives who are eager to reform public services, for instance). Proposed policy changes that work best encapsulate not only internal auditing elements but also the related elements of accountability, such as sound control environment, risk management, monitoring, and transparency. Success is more likely if the mandate is owned by a powerful executive.

Legal Framework

An audit charter needs to be put into effect by the authorized body—the city council or executive board. The charter should

- Provide simple definitions of internal audit, objectives, mission, operations to be audited, the meaning of chief executive officer and auditors, status, duties, and responsibilities;
- Clarify who will have authority over the budget of the internal audit unit;
- Define the methods to be used in appointing a chief auditor and individual auditors;
- Make clear the qualities and professionalism required for the internal auditors;
- Outline auditing standards and certification processes; and
- Name and explain the types of audit and audit reports, scope of audit, audit schedule, records, and the authorized bodies who will be receiving and following up on the audit reports.

As with internal control, the MOF (or Treasury or external auditor) might play a role in setting the framework and monitoring its effectiveness to achieve uniformity of audit standards across the country.

Chief Auditor

An experienced person who has qualities that fit the charter should be appointed as the independent chief auditor by either the executive board or the legislative body. The chief auditor ensures that ordinances are in place to administer the internal audit standards, ethics rules, and audit work. The chief auditor ensures that internal auditors are hired, that they operate in accordance with these regulations, and that audits are conducted as required in the charter. Audit results are communicated by the chief auditor to senior management so senior management can address the advised reinforcements. The appointment and removal of the chief auditor by an executive should be subject to legislative confirmation to negate any partisan influence on his or her independence.

Independence

Senior management and local politicians should not interfere with any decision on hiring and firing of internal auditors and the scope, design, and areas of audit work; all of these are subject to review by the legislative body. Internal auditors should be invested with full, free, and unrestricted access to all finance records, personnel records, contracts, documents, and reports.

Management should develop a rapport with the audit unit to negotiate, if necessary, the audit results. Open support proclaimed by management (perhaps by way of an internal circular) that delineates employee behavior regarding the audit work and audit results might be a great help. While audit independence is ensured by legal statute, it takes time for the audit culture to be completely absorbed within an organization.

Audit Committee

In some instances, an audit committee is in place to consult with the chief auditor regarding the audit results and to follow up on the control reinforcements. The committee facilitates communication of the audit results between the executive and the chief auditor. Additionally, the executive may have special requests that internal audit identify pitfalls and shortcomings in a particular program; the committee assists in voicing such requests. The audit committee preferably includes representatives from senior management, budgetary and accounting officials, legislative representatives, and the head of internal audit. Members of the committee, therefore, should be assigned by the legislative body, and at least one member should be appointed from among members of that body.

Audit Scope and Work

The auditors should be directed to perform compliance, financial, and performance audits in all departments, offices, activities, and programs of a local entity. Limitations on this scope would undermine the effectiveness of internal audit and cripple expected outcomes. Thus, the audit should cover all programs regardless of internal boundaries or geographical restrictions; and the internal auditors should be able to conduct audits not only at headquarters but also in chapters, subsidiaries, government-run enterprises, and related agencies.

Annex 6A.4: Basic Elements of Internal Audit

In its "International Standards for the Professional Practice of Internal Auditing," the IIA states, "Internal auditing is an independent, objective assurance and consulting activity designed to add value and improve an organization's operations. It helps an organization accomplish its objectives by bringing a systematic, disciplined approach to evaluate and improve the effectiveness of risk management, control, and governance processes" (IIA 2005: 10). Reflecting on this definition, Diamond (2002) argues that the broad view of the role of internal audit certainly places it more centrally as an important element of public financial management. Moving beyond a narrow compliance standpoint, this renewed approach embraces a wider definition of internal control, with more emphasis on management controls and information and communications processes.

This broad definition strikes initially at four critical points that demand further explication: independence, objective assurance, added value, and a systemic, disciplined approach.

Independence

According to Van Gansberghe, "Internal audit must contribute positively to the management, while at the same time not becoming its servant but faithfully report on the status to the board or other equivalent governing body" (Van Gansberghe 2005: 1). Audit should be isolated from any intervention posed against its objectivity. Such threats may stem from a variety of sources, such as political or administrative pressures to reduce the ability of auditors or to change the course of a particular audit. The threats might also come under different forms, such as budget reductions, limited supplies and facilities, and dismissal from the office. A concrete audit charter to strictly bind all parties is considered the most effective way to reduce the outside influences on audit. Similarly, personal misbehavior (misuse, graft, and bribery) undoubtedly can impact the audit's independence and objectivity. A code of ethics, therefore, is indispensable to internal audit in providing a safeguard against such illicit actions.

The IIA points to an organizationally independent internal audit for privately held entities governed by an executive board and run by a chief executive officer (CEO). In this sense, internal auditors are obliged to report to the CEO, who will reinforce the recommendations; however, the board—not the CEO—holds the power to hire, fire, and administer the internal auditors and the audit work.

In public sector institutions, the organizational structure of internal audit displays variations that highlight two outstanding issues regarding objectivity: statutory independence and budgetary independence. Driven by ideology and efforts to prevent corrupt behavior, senior management often becomes eager to intervene in the audit reviews, the scope of work, and the results. To prevent such attempts, the status of internal audit should be adjusted so it can carry out its function effectively. The chief auditor should hold an adequately powerful position to be isolated from such influences. The chief auditor is given responsibility to facilitate the effective discussion and negotiation of the results of internal audit with senior management. He or she ensures that the audit results are reflected in managerial action. Also, the chief auditor is obliged to take measures to keep individual auditors from getting involved in any managerial operations, biased reviews, and the potential for conflict of interest. The chief auditor prepares the annual work schedule to make sure that no internal auditors are embedded in a particular department for an extended time that might compromise the arm's-length relationship.

A second concern is related to the budget of the internal audit unit. So long as it is subject to legislative oversight, the funds allocated to the audit unit should be determined by the unit itself rather than any other service level. Otherwise, any management that feels threatened may exploit budget-making power as a way to limit the scope and effectiveness of audit work.

Objective Assurance

After evaluating the organization's programs, systems, and processes, the internal auditor is required to deliver an audit report that has a precise conclusion based on robust evidence. An internal auditor is bound by the organization's legal framework, objectives, and performance criteria to assess available evidence with an appropriate methodology and to provide a written assessment. An auditor can rely on common sense to reach a concrete conclusion where inadequate evidence exists. However, the auditor should remember that he or she is neither a prosecutor with the authority to arraign someone nor a judge able to reprimand an illicit act. Instead, the auditor needs to consider whether the public's money has been or is being used in accordance with the performance framework and legal statutes. The audit engagements normally involve three parties: auditee, or persons who have a degree of responsibility regarding the activity in question; auditor, or persons assessing the activity in question; and senior management, or persons who need to address the recommendations of the written audit assessments (IIA 2005).

Added Value

Internal audit is intended to provide value to the organization by improving opportunities to meet the organizational objectives by identifying operational improvements, and by mitigating risks through objective assurance. Evolving features of internal auditing have brought some modifications to the definition of added value. For example, in a traditional approach, savings from the loss endured in public programs—plugging the hole—was a fundamental goal, compared with the present where delivering services effectively, efficiently, economically, and ethically have emerged as primary goals.

A Systematic, Disciplined Approach

Internal audit is carried out in a way that, with some exceptions, produces similar conclusions for similar engagements and actions. Audit services need to be protected from personal bias and guided by audit standards. Because there are similar types of irregularities and misconduct worldwide, IIA first published audit standards in 1978 in an effort to streamline the process of evaluating entities. Some countries have followed up by issuing government auditing standards, such as the GAO in the United States. This effort is commendable because a unified method used in governmental auditing enormously helps to facilitate public program assessment by explaining the means to be applied and the ends to be achieved. For local authorities, internal audit guidelines are essential to helping assigned auditors who may be struggling to understand where to start in an engagement and how to handle the financial and performance audits.

Annex 6A.5: Importance of Risk Management

An effective internal control cycle is a dynamic process within which the administration should be continuously ready to address the arising risks and issues. Risk assessment is therefore central to internal control because it enables management to identify and mitigate potential risks. Without recognizing perceived risks, the financial management system of a local government would remain vulnerable to both external circumstances (for example, economic shocks, monetary devaluation, high inflation, or policy changes by the central government in taxation or in the transfer formula) and internal conditions (budgetary deficits, irregularities in earmarked funds, poor pension fund management, overborrowing, or overspending in capital projects, for instance). Characteristics of risk vary from one set of circumstances to another. However, commonly acknowledged risks may arise in any type of public organization—corruption, misuse, fraud, systemic and individual errors, waste, mismanagement, inefficiencies in budget and accounting, unreliable financial records, inadequate ethical values, insufficient managerial oversight and monitoring, and various failures in exercising budgetary power and in generating reliable information.

In addressing potential risks, INTOSAI's guidelines (2004) for internal control standards propose a four-phase risk assessment model: identify the risks, evaluate the risks, assess the "risk appetite,"[16] and develop responses. The model includes actions for identifying and countering risks; it also includes actions for detecting and fixing deficiencies within the internal control system. Risk management, therefore, plays a secondary but still important role for developing the right internal control mechanisms.

A precise response for preventing harmful impacts is appropriate in a sound risk assessment system. The response varies from eliminating the risk and its causes, to treating the risk, to tolerating it to a certain degree. After all, it is management's responsibility to determine the severity of a risk, the organization's desire to mitigate the perceived risk, the magnitude of the response, and the scope of preemptive actions for future risks.

Notes

The authors gratefully thank Roumeen Islam, Richard Allen, Anwar Shah, Michael Schaeffer, Pierre Prosper Messali, Mozammal Hoque, Rafika Chaouali, and Yesim Yilmaz for their valuable comments and contributions.

1. Internal control and audit are not necessarily stand-alone management tools; they can be effective only to the extent that accounting and governance systems operate well. Internal control and audit functions should be established and aligned with broader governance reforms, such as strategic planning, accounting, budgeting, medium-term expenditure framework, procurement, reporting, external audit, public debt, and asset management.
2. The literature on internal control and audit is scarce and it concentrates on such practices at the central government level. For example, International Monetary Fund and World Bank staff studies on internal control and audit highlight the significance of internal audit in central governments (Diamond 2002; Van Gansberghe 2005) and take no notice of their importance at the local level.
3. Only 3 out of 10 cantons in the Federation of Bosnia and Herzegovina—Sarajevo, Tuzla, and Bihac—have recently introduced internal control and audit functions to strengthen the line of defense against waste and corruption (World Bank 2003a).
4. The public sector has borrowed contemporary internal control practices from the private sector. The Committee of Sponsoring Organizations of the Treadway Commission (COSO) is a voluntary private-sector organization established to improve the quality of financial reporting through business ethics, effective internal controls, and corporate governance. In 1992, COSO published its "Internal Control–Integrated Framework," a flagship of internal control guidelines. This framework consists of five components: (a) control environment, (b) risk assessment, (c) control activities, (d) information and communication, and (e) monitoring. For more information, see http://www.coso.org.
5. INTOSAI is the professional organization of supreme audit institutions in countries that belong to the United Nations or its specialist agencies. INTOSAI's published guidelines incorporate a detailed analysis of internal control, definition, objectives, control environment, risk assessment, control activities, monitoring, roles, and responsibilities. Although adopting these guidelines is not mandatory for member countries, the INTOSAI standards should be a guiding principle in creating internal control systems at all levels of government, including the local level. For more information, see http://www.intosai.org.

6. According to INTOSAI, the objectives of an internal control system are (a) executing orderly, ethical, economical, efficient, and effective operations; (b) fulfilling accountability obligations; (c) complying with applicable laws; and (d) safeguarding resources against loss, misuse, and damage (2004).

7. Internal control has inherent limitations, and does not necessarily provide an *absolute assurance*. Indeed, only a *reasonable level of assurance* is attainable, equating to a satisfactory level of confidence under given considerations of costs, benefits, and risks (INTOSAI 2004).

8. Internal audit is not a recent issue for corporate governance. The Institute of Internal Auditors (IIA) was formed in 1941 to promote auditing in privately held companies to help developing corporate structures foresee future risks and protect companies from failure. Since then, the IIA has been the prime catalyst of internal audit practices by publishing auditing standards, issuing professional certificates, and delivering training programs. Currently, the IIA is involved in various activities, ranging from publishing reports and studies on governmental audit, to upgrading standards through increased attention to public sector dynamics, to actively organizing seminars and workshops for representatives from various government departments. For more information, see http://www.theiia.org.

9. For more information, see http://www.auditorgen.state.pa.us.

10. For more information, see http://www.philadelphiacontroller.org.

11. For more information on the New York City Office of the Comptroller, see http://www.comptroller.nyc.gov.

12. For more information on the mandate of the regional audit chambers, see http://www.intosaiitaudit.org/mandates/mandates/Mandates/France.html#France_H6.

13. For more information on the role of the Audit Commission, see http://www.audit-commission.gov.uk/.

14. The U.S. Sarbanes-Oxley Act of 2002 requires organizations to adhere to internal control adequacy, with serious consequences for noncompliance. The U.S. Securities and Exchange Commission, accountable for enforcement of Sarbanes-Oxley, recognizes only the COSO framework as an acceptable model for control.

15. The European Commission (2002) has elaborated the "principle of segregation of duties" within a framework for financial regulation (No. 2343/2002).

16. Risk appetite is "the amount of risk to which the entity is prepared to be exposed before it judges action to be necessary" (INTOSAI 2004: 25).

References and Other Resources

Allen, Richard, and Daniel Tommasi. 2001. *Managing Public Expenditure: A Reference Book for Transition Countries*. Paris: Organisation for Economic Co-operation and Development/Support for Improvement in Governance and Management (OECD/SIGMA).

Arlia, Alejandro. 2005. "Argentina: From 'Funny Money' to 'Fiscal Responsibility.'" *Federations* 4 (4): 19–20.

Chartered Institute of Public Finance and Accountancy. 2000. "Code of Practice for Internal Audit in Local Government." CIPFA, London. http://www.cipfa.org.uk.

Commission on Audit, Republic of the Philippines. 2003. "Strengthening of Accountability in Poor Local Government Units–Audit Component." Local Government Units Review and Assessment Report, World Bank IDF Grant No. 27436, Manila.

COSO (Committee of Sponsoring Organizations of the Treadway Commission). 1992. "Internal Control–Integrated Framework." http://www.coso.org.

Diamond, Jack. 2002. "The Role of Internal Audit in Government Financial Management: An International Perspective." Working Paper 02/94, International Monetary Fund, Washington, DC.

European Commission. 2002. Regulation Number 2243/2002, "Official Journal of the European Committees." http://www.europa.eu.int.

IIA (Institute of Internal Auditors). 2005. "International Standards for the Professional Practice of Internal Auditing." Institute of Internal Auditors, Altamonte Springs, FL. http://www.theiia.org.

———. 2006. "The Role of Auditing in Public Sector Governance." Institute of Internal Auditors, Altamonte Springs, FL http://www.theiia.org/download.cfm?file=3512.

INTOSAI (International Organization of Supreme Audit Institutions). 2004. "Guidelines for Internal Controls Standards for the Public Sector." Internal Controls Standards Committee, Brussels, Belgium. http://www.intosai.org.

Khan, Asmeen, and Rajiv Sondhi. 2005. "Reforming Local Financial Management and Accountability in Indonesia." PowerPoint presentation. http://www1.worldbank.org/publicsector/decentralization/March2005Seminar/Seminar.htm.

Lapointe, Jacques. 2004. "An Audit Transformation." *Internal Auditor* (October): 62–6.

Madsen, Johannes Stenbaeck. 2003. "Capacity Development in Internal Audit: A Case Illustrated Approach to Developing Internal Audit Capacities." PowerPoint presentation at PFM Capacity Development Course, World Bank, Washington, DC, May 3–5.

Mountfield, Edward, and Christine P. W. Wong. 2005. "Public Expenditure on the Frontline: Toward Effective Management by Subnational Governments." In *East Asia Decentralizes: Making Local Government Work*, 85–106. World Bank: Washington, DC.

National Audit Office of China. 2004. "Audit and Investigation Findings on the Tax Collection and Management." Report No. 2004-04 (Serial No. 05), Beijing. http://www.cnao.gov.cn/main/articleshow_ArtID_917.htm.

NSW (New South Wales) Department of Local Government. 2005. "Internal Audit Discussion Paper." Circular No. 05/33, Australia.

OECD/PIFC (Organisation for Economic Co-operation and Development/Public Internal Financial Control) Expert Group. 2004. "Internal Control Systems in Candidate Countries," vol. 2. Working Group on Audit Manuals, Vienna. http://www.sigmaweb.org.

OECD/SIGMA (Organisation for Economic Co-operation and Development/Support for Improvement in Governance and Management). 2004. "Assessment Report: Albania Internal Financial Control." Paris. http://www.sigmaweb.org.

Schaeffer, Michael. 2005. "Local Government Accountability: Challenges and Strategies." Decentralization Thematic Group, World Bank, Washington, DC.

Subramanian, P. K. 2005. "FM Diagnostics in Indian Local Governments: Innovations and Challenges." Presentation at World Bank Course on Local Budgeting and Financial Management, March 29–30. http://www1.worldbank.org/public sector/decentralization/March2005Seminar/Seminar.htm.

Swedish Government Official Reports. 1998. "Local Government Auditing Inquiry." SOU:1998/71, Stockholm.

———. 2004. "Examining and Determining Accountability in Local Governments." SOU:2004/17, Stockholm.

U.S. GAO (United States General Accounting Office). 1999. "Government Auditing Standards." U.S. GAO, Washington, DC. http://www.gao.gov.

Van Gansberghe, Cecilia Nordin. 2005. "Internal Audit: Finding Its Place in Public Finance Management." World Bank Institute, Washington, DC.

World Bank. 2002a. "Argentina: Country Financial Accountability Assessment Report." Latin America and the Caribbean Region Financial Management and Accountability Team, World Bank, Washington, DC.

World Bank. 2002b. "Bosnia and Herzegovina: Country Procurement Assessment Report." Report No. 24396, World Bank, Washington, DC.

———. 2003a. "Bosnia and Herzegovina: Country Financial Accountability Assessment Report." Report No. 26927-BA, World Bank, Washington, DC.

———. 2003b. "Decentralizing Indonesia: A Regional Public Expenditure Review Overview Report." Report No. 26191-IND, East Asia Poverty Reduction and Economic Management Unit, World Bank, Washington, DC.

———. 2003c. "Philippines Improving Government Performance: Discipline, Efficiency and Equity in Managing Public Resources." Report No. 24256-PH, World Bank, Washington, DC.

———. 2004a. "Decentralization in the Philippines: Strengthening Local Government Financing and Resource Management in the Short Term." Economic Report No. 26104, World Bank, Washington, DC.

———. 2004b. "India Karnataka State Public Financial Management and Accountability Study." Report No. 28607-IN, World Bank, Washington, DC.

———. 2004c. "Pakistan NWFP Provincial Financial Accountability Assessment." Report No. 27706-PAK, Financial Management Unit, South Asia Region, World Bank, Washington, DC. http://www1.worldbank.org/publicsector/decentralization/ March 2005 Seminar/3Lee/World%20Bank%202004%20NWFP%20Provincial% 20Financial%20 Accountability%20Assessment%202004.pdf.

———. 2004d. *World Development Report: Making Services Work for Poor People.* Washington, DC: World Bank.

———. 2005a. "Colombia: Country Financial Accountability Assessment Report." Report No. 31915, World Bank, Washington, DC.

———. 2005b. *East Asia Decentralizes: Making Local Government Work.* Washington, DC: World Bank.

———. 2005c. *State Fiscal Reforms in India: Progress and Prospects.* New Delhi: Macmillan India Ltd.

7

External Auditing and Performance Evaluation, with Special Emphasis on Detecting Corruption

AAD BAC

Internationally, the number and importance of policy areas over which local governments have authority range widely. The extent of decentralization in a country is based somewhat on the trust central government has in local government. The population of local government jurisdictions also ranges widely. In some countries, local jurisdictions are still small. In others, scale increases have started, leading to reasonably large entities. Both factors have consequences for the size of bureaucratic organizations, the corresponding capacity of management, the awareness and quality of accountability, the presence of inspection and auditing, the architecture of auditing structures, and the quality of auditing.

This chapter provides an overview of auditing factors relevant to local government:

▪ What makes auditing in the government area special
▪ The object of audit
▪ The scope of the audit
▪ The users of audits

- The auditor
- The auditee
- The audit
- The auditor's reporting

What Makes Auditing in the Government Area Special?

The auditing profession is generally dated to the middle of the 19th century. The oldest professional body, in Scotland, dates back to about 1850. Economic development boomed around that time as a result of the industrial revolution. Business entities grew and the "distance" between owners and managers increased. This called for supervision relationships supported by independent audit. Although several large companies operated before this period (for example, the colonial trading companies in the 16th and 17th centuries in the United Kingdom and the Netherlands), this reason for the advent of independent auditors in the private sector holds in general.

Conversely, examples of complex mandate structures calling for comprehensive systems of specific auditing measures can be found, specifically in the government arena, in China (Center for International Accounting Development 1987) and Babylon (Holy Bible, Daniel 6: 2–3) as early as 500 BCE. The old Chinese Empire as well as the Babylonian Empire controlled extended areas and badly needed, within the possibilities of that time, control instruments. During the following ages, auditing agencies developed and evolved.

There are more differences between auditing in the government sector and auditing in the private sector than their historic origins. In the private sector, the primary audit output is an opinion about whether stakeholders of the reporting entity are being provided with a true and fair view of the accounts. This opinion, as a short form auditor's report, is published together with the financial report. A long form auditor's report may serve the board of directors' (or in the European continental structure, the board of supervisors') approval process as the board performs its supervisory function over the executive. The auditor's opinion is primarily intended to serve the anonymous public who make use of the entity's financial reports.

In the public sector, an auditor's opinion is also intended to serve the general public, but only secondarily. Because of the environment in which the auditor's opinion functions (taking democracies as a reference), the public is represented by an elected legislative body. The primary purpose of an auditor's opinion here is to serve the formal supervisory procedure in the democratic process. The short-form auditor's report (with an overall opinion) and the long-form auditor's report (with detailed findings) go together in, for example, municipal council meetings concerning financial reports and their approval by the supervisory authority.

Other differences in audit between the private sector and the government sector come from environmental factors and task-related factors.

Environmental Factors

The first difference attributable to environmental factors is the importance government organizations attach to truth and to lawful conduct. If the government itself does not comply with laws and regulations, how can it expect citizens to do so? Government intervenes in society through its laws and regulations. Citizens are thus entitled to expect lawfulness and fairness in return. The result is that the audited government organization's environment is a mass of legal rules. This set of legal rules is supplemented by "rules of unwritten law," stemming from customary law and principles of decent public administration.

Complying with laws and regulations is an important culture-determining factor in government organizations. Well-conducted audits in government organizations have to be based on a solid knowledge and understanding of this characteristic of official organizations as well as of its implications.

The same holds true for a second important culture-determining factor of government organizations—the continuous interaction between the official organization (the bureaucracy) and the political organization (the executive authority and the legislature). The two are complementary, and together perform the tasks of public administration.

Decision-making processes in business are predominantly determined by technical and scientific factors concerning the primary process of the entity and economic limiting conditions. Thus, business administration is concerned with technical scientific rationality and economic rationality.

Decision-making processes in government are much more complex. In addition to the technical scientific rationality and the economic rationality, there is also the legal rationality, and because of the allocation role of government, the political rationality. Additionally, the economic rationality in the government sector has both microeconomic and macroeconomic components.

In government decisions these four rationalities have to be brought into balance. The technical scientific, the legal, and the economic rationalities are the responsibility of the bureaucracy, and the political rationality—the decisive one for bringing balance—will come from the political organization. The auditor should be aware of this characteristic of public sector audits.

Task-Related Factors

Government success cannot be measured by the bottom line of the income and expenditure statements, as success is measured for private sector entities. Government organizations do not have income acquisition as a goal. They have, on the contrary, an income-spending goal. So performance has to be measured by means of other criteria. Thus, government auditing has a wider objective than in the private sector. Auditing the accounting system of a government organization is important not only for assessing its financial reports, but also for obtaining information used as inputs into decision making.

If performance cannot be measured easily, which is often the case, it becomes important to review the process leading to the outcomes, as well as the elements used in the process. The accounting system is important because of the information it contains on these elements, the raw material for decisions. This justifies a specific audit on the implicit quality of the accounting system for this purpose.

Another consequence is the need for attention to processes—acquisition of resources (economy), use of resources (efficiency), and satisfaction of needs of society (effectiveness). Therefore, in addition to the usual audit of financial statements, government audits will also include financial management audits and "regularity" audits, which assess compliance of transactions with laws and regulations.

The same holds true with respect to policy-execution management in, for instance, value-for-money audits, which assess efficiency and effectiveness.

In an organization without automatic external warning signals, like market signals in the private sector, the internal control system becomes crucial. Of course, the internal control system naturally receives an auditor's attention, because a good internal control system helps the auditor perform an efficient and effective audit. However, the internal control system is often the only cautioning instrument available to the government organization itself. Thus, the quality of the internal control system is a key precondition for solid government performance. That is why government auditors are often required to audit the internal control system.

Audits in the government sector, therefore, are concerned not only with the presentation of results (true and fair view), but also with the content of activities, and with control measures. Later in this chapter, when dealing with the scope of audit, these three audit types will be discussed more extensively.

Another specific aspect of auditing in the government sector concerns materiality. (Inaccurate or incomplete information is "material" if economic or political decisions would have been different had the users of the information been aware of its inaccuracy or incompleteness.) In private sector audits materiality has an absolute (a specific amount) and a relative (a proportional) aspect and also some undetermined qualitative component (emotional reactions of users that lead to different decisions, but not based on absolute or relative quantifiable factors). This is true in the government sector, too, but experience shows that materiality criteria cannot just be taken from the private sector shelf.

The fact that citizens perceive government as belonging to them, where their money, or part of their money, is spent or wasted, has consequences for the materiality criteria. There is hardly any evidence for the assertion that this has consequences for the perception of materiality, but it is believed plausible by many people. The government sector thus encounters stricter (lower) amounts for absolute materiality, stricter (lower) percentages for relative materiality, and greater sensitivity to political (qualitative) materiality, especially with respect to fraud. The greater sensitivity to fraud in government organizations, can, according to a study by the Dutch professional body of accountants, be explained by the perceived injustice when innocent citizens have to bear the consequences of government managers being unable to prevent fraud in a government organization (Royal NIVRA 1969/1970: 71). (The money is gone and can no longer be spent for the good of the citizenry.) In a private sector company, responsibility and consequence remain more in each other's neighborhoods, so feelings of being taken advantage of are lower.

The Object of Audit

Audits may occur in situations in which certain institutions have the power to transfer accountability to other institutions or persons. Audits are necessary when mandatory supervision cannot be made effective without the help of professionally trained auditors. The audit has to be as objective as possible, presenting findings to a certain level of detail and providing an overall judgment based on those findings. Subjectivity, inherent to the supervisory function, implies weighing the seriousness of findings and whether sanctions should be applied based on them. This is a responsibility that the auditor does not and should not have. So, audit is subordinate to supervision. The object of the audit will be defined by existing supervisory structures, the supervisors who want to make use of the auditor's services, the accountability documents that exist, and so on.

Sometimes, full cash accounting will be in place and reporting will be restricted to a budget-execution document. In other cases, accounting and financial reporting will be more sophisticated and will consist of a balance sheet and a statement of income and expenditure. In still other cases, the statement of income and expenditure will be in the form of a budget-execution document and be functionally specified; sometimes, when the statement of income and expenditure is categorically specified, it goes together with such a budget-execution document.

Generally, audits focus on documents. Auditing can be broadly defined as "the systematic review or examination of the assertions or actions of a third party to evaluate conformance to some norm or benchmark" (Gauthier 2001: 335). Auditing activities in government often involve performance auditing. Performance audits aim to measure a government's success in executing its functions for society. Another example of an audit in government is the audit of the orderly and verifiable financial management of the executive management of government organizations. The definition above misses a third audit category—the audit of systems, for instance, the audit of the internal control system. Internal control systems need to be audited to be able to judge the management of the organization's in-control statement, or, if no such statement is required, to be able to report on that subject in the long-form auditor's report.

The Scope of the Audit

This section covers a series of different perspectives from which the scope of the audit in government can be addressed. The following types of audits will be reviewed:

- Compliance with financial reporting laws and regulations—regularity
- Compliance with budget laws
- Compliance with laws and regulations regarding the content of policy areas and programs
- The soundness of accounts
- The true and fair view of financial reports
- Orderly and verifiable financial management
- Abuse or improper use of laws and regulations
- Fraud and corruption by politicians or government officials
- Performance

Compliance with Financial Reporting Laws and Regulations

Government financial reporting and budgeting are generally regulated, as they are in the private sector. Laws and regulations for financial reporting in the private sector are typically unsuitable for application in the public sector.

Financial reporting in the public sector occurs not only ex post, as in the private sector, but also ex ante, because the public sector budget is a public document disclosing the political choices for allocation of resources. The democratic requirement for transparency in government planning and resulting financial consequences means the budget has to be publicly available for the citizenry. Therefore, laws and regulations regarding financial reporting in the public sector generally start with the budgeting process and the structure of the information in the budget documents. This is the first reason why laws and regulations regarding financial reporting for the public sector have to be different from those for the private sector.

A second is found in the fact that the government sector operates under different economic conditions than the private sector. Private sector entities are guided by economic principles and market discipline. The primary goal of a company is to attain an income greater than the cost of production of goods and services. Management's actions should result in an increase in the company's capital. The profit and loss account reports the increase of capital realized in a certain year. The balance sheet presents the accumulated financial success through the end of the year. A healthy balance sheet together with continuing successful operations revealed by the profit and loss account depict a successful company and should result in a strong position in the capital markets and on the stock exchange.

Government entities also operate according to economic principles, but there is no market, so there is no market discipline and the primary goal is not to realize an income over cost of "production" of goods and services, but to realize the maximum possible usefulness to society from limited resources coming from taxes and other levies. In exceptional cases, goods and services provided by government entities can be priced, but they need not and often are not priced on the basis of their cost of production or on their defrayal. Therefore, the income and expenditure accounts of government entities are not merely reports of increases in capital, but documents with implicit importance. Thus, the income and expenditure account is the more dominant document of the financial report and the balance sheet is necessary simply to link subsequent years. For this reason, the income and expenditure account of a government entity is specified functionally, according to the policy areas to which available resources have been allocated.

In contrast with the private sector, the bottom line of the income and expenditure account of a government organization should not present as high a figure as possible, but some amount close to zero, meaning that the government's mandate has been successfully executed and the citizenry has not been overtaxed.

A third difference comes from the fact that success in government entities is not expressed in financial terms combining all activities, but consists of a series of different performance indicators; thus, performance has to be presented in a different way. Laws and regulations regarding financial reporting in the public sector often contain regulations regarding the expression of performance. The notes to the accounts will be more extensive than is necessary in financial statements of private companies.

Although there are additional differences, it is sufficient to conclude that different sets of laws and regulations regarding financial reporting in the private sector and the public sector should be in place, regardless of the usefulness of harmonization (Bac 2005).

Around the world, three headstreams of regulating financial reporting in the public sector are emerging:

▨ First, many countries regulate budgeting and financial reporting in public law. In such cases, the legislature has reserved the standard-setting role for itself.

▨ Second, a number of countries have instituted relatively independent boards with the authority to set standards for financial reporting by central or lower government (or both). In some cases, this authority is vested in the professional body of accountants in that country.

▨ Third, some countries have chosen the same standard setter for both the private sector and the public sector. These standard setters operate with varying inclinations toward harmonization with, for instance, the private sector or with other countries.

The International Public Sector Accounting Standards form an authoritative set of standards tailored to the public sector, upon which national standard setters can draw (IFAC 2006).

Financial reports must comply with the laws and regulations regarding their composition. Auditors in private as well as in public practice typically insert an explicit sentence in the opinion paragraph stating that the financial report complies with applicable laws and regulations regarding financial reporting.

To render judgment, the auditor has to execute the auditing program. The auditor first has to acquire sufficient knowledge of these laws and regulations and their interpretation. Auditors can facilitate uniformity in audit quality by drawing up questionnaires regarding the laws and regulations applicable to the financial reports of certain government entities. Findings from such audits will concern noncompliance with certain details of the applicable laws and regulations. Consequences based on the auditor's judgment in the short-form auditor's report will not often occur. The auditor's long-form report, however, provides a basis for the reporting of such noncompliance to the supervisory authority of the government entity under audit.

Compliance with Budget Laws

Economic processes in the private sector are controlled by the market mechanism. According to economic theory, the relation between demand and supply determines prices. In the public sector, such an automatically correcting mechanism is not available. In the public sector, even in ancient times, budget mechanisms were developed to control the financial consequences of administrative processes. Especially in democracies, the budget conveys the outcome of the executive's allocation processes, as approved by the representatives of the electorate.

Audits of compliance with budget laws are actually performed throughout the year. Every transaction must comply. For each transaction, the following must be known:

- In which year is it budgeted?
- To what program does it refer?
- How much was budgeted?

If the transaction is permitted after considering these three factors, budget law compliance has been fulfilled. A budget overrun occurs if the total amount spent for a certain program in a budget year exceeds the amount originally allocated or the supplement budgeted for that program.

Noncompliance can take several forms:

- The transaction took place in a year other than the one in which it was budgeted, although the budget capacity in that year remained unused.
- The transaction was accounted for in a program other than the one to which it belonged.

- The real expenditure was higher than budgeted, but was compensated for by related higher income.
- A budget overrun occurred because the expenditure did not fit within the framework of the program, but it could not be detected and reported earlier (for example, open-end arrangements, definitive settlements of a subsidy, write-offs of irrecoverable amounts).
- A budget overrun fit within the framework of the program but was not reported earlier by mistake (for example, additional work ordered, or shortcomings during execution).
- A budget overrun did not fit within the framework of the program. Resources were spent on other purposes than intended by the legislature.
- A budget overrun involves expenditures that after investigation proved to have been illegal.
- The budget was not overrun, but performance of the function for which the expenditure was allocated was lacking.
- Capital cost was too high because the investment budget was overrun.

The seriousness of these irregularities varies. In some cases, it is a matter of correcting a mistake; in others, the expenditure can be approved afterwards; and in still others, managers have to be blamed. If it is not a matter of correction, if the expenditure cannot be approved retroactively, or if it is a case of reproachable action, findings will have to be reported to the supervisory authority in the long-form auditor's report.

So far, this section has dealt with the first criterion of compliance, budget compliance. Before bringing a transaction to a budget, however, a number of other criteria have to be met:

- *The calculation criterion.* Amounts have been correctly calculated.
- *The value-dating criterion.* The moment of payment and recognition is correct.
- *The delivery criterion.* Received goods and services conform to contracts.
- *The addressing criterion.* The person or organization to which payments are flowing is correct.
- *The completeness criterion.* All income due is accounted for.
- *The acceptability criterion.* The transaction complies with the activities of the entity and, more specifically, with the program budget, and an acceptable balance between cost and performance is attained.
- *The budget criterion.* Financial transactions based on compliance with the foregoing criteria have to fit within the framework of the authorized budget as well as within the described and authorized program.

Two additional criteria refer to regulatory and legal compliance, but they belong to the next section. For reasons of completeness they are mentioned here, but elaborated upon later.

- *The conditions criterion.* Further conditions required at the execution of financial management actions have been met.
- *Abuse and improper use criterion.* The internal check on accuracy and completeness of data rendered with respect to the use of government programs has been made, to prevent abuse. The internal check on whether third parties to government programs have not taken actions contrary to the purpose of the program has been made, to prevent improper use.

Compliance with Laws and Regulations Regarding the Content of Policy Areas and Programs

Laws and regulations apply to many government activities, especially ones that involve "nonexchange transactions." In exchange transactions, equal value is given in exchange for received goods and services. In nonexchange transactions, laws and regulations determine the right to receive goods and services without (or with limited) consideration. Examples of nonexchange transactions include transfers, taxes, and levies on the income side, and transfers, subsidies, and social policy payments on the expenditure side. This is where the conditions criterion of compliance, mentioned in the previous section, comes into play.

The same is true for the abuse and improper use criterion. Government services for which no equal value has to be paid, and transfers, are subject to abuse and improper use. Users may try to get such services by giving false information. The problem with improper use is that laws and regulations inadvertently open up possibilities for certain categories of users to get the services legally, although clearly the laws and regulations never intended to do so. Improper use can only be stopped by improved legislation and regulation.

All laws and regulations have to be complied with for every transaction, and there is no limit to management's responsibility to comply. So the internal control system must be adequate for the task.

Whether this also applies to auditing for compliance leads to different answers. Some countries require the auditor to include the complete set of applicable laws and regulations in the audit, regardless of the degree of relevance. This is especially the case in countries where, by tradition, audits have a more legal orientation. In other countries with a more economic view of audit, audit can be limited to that part of laws and regulations with clearly retrievable and direct financial consequences.

Auditors in the public sector must acquire sufficient knowledge of applicable laws and regulations and, depending on the circumstances, such knowledge may be limited to the part with clearly retrievable direct financial consequences. Responsible auditors have to disseminate this knowledge across their staff to ensure that this aspect receives adequate attention in the auditing process. The laws and regulations have to be part of the audit criteria that must be fulfilled in the audit process.

Noncompliance invalidates a transaction and qualifies it as illegally made. Such findings will be reported on the long-form auditor's report, and may, if in sufficient number and materiality, develop to a qualification in the short-form auditor's report.

The Soundness of Accounts

In many countries, the financial accounts come from a cash-based accounting system. This often means that a balance sheet does not exist. In some situations, a modified cash accounting system may be used that includes some kind of balance sheet; however, the auditor will not usually express an opinion on whether the accounts present a true and fair view.

In countries where the architecture and structure of government auditing are dictated by the legal environment, cash accounting presents another reason for an audit directed toward a compliance objective rather than toward a fairness objective. Assurance that laws and regulations are being complied with is needed more than assurance that the statements are providing a true and fair view. Audits with a compliance objective apply stronger materiality criteria than audits with a fairness objective.

The first three elements of compliance, as outlined in the previous three sections, provide an auditor the opportunity to express the opinion reached on budget compliance, on compliance with laws and regulations relating to specific policy areas and programs, and on compliance with accounting and reporting demands based on formal legislation or accounting standards. A practical problem arises with respect to the lack of congruence among these three compliance requirements, because compliance with laws and regulations regarding financial reporting or accounting standards and compliance with budget laws both concern the financial accounts, while compliance with laws and regulations regarding the content of policy areas and programs concerns the individual transactions reported in the financial accounts. The consequences thereof will be dealt with in the final section of this chapter, on the auditor's reporting.

The True and Fair View of Financial Reports

When the accounting regime leans more toward modified accrual or full accrual instead of cash, the auditor's assignment is to come to an opinion on the true and fair view of the financial reports. Accrual accounting yields financial reports consisting of a balance sheet and an income and expenditure statement, together with accompanying notes. More ambitious accounting and reporting regulations often accompany a more ambitious view of the role of auditing. As may be clear from the preceding section, the audit of the accounts is the epitome of the compliance audit. Although information quality may be part of the financial reporting laws and regulations, such regulations demand different compliance answers than the majority of other accounting regulation, because they require judgments to be made, first, by the reporting entity's chief accounting officer and second, by the auditor whose opinion is asked on the results. The reporting entity and the auditor have to ask themselves how the information needs of stakeholders can be served best.

In extreme cases, chief accounting officers may feel forced to deviate from regulations in the interest of the quality of information given to users. The more tailored the accounting regulations, the less reason can be found to let a "true and fair override" become part of it. If a true and fair override is allowed, it has to be accompanied by a "comply or explain" obligation. In most cases, the questions about information quality deal primarily with the extent to which the notes elaborate on factors such as performance, reasons for underperformance or budget overruns, and the like. The way these quality questions are dealt with is explicitly the concern of the government auditor. The overriding question the government auditor has to ask is whether the information given in the financial report contributes to optimal supervision by the legislature, which is a more far-reaching question than strict compliance with applicable formal requirements.

Orderly and Verifiable Financial Management

Another possible frequent object of audit in government organizations is the existence of sound and verifiable (auditable) financial management. Because government organizations often operate under conditions in which external warning signals are lacking and performance indicators are difficult to define, the awareness that financial management has been sound can be comforting to responsible politicians and representatives. The financial management audit can hardly be expected to be comprehensive each year—it is too complex and too broad. So, often, there is a difference in the frequency with which processes or departments of the government are submitted to this type of audit. Processes or departments of essential importance and high risks are audited frequently, processes or departments of great importance and average risks are audited less frequently, and processes and departments with low risks are audited even less frequently. In setting these priorities, of course, the right for follow-up audits on improvements deemed necessary in former audits should be reserved. Laws and regulations should define the minimum audit frequency for every process or department.

Financial management audits might cover the following aspects:

- Budget preparation in accordance with instructions of the executive
- Acceptable estimates
- Budget structure in compliance with the law
- Budget process in compliance with the law
- Architecture of budget accounting system
- Accounting systems and internal control
- Safety, continuity, and verifiability of the budget system
- Safety, continuity, and verifiability of systems in general
- Efficiency of the budget system
- Efficiency of systems in general
- Effective budget control
- Supervision structure
- Feedback systems
- Timely updating of budgets
- Accurate and complete collection of taxes
- Feasibility and verifiability of new laws and regulations
- Acceptability of commitments
- Acceptability of contracts
- Structure of the accounting system
- Timeliness of accounting transactions
- Registration of performance information
- Materials management
- Inventories
- Efficient risk management
- Frequent screening of risk indicators

Abuse or Improper Use of Laws and Regulations

Transfers and nonreciprocal transactions are especially susceptible to abuse or improper use of laws and regulations. Abuse implies illegal transactions. Improper use implies transactions being formally lawful, but obviously contrary to the intentions of the legislature.

The accountable executive has to ensure that policies aimed at preventing and fighting abuse and improper use are in place. Of course, specific circumstances have to be taken into account. Even if a defined policy has been qualified as sufficient and is consistently applied, uncertainty regarding the figures in the financial statements may still remain because it is impossible to verify all the third-party information constituting the basis for these figures. Such uncertainty is inherent in financial management and should be qualified as acceptable or tolerable uncertainty in the financial statements. If adequately disclosed, these uncertainties need not play a role in the auditor's opinion. If possible, the disclosure should be quantitative.

The auditor will have to assess the internal control measures aiming at verifying third-party information. If the audit proves that internal control has been deficient or absent, clearly financial management in this respect has been insufficient. Thus, figures in the financial statements have a higher risk of being incorrect than the inherent and unavoidable level of uncertainty. This may be reflected in the auditor's opinion on the financial statements and on the quality of financial management.

Fraud and Corruption by Politicians or Government Officials

Fraud

The possibility that auditors can detect fraud and corruption is limited, because they generally do not have the same authority and instruments as, for instance, police and intelligence officers do. But there is certainly a role for auditors in this area. Auditors can be most effective in detecting areas where the risk of fraud and corruption is high. Sometimes, their work may bring to light actual cases of fraud and corruption, but that is generally not an explicit goal of their work, and even when it is, their capacity is still limited.

A distinction must be made between the effects of fraud on the financial statements under audit, and the simple occurrence of fraud. Auditors can be responsible for detecting fraud that leads to a material misstatement in the financial statements. Their audit program should be developed sufficiently to find fraud extensive enough to result in material misstatements.

However, the auditor is generally not able to compensate for failures in the internal control system resulting from cooperation of key staff members, because the auditor may not be able to find any traces of some transactions or interventions in the accounting system of the entity. This circumstance is sometimes called the axiomatic reservation. In such cases, the auditor is dependent on accidentally emerging signals that may indicate possible fraud.

IFAC (2004) makes explicitly clear that the auditor, in planning and performing the audit to reduce audit risk to an acceptably low level, should consider the risks of material misstatements in the financial statements from fraud, where fraud is distinguished from errors by being intentional. The risk of not detecting a material misstatement resulting from fraud is higher than that of not detecting errors because fraud may involve sophisticated and carefully organized schemes designed to conceal it. Therefore, the auditor and the audit team should maintain an attitude of professional skepticism throughout the audit, recognizing the possibility that a material misstatement due to fraud could exist, notwithstanding the auditor's possible past experience with the entity about the honesty and integrity of management and those charged with its governance or supervision.

When obtaining an understanding of the organization and its environment, the auditor should assess risks by making inquiries about management's position, risk awareness, role modeling on fraud, and the like. The oversight and supervision structure of the organization is also important.

The auditor should be alert that information obtained about unusual or unexpected relationships may indicate risks of material misstatements due to fraud.

Risks of fraud should especially be considered when opportunities such as the following are in place:

- Significant related-party transactions not in the ordinary course of operations of the entity
- Significant, unusual, highly complex transactions, posing difficult "substance over form" questions
- Ineffective monitoring by management or supervisors
- Complex or unstable organizational structure
- Deficient internal control components
- Inadequate attitudes, lacking codes of ethical standards
- Large amounts of cash on hand or processed
- Easily convertible assets

The auditor may become aware of the possibility of fraud by circumstances such as the following:

- Discrepancies in the accounting records, such as transactions not completely, not timely, or improperly recorded; last minute adjustments significantly affecting the financial statements; inadequate authorizations; tips or complaints

- Conflicting or missing evidence, such as missing documents; unexplained items on reconciliations; inconsistent, vague, or implausible responses to questions; differences from confirmations of balances
- Difficult or unusual relationships between auditor and auditee, such as denial of access to information or unwillingness to cooperate, undue time pressure, delays in providing requested information, unwillingness to address identified weaknesses in internal control

Once the auditor has become aware of existing fraud risks or has received signals indicating the possibility of fraud, he or she must respond to the situation. A variety of specific responses could be used, depending on the types or combinations of fraud risks. Examples of such responses include the following:

- Performing tests on a surprise or unannounced basis
- Conducting inventory nearer to year end
- Altering the audit approach
- Physically observing operations and procedures
- Performing a detailed review of year-end adjusting entries and investigating any appearing unusual in nature and amount
- Performing substantive analytical procedures using disaggregated data
- Performing computer-assisted techniques such as data mining to test for anomalies in a population of data
- Seeking additional audit evidence from sources outside the entity being audited, including using experts
- Reviewing the propriety of large and unusual expenses

Sometimes government auditors' assignments insist on more attention to fraud than that materially influencing the financial statements, because fraud damages the trust of the citizenry in the government and its apparatus. Therefore, more strict materiality criteria are often assigned to the detection of fraud in government organizations, compared with the materiality criteria sufficient to serve the auditor's responsibility to detect material misstatements in the financial statements.

Corruption

With respect to corruption, regular auditors are limited by their skills and authority. Of course, auditors can be given more authority, comparable to police and intelligence officers, and can be educated for these tasks. Auditors can play an important role in discovering areas where the risk of corruption is high. They also can be very useful in testing the level of organizational resistance to corruption.

A distinction has to be made between vulnerable activities on the one hand and vulnerable processes and vulnerable positions on the other. Examples of vulnerable activities can be found where staff or managers deal with

- Handling cash (authorization, collection, or disbursements, especially of nonreciprocal transactions);
- Ordering commitments;
- Buying, keeping, or using capital goods, or other goods and services;
- Handling confidential information;
- Handling licenses and identification cards; and
- Managing supervision and enforcement.

The degree of vulnerability from activities is determined by the consequential damage they could bring about. Consequential damage can be looked upon from several points of view, including the following:

- Financial losses for the organization
- Waste of tax money
- Loss of prestige and harm to citizenry's trust in government
- Negative influence on the working team atmosphere, tension, and deterioration of morale
- Political administrative implications, and so on

Thus, risks of vulnerability can be qualified as serious or even extremely serious. It is important to make an inventory of vulnerable activities to be able to judge the sufficiency of internal control measures developed to defend the organization against the identified risks. Comparable inventories have to be made for vulnerable processes and vulnerable positions. Special attention has to be given to those vulnerable activities, processes, and positions that have been qualified as very important.

The level of organizational resistance to possible corruption is especially determined by the organizational structure resulting from the set of formal rules, procedures, prescriptions, working instructions, policies, and the like. Questions to answer will be whether the risks coming from vulnerable activities, processes, and positions are "covered" by rules, measures, and policies; whether the quality of such rules, measures, and policies is sufficient; and whether staff actually know and apply such rules, measures, and policies. Rules, measures, and policies have to be documented to

- Give staff clarity about how to deal with vulnerable activities,
- Promote uniform procedures, thus preventing arbitrary actions,
- Provide control elements making vulnerabilities testable, and
- Create avenues for staff and management to talk to each other about their conduct.

Examples of such rules, measures, and policies include the following:

- Recruitment and orientation policy for staff
- Availability of clear and comprehensive descriptions of staff functions
- Segregation of duties
- "Four-eyes principle" (requiring that business be conducted using two people)
- Job rotation
- Acceptance of presents
- Acceptability of additional functions or jobs
- Policies toward whistle-blowers
- Availability of a confidant for integrity matters

The lack of such rules, measures, and policies generally indicates integrity risks.

The quality of such rules, measures, and policies can be judged by a series of factors, such as

- Actuality (when updated last? with what frequency?)
- Comprehensibility (readable and easily understood?)
- Unambiguousness (not subject to multiple interpretations?)
- Enforceability (sufficiently discrete to be enforced?)
- Feasibility (can they be practically applied?)
- Comprehensiveness (sufficient scope and sufficient detail?)
- Consistency (are they not reciprocally contradictory?)
- Legal sustainability (are they durable?)

Performance

"Value for money audit," "comprehensive audit," "3-E audit," "performance audit," "evaluation," and the like are all synonyms. The need for this kind of audit emerges in situations in which it is difficult to define performance. The audit object can be management systems and practices, management's reporting on performance, or performance itself (Leclerc and others 1996).

These kinds of audits are much less consolidated than financial audits. The planning phase of these audits contains many more undefined elements than auditors are accustomed to in regular audits.

When a comprehensive audit is planned, an audit approach has to be chosen: management systems, management reporting on performance, or performance itself. The course depends on the government organization under audit, and may also be influenced by the type of policy area or program to be audited. The planning starts with a determination of whether there is any recognizable performance. If not, management systems will be chosen. If performance is recognizable and amenable to reporting, management representations will be chosen. Sometimes, performance is recognizable but not so easily measurable that frequent reporting by management can be expected, for instance, if the measurement cost is high. Then, performance will be investigated and measured to the extent possible at the time of the audit. Next, the performance itself together with the measurability of it will be audited and reported on.

Understanding the organization is key when executing a comprehensive audit; otherwise, the auditor cannot know what should be examined, and which conclusions have to be drawn. If knowledge of this kind is not present, it must be acquired before being able to adequately plan the audit.

The scope has to be defined—will it be the whole organization or only some divisions or branches, or perhaps functions. Unlike financial audits, there is no clear-cut general definition of the scope.

Depending on the audit object, especially in this type of audit, the possible degrees of assurance that can be offered by the auditor may vary. Thus, the intended degree of assurance ("moderate" or "reasonable") has to be defined in advance.

In many comprehensive audits, the audit criteria—the yardsticks against which actual performance will be assessed—have to be defined. Sometimes, negotiations with the auditee about the audit criteria have to be undertaken to prevent unfruitful discussions following completion of the audit about the reasonability of the audit criteria.

Another point of attention will be defining the significance of findings during the audit. Like the level of assurance, the defined measurement of the significance of findings will influence the amount of work to be done, the opinion to be drawn, and the relevance of the reports generated.

The auditor has to define how much evidence will be needed for conclusions to be drawn at the intended degree of assurance. The auditor has to plan how to collect this evidence and where to get it.

The Users of Audits

Possible users of the outcome of the audits can vary, depending on the case, the circumstances, and the legislation. This section will address three categories of users: legislative bodies, supervisory authorities, and the public in general.

The primary user of the outcome of audits in government organizations is the legislative body, made up of elected members representing the citizenry. The legislative body is closest to the ideal representation of all stakeholders of local government, although some stakeholders may not be represented. Creditors may come from other cities and staff may reside elsewhere. Nevertheless, in general, the legislative body represents the majority of stakeholders. In the private sector, the auditor's report, along with the multipurpose financial report, is directed to the anonymous stakeholders in general. In contrast, in the government sector the financial report is primarily meant for the supervisory function of the legislature.

In the government sector, local government regularly undergoes supervision by a higher level of government. This supervisory authority may be the province, the state, or the central government. The objective of supervision will, at a minimum, be to ensure sound financial management at the local government level, but in some jurisdictions will also encompass some kind of supervision on policy making or policy execution, or both. The local government financial report will always be necessary to this supervision.

Only then will the financial reports, and the auditor's report, begin to serve as a means to inform other specific stakeholders. At this point, the situation in the government sector again begins to resemble the situation in the private sector.

The Auditor

The auditing role can be fulfilled in a series of ways. In some countries, the supreme audit institution has authority to act at the lower levels of government. The supreme audit institution is often a constitutional body and is generally independent of government. In federal states, the subnational government sometimes performs an intermediate role—from there downward, there is a hierarchy toward lower levels of government. Regional audit institutions are often a part of such situations. In such cases, the audit of lower levels of government is often constitutionally assigned to these regional audit institutions. In decentralized unitary state models, the local governments are constitutionally relatively independent of higher-level governments. The subsidiarity principle is at work in such a model, according to which everything that can be dealt with nearer to the electorate should be assigned to that level of government. If policy inherently will concern a greater area than the jurisdiction of a local government, it will be dealt with at the next higher level, and so on. This implies that the local government audit is also organized at the local level. This can be done using local audit institutions, but also by assigning audits to chartered accountants from private firms.

Sometimes, no formal audit is instituted at the local government level; the role is integrated into the supervisory relationship, in which case it takes the form of inspection by higher-level government bureaucrats.

Auditors in the government sector as well as in the private sector need a code of ethics containing values and principles guiding the daily work of all auditors, including the main responsible auditor, executive audit officers, and all other staff involved in audit work. Because of national differences of culture, language, and legal and social systems, a code of ethics has to be developed for each country (INTOSAI 1998).

An outline of ethical standards follows.

- The conduct of auditors should be beyond reproach at all times and in all circumstances; otherwise, they could put the integrity of auditors, the validity and quality of their work, and the reliability and competence of the auditing institution in doubt.
- The authority audit work can only exist when auditors are looked upon with trust, confidence, and credibility. The auditor promotes this by adopting and applying the ethical requirements of the concepts embodied in the key words integrity, independence and objectivity, confidentiality, and competence.
- Integrity is the duty to adhere to high standards of behavior, honesty, and candor, in work as well as in relationships with auditees and auditees' staff, acting legally and fairly, not just in form but also in the spirit of auditing and ethical standards.
- Independence from the audited entity and other outside interest groups is indispensable. An auditor's independence should not be impaired by personal interests, by external pressure or influences, by prejudices, by recent employment, by financial involvement, and so on.

- Objectivity in dealing with issues and topics under review and impartiality in all work conducted, particularly in reports, is essential. Reports should be accurate and objective. Conclusions in opinions and reports should be based exclusively on evidence obtained and assembled in accordance with auditing standards and not on views of the audited entity and other parties.
- Independence and impartiality should be practiced in fact as well as in appearance.
- Especially for auditors operating in the government sector, it is key to maintain political neutrality, both actual and perceived. Auditors in the government sector work closely with legislative authorities, the executive, or other government entities. Entering into political activities may lead to personal conflicts and diffuse situations.
- Auditors should be aware of the risk of conflicts of interest when they enter into other services to auditees than audit alone, such as advice. They should refuse gifts; avoid relationships with managers and staff of the audited entity that may influence, compromise, or threaten their ability to act; and be seen to be acting independently.
- Auditors should embrace professional secrecy and not disclose any information obtained in the auditing process, except for the purpose of their assignment. Nor should they use this information for personal benefit.
- Lastly, the auditor is obliged to be competent, not to accept assignments beyond his or her competence, and to maintain competence by means of professional development and continuous education.

The Auditee

The auditee may differ among countries. Again, taking democracies as a reference, ultimately parliament, and at the local government level the legislative body containing the elected representatives of the population, will be the supervisory authorities. So the most logical auditee is the level for which the legislative body is accountable. This is the executive body of a local government. The political executives bear the highest responsibility for government activities and will have to present their accounts together with an auditor's report. But sometimes the distance from the executive to the level of policy execution is great. What to do with the responsibility of bureaucrats?

In many countries, public law states that the political executive bears all responsibility for the government's activities and actions, regardless of the fact that failures and mistakes often are made at the official level by bureaucrats. Although this circumstance will be denied by no one, the political executive alone will stand before the legislature and answer for government activities, government performance, government failures, and the like. The political executive in this model is seen as the top management level of government.

In other countries, the possibility that officials belonging to the bureaucracy may take reproachable actions is more clearly recognized. In such countries, public law opens the possibility for the legislature to call bureaucrats to answer for government activities, government performance, and government failures, to the extent of their responsibility. Although the political executive in this model still is seen as the top-management level of government, some space is created for bureaucratic accountability.

In some countries, the above model has been adapted to clearly separate the government as policy maker (or "buyer" of government services on behalf of the citizenry) from agencies where these services are "produced." Accountability of the government as policy maker is in this model an obligation of the political executive, while accountability for the producing agencies is required from the bureaucratic managers of the agencies.

Depending on the model valid in a country, the auditee can be the political executive, the bureaucratic manager, or both.

The Audit

The audit has to be performed according to authoritative auditing standards. The Generally Accepted Government Auditing Standards published in the "Yellow Book" of the U.S. Government Accountability Office could serve as a reference. The "Auditing Standards" issued by the Auditing Standards Committee of International Organizations Supreme Audit Institutions may be even more authoritative (INTOSAI 1992, amended 1995). Although they have not been tailored to apply to local government situations, there should be little difference in auditing standards for central government and lower government assignments.

The INTOSAI auditing standards consist of four parts:

- Basic principles
- General standards
- Field standards
- Reporting standards

These four parts are detailed in an extensive document (INTOSAI 1992, amended 1995). The lead topics from this document are listed below. (INTOSAI's reporting standards are less government specific, thus not covered in this section. Reporting as a function of the audit is covered in the final section of the chapter.)

Basic principles

The basic principles stipulate the importance of

- Compliance with auditing standards;
- Professional judgment where auditing standards seemingly are not applicable;
- An effective working accountability process;
- Adequate information, control, evaluation, and reporting systems;
- Acceptable accounting standards and specific and measurable objectives and performance targets;
- Consistency in application of acceptable accounting standards resulting in a fair presentation of financial position and results;
- Adequate systems of internal control;
- Full access to all relevant data on a legislative basis;
- Unlimited audit mandates; and
- Continuously striving for improvement of techniques for auditing the validity of performance measures.

General standards

The general standards relate to the quality of the instruments the auditor is using and standards with ethical significance. The first category refers to the requirement of policies and procedures to

- Recruit personnel with suitable qualifications;
- Develop and train audit staff to enable them to perform their tasks effectively and to define the basis for the advancement of auditors and other staff;
- Prepare manuals and other written guidance and instructions concerning the conduct of audits;
- Support the skills and experience available within the audit organization and identify the skills that are absent; provide a good distribution of skills to auditing tasks and assign a sufficient number of persons for the audit; and have proper planning and supervision to achieve its goals at the required level of due care and concern; and
- Review the efficiency and effectiveness of the auditor's internal standards and procedures.

The standards with ethical significance cover

- Independence;
- Avoidance of conflicts of interest;
- Competence requirements; and
- Due care and concern in complying with INTOSAI auditing standards, which implies due care in planning, specifying, gathering, and evaluating evidence, and in reporting findings, conclusions, and recommendations.

Field standards

The field standards in government auditing require

- The auditor to plan the audit in a manner ensuring that an audit of high quality is carried out in an economic, efficient, and effective way and in a timely manner;
- The work of audit staff at each level and audit phase to be properly supervised during the audit, and documented work to be reviewed by a senior member of the audit staff;
- The auditor, in determining the extent and the scope of the audit, to study and evaluate the reliability of internal control;
- The auditor, in conducting regularity audits, to make a test of compliance with applicable laws and regulations; the audit plan should provide reasonable assurance of detecting errors, irregularities, and illegal acts, with a direct or an indirect and material effect on the financial statements;
- The auditor, in conducting performance audits, to make an assessment of compliance with applicable laws and regulations; the audit plan then should provide reasonable assurance of detecting illegal acts that could significantly affect audit objectives; the auditor should also be alert to situations or transactions that could be indicative of illegal acts with an indirect effect on the audit results;
- The auditor, after getting any indication that an irregularity, illegal act, fraud, or error, with a possibly material effect on the audit, may have occurred, to extend audit procedures to confirm or dispel such suspicions;
- The auditor to obtain competent, relevant, and reasonable evidence to support the auditor's judgments and conclusions regarding the organization, program, activity, or function under audit;
- Auditors, in regularity audits or in other types of audits when applicable, to analyze the financial statements to establish whether acceptable accounting standards for financial reporting and disclosure are complied with, to

such a degree that a rational basis is obtained to express an opinion on financial statements.

The Auditor's Reporting

Government organizations are income-spending organizations for which a positive bottom line is not the indicator of success. Success needs to be displayed in every policy area, and will be measured in various ways.

Thus, the supervisory procedure is more complicated than in a private company, making a long-form auditor's report indispensable in government organizations. Long-form reports provide auditors the opportunity to present information about findings for each policy area. This makes it possible for legislatures to extend their supervisory function to all areas of policy execution implemented by the executive.

This does not imply that a short-form auditor's report would not be useful in the government environment. On the contrary, the representatives can use the comprehensive judgment of the auditor when the long-form report may consist of a series of findings that could convey the wrong idea about the overall view. So the auditor's professional support can be very helpful.

Moreover, the financial statements are also presented to the public, which does not have to approve and can limit itself to an overall view. The short-form auditor's report will suffice here. However, the long-form report will, for democratic and transparency reasons, generally also be published.

Although the short-form auditor's report is serviceable, experience indicates that users would like a comprehensive report. Thus, the audit opinion should explicitly cover the fair view, as well as the regularity, and sometimes even the quality of internal control. These aspects of the supervisory procedure require distinct types of opinions. In some cases, the auditor's opinion about the quality of management assertions is wanted, while in other cases, the auditor's opinion about conduct or systems is wanted. Combining these different types of opinions in one short-form auditor's report can only end up confusing the users.

With recent developments in financial reporting in both the private and government sectors, management is gradually accounting for more than in the past. Partly because of governance discussions, management assertions about being in control and about compliance with laws and regulations are becoming more and more usual. The advantage for auditors and their reporting is that if such management assertions are to be usual and mandatory parts of the financial statements, a material shortcoming in control or in legality, unless adequately disclosed in the accounts or the notes to them, will be classified as a shortcoming of the accounts and thus a possible reason for a qualified opinion for the accounts as a whole.

References

Bac, Aad D. 2005. "Perspectives of Harmonization in Government Accounting." In *Mélanges en l'honneur du Professeur Jean-Claude Scheid, comptabilité, recherche comptable et profession comptable*, ed. Evelyne Lande, 93–100. Paris: Conservatoire des Arts et des Métiers.

Center for International Accounting Development. 1987. *Accounting and Auditing in the People's Republic of China: A Review of its Practices, System, Education and Developments*. Richardson, TX: Center for International Accounting Development.

Gauthier, Stephen J. 2001. *Governmental Accounting, Auditing, and Financial Reporting*. Chicago: Government Finance Officers Association.

IFAC (International Federation of Accountants). 2004. "ISA 240: The Auditor's Responsibility to Consider Fraud in an Audit of Financial Statements." Effective December 15, 2004. IFAC, New York.

———. 2006. *Handbook of International Public Sector Accounting Pronouncements*. New York: IFAC.

INTOSAI (International Organization of Supreme Audit Institutions). 1992, amended 1995. "Auditing Standards." Issued by the Auditing Standards Committee of the XIVth Congress of INTOSAI in 1992 in Washington, DC, and amended by the XVth Congress of INTOSAI 1995 in Cairo, Egypt.

———. 1998. "Code of Ethics and Auditing Standards." Auditing Standards Committee, Stockholm.

Leclerc, Guy, W. D. Moynagh, J.-P. Boisclair, and H. R. Hanson. 1996. *Accountability, Performance Reporting, Comprehensive Audit: An Integrated Perspective*. Ottawa: Canadian Comprehensive Audit Foundation–FCVI Inc.

Royal NIVRA 1969/1970. "Controle van Overheidsrekeningen (The Audit of Governmental Financial Statements), Rapport van de Commissie Toepassing Beroepsregelen inzake enkele vraagstukken, welke bij de controle van overheidsrekeningen van belang zijn te achten (Report of the Committee Application Professional Standards regarding some topics deemed of interest when auditing governmental financial statements)." *de Accountant* 76 (2): 71–82.

Index

Boxes, figures, notes, and tables are indicated by b, f, n, and t, respectively.

CPSIA information can be obtained at www.ICGtesting.com
Printed in the USA
BVOW040206180912

300729BV00005B/25/P

9 780821 369371